STRANGE,
SPOOKY
AND
SUPER-
NATURAL

ALSO BY MIKE BROWNE

Murder, Madness and Mayhem

CURIOUS TALES OF FASCINATING
PEOPLE, PLACES AND THINGS

STRANGE, SPOOKY AND SUPER- NATURAL

MIKE BROWNE

Collins

Published by Collins, an imprint of HarperCollins Publishers Ltd

First edition

HarperCollins books may be purchased for educational, business,
or sales promotional use through our Special Markets Department.

HarperCollins Publishers Ltd
Bay Adelaide Centre, East Tower
22 Adelaide Street West, 41st Floor
Toronto, Ontario, Canada
M5H 4E3

www.harpercollins.ca

Library and Archives Canada Cataloguing in Publication

Title: Strange, spooky and supernatural : curious tales of fascinating people,
places and things / Mike Browne.
Names: Browne, Mike, author.
Description: Includes bibliographical references.
Identifiers: Canadiana (print) 20240416295 | Canadiana (ebook) 20240416317 |
ISBN 9781443470490 (softcover) | ISBN 9781443470506 (ebook)
Subjects: LCSH: Curiosities and wonders.
Classification: LCC AG244 .B76 2024 | DDC 001.94—dc23

Printed and bound in the United States of America

24 25 26 27 28 LBC 5 4 3 2 1

Curiosity, when it ventures into the realm of the macabre, becomes an insatiable hunger for the forbidden, compelling us to confront the shadows within.
—OSCAR WILDE, *The Picture of Dorian Gray*

'Tis strange—but true; for truth is always strange;
Stranger than fiction; if it could be told,
How much would novels gain by the exchange!
How differently the world would men behold!
—LORD BYRON, from *Don Juan,* canto XIV, stanza 101

CONTENTS

Foreword

WHEN YOU HAVE a passion for life's mysteries, you often end up aligning with others who feel the same calling for a deeper under-standing. In short, that's how Mike and I found one another, and we met over one very specific story, known as the Amherst Mystery in Canada's Maritimes. The Amherst Mystery—the tale of Esther Cox and the exploitation of her alleged psychic gifts—stands as a warning to all those who step into the role of paranormal storyteller. After working in the parapsychology field for many years, I have learned that intention, care, representation, facts and personal truth all play a role as we attempt, in our human way, to get to the bottom of this paranormal journey. The more we dig, the deeper the journey becomes and the more we as humans come to realize . . . there is no bottom. We explore paranormal phenomena through science, sto-ries and art in the best way we can and use our physical abilities to explore the evidence we have, expressing it through many tried and true avenues. Our podcast, *Supernatural Circumstances*, has become an avenue for Mike and me to ride this winding train for ourselves; it has allowed us to explore these stories from the perspective of our guests, but also from the perspective of one another. Through this exploration, I have come to realize that in this human adventure, we must travel down this road of spirituality and high strangeness using whatever mode of expression we feel most akin to, and if you've picked up this book, then congratulations: You've just bought your train ticket.

The paranormal and psi have always had a strong influence on popular culture: *Ghostbusters, Supernatural, Doctor Who, The X Files, Stranger Things* and, even earlier, comics such as *Doctor Strange, Scooby-Doo, Casper the Friendly Ghost* and more. These paved the way for reality hits like *Ghost Adventures, Most Haunted* and other staged reality shows designed for thrills and entertainment. Movies inspired by games such as *Silent Hill* have touched on some very prominent ideas in current parapsychological research, such as the idea of frequencies and planes of existence. The film *Silent Hill* and the series *Stranger Things* explore the idea that there are intelligences beyond what we are capable of seeing within the human spectrum of vision. Only when conditions change and that frequency of vision is expanded will we gain access to these other realms of existence. The storytellers, it seems, are slowly catching up to the science, but not in any way that appears to make much difference.

As a veteran parapsychology researcher for over 20 years, I believe the television shows and books that feature ghost hunters running around with shaky cameras and exaggerated claims have unfortunately cheapened the reality of serious investigators and scientists who genuinely seek to study new phenomena and assist people who are in trouble. Many don't realize that when someone like me gets a call, the stories are deep and multi-layered: People are often on the verge of divorce, losing their homes or having severe emotional crises.

While many books and other mediums further the idea that some quick ritual will "cure" the home or business of its problems, they often make parapsychology stories extremely one-dimensional in the process. Much of this subject is therefore buried in cheap thrills and frightening fantasies, obscuring the truth of the story itself and many times blurring the best part of the real deal. Reducing these incredible encounters to simple campfire stories is something we desperately want to change as podcasters and researchers ourselves.

Scientifically, we have moved far past the argument of whether or not a phenomenon exists: The focus has become "Why is it happening, and how do we understand it?" These two important questions have fuelled the paranormal passion that Mike and I share.

It is a rather new thing for humanity to begin extending this art of storytelling to *real-life* stories of the paranormal, and this can either run us into trouble or become a mode of truthful expression: We have the ability to enhance, elaborate, examine and even lie about stories depending on the outcome the writer wishes to achieve. It takes a unique individual to be able to hear human stories and then retell them in a way that allows the audience to examine the content. Mike Browne is one of those rare people. In many cases, even folkloric stories can be examined to discover a truthful reality, and without the storyteller, these stories are forgotten and lost to our busy and sometimes controversial history. This is, perhaps, the very importance of storytellers themselves—they are the preservers of time past and the keepers of the stories of ages. However, they can also serve as a platform to stand on and a ladder to climb for those who are traversing forward in this field of parapsychology.

How we tell a story can say much about a person and less about the subject, and nowhere do we see that more than in the case of paranormal reporting. How someone decides to tell a story has the ability to allow the audience to draw their own conclusions and encourage critical thinking, or to shut down discussion with rhetoric and criticism. It can spark wonder and imagination, or it can frighten us to never inquire into a subject ever again. Whether we are creating a podcast, writing a book or presenting a show, this is always in the forefront of a researcher's mind.

While much of parapsychology is up for debate, one thing that isn't is that we tend to align with other people for reasons we don't always initially understand. After keeping in touch after my *Dark Poutine* interview, Mike and I soon began to realize a piece of that purpose, and our podcast, *Supernatural Circumstances*, was born. As two self-proclaimed (and very proud) nerds, we both felt that the science and research of the parapsychological field were being horribly overlooked and overshadowed by flashy television shows and ghost hunters who based few or none of their methods and theories on research or fact. In the same turn, the parapsychology world was stuck in the academia rut of white papers and complicated words, and most people either had no interest in reading them or simply couldn't understand their relevance. We decided to change that, and I knew Mike was the perfect partner with whom I could journey forward.

Mike's down-to-earth approach, without a doubt, is the perfect match for my passionate knowledge and reaches people beyond the true crime genre, offering them a key to a door that many have longed to open for years but weren't sure how. Everyone, we have learned, has a story, even if they don't know it. Through *Supernatural Circumstances*, we have been able to talk to the greatest minds and the most interesting people, as well as hear both the research of the most advanced organizations and the fantastic experiences of the common individual. Greatness, we have discovered, is often revealed in the anomalous encounters we don't expect, and these aren't always experienced by famous channellers or studious scientists in white coats but by the everyday person who is aware enough to recognize when something is magical.

Mike is someone who sees the magic in the small things: daily meditation, finding joy in the subtle everyday things, and recognizing that the little we know as a species is actually not a fault but the beginning of the adventure. This point of view is something we both share and have become passionate about sharing with others. I have been so fortunate to experience this journey with Mike and all of the incredible people we have interviewed, many of whom we now call good friends. These fabulous stories and rich information are passed down to others through Mike's specialty: storytelling. His relatable and humble way of allowing a story to compassionately unfold is the very thing that will make the readers of this book unable to put it down. The story keepers of our time are the folklorists of the modern day and must never be taken for granted. It is the crucial process of retelling, no matter what the format, that allows us as humans to hold on to tales that offer us clues into our future. They aren't simply a representation of outdated ideas or silly stories, but rather information we may otherwise forget that allows us a fuller understanding of where we are going.

As *Supernatural Circumstances* continues into its next season and beyond, I can't help but look forward to continuing this journey with Mike Browne, and I hope everyone who picks up this book will feel the same way. Once a person delves into these stories in a meaningful way, one can't help but be touched by them. However, a word of warning: Seeing the world differently is an inevitable consequence of indulging in the following pages. But if you're ready and open, and you know in your heart there is more to this world than meets the eye, this book will only add more questions, answers and passion to your inevitable and unending journey. So settle in for a look at some of the world's most terrifying, inspiring and utterly fascinating supernatural tales.

—MORGAN KNUDSEN, co-host of *Supernatural Circumstances*

A LIFETIME OF OBSESSION
WITH THE WEIRD

THROUGHOUT MY LIFE, I've been drawn to the outer edges of human experience—bizarre creatures, hauntings, extreme human feats, medical anomalies and unexplained phenomena. For as long as I can remember, I have been obsessed with death and the possibility of an afterlife. I'm unsure when it started or the catalyst, but it is likely a confluence of things.

Very early in life, the thought of death—and things related to it—terrified me. It still does. So, of course, there will be a chapter in this book about that. I devoured stories about ancient Egypt during the day, and then at night, I was terrorized by slow-moving mummies lumbering toward me, powerless to escape their relentless pursuit. My fear of death has informed my interest in the afterlife, the occult, horror and true crime.

I grew up in Nova Scotia, Canada, and my curiosity was nourished through the local lore, oddities and curiosities that richly colour the province's folklore. A stone's throw away from my hometown of Bridgewater, Oak Island's famous Money Pit exerted a strong pull on my youthful imagination. This mysterious spot, steeped in tales of hidden treasures and relentless treasure hunters since the 1700s, filled me with awe and wonder. This local enigma was my first encounter with the unexplained, a story I would later explore in depth in my first book, *Murder, Madness and Mayhem*. It was the first story, but far from the last, in my collection of tales.

Nova Scotia's inextricable relationship with the sea means many of its mysteries have a nautical theme: the ill-fated *Titanic*, the infamous ship graveyard of Sable Island. These tales, each a fascinating maritime mystery, found their way into my bedroom—posters and maps adorning my walls, volumes on my bookshelves, their compelling tales filling my dreams.

One of my favourite Nova Scotian nautical-themed stories is that of the *Mary Celeste*, a famous ghost ship that was found abandoned in 1872. The brigantine was built in Nova Scotia and named *Amazon* before being sold to an American owner and renamed. On its fateful voyage, it set sail from New York City to Genoa, Italy, on November 7, 1872, with Captain Benjamin Briggs, his wife, his daughter and a crew of seven. The ship encountered harsh weather, but the last log entry suggested nothing unusual.

On December 5, the *Dei Gratia* found the vessel adrift near the Azores, 400 nautical miles (740 kilometres) away, with no one aboard. The ship was in seaworthy condition, with its cargo intact and personal belongings undisturbed, but the lifeboat was missing. The crew of the *Dei Gratia* sailed the *Mary Celeste* to Gibraltar, where an investigation found no evidence of foul play.

Theories about the abandonment have ranged from mutiny and piracy to supernatural occurrences, none of which have been substantiated by evidence. One plausible explanation is that Captain Briggs might have thought the ship was sinking because of a malfunctioning pump and a faulty reading from the sounding rod used to check water levels in the hold. This could have led to a hasty evacuation onto a longboat that later met with disaster.

Despite its mysterious history, the *Mary Celeste* continued to be used until 1885, when it was intentionally wrecked as part of an insurance fraud. The intrigue around the ship was further fuelled by a fictional story published by Arthur Conan Doyle in 1884, but the true fate of its passengers and crew remains one of the sea's unsolved mysteries.

Beyond the sea, the province's lore includes other curiosities, such as the famous Cox family haunting in Amherst, near the New Brunswick border. From the unseen presence beneath Esther Cox's bed to the unexplained noises, illnesses, flying objects and fires, perhaps caused by a malevolent poltergeist, this tale remains a captivating part of the region's folklore.

Thanks to my father's subscription to *National Geographic*, my appetite for the strange and the supernatural extended beyond my province. Those magazines, filled with captivating stories and eye-opening facts, became my window to a world brimming with curiosities.

In the pre-internet age, my resourceful nature also led me to the local bookstore, Sagor's, where I dove into books like *The Guinness Book of World Records*, which fed my fascination for extreme human accomplishments. Yet the stories of peculiarities, like the giant Robert Wadlow, whom you'll learn more about later, truly gripped me.

Among my treasured finds from the Scholastic catalogue was a book about Eric Weiss, better known as Harry Houdini. His death-defying stunts as a magician and his quest for a connection with the afterlife resonated with me, nurturing my healthy skepticism of and fascination with the mysterious.

I also watched 1980s-era television shows like *Real People*, *That's Incredible!*, *Creepy Canada*, *In Search of . . .*, *Ripley's Believe It or Not!* and *Unsolved Mysteries*, which further fed my obsession with the strange and wonderful. I can still recall the days spent in front of the "idiot box," as my parents called it, eyes wide with wonder, my heart racing, as I pondered the amazing stories on the screen.

One story I've always remembered is that of Roy Sullivan, a park ranger at Shenandoah National Park in Virginia, who holds the Guinness World Record for most lightning strikes survived. Sullivan was struck by lightning seven times throughout his life, earning him the nickname "Spark Ranger."

Sullivan's first encounter with lightning occurred in 1942, in a fire tower without lightning rods, where a strike burned a strip down his right leg and removed his big toe. The second incident occurred in 1969 when lightning hit some trees near his truck, rendering him unconscious and burning off his eyebrows and eyelashes. The third strike occurred in his home garden, where lightning from a transformer hit his shoulder. The fourth and fifth encounters, in which Sullivan was set on fire and had a shoe knocked off by the force, happened while he was at work. The sixth strike occurred while he was walking in the park, prompting his retirement five months later. The seventh and final strike happened when he was fishing, causing burns and partial hearing loss. Despite the astronomical odds against such frequent strikes, no one ever witnessed these incidents, leading to doubts about their veracity. Sullivan later died from a self-inflicted gunshot wound in 1983.

I was adopted, so genetics and heredity have always fascinated me. Another story that drew me in was that of identical twin brothers Jim Lewis and Jim Springer, who were separated at birth. They were adopted by different families in Ohio in 1940. Unaware of each other's existence, they led strikingly similar lives. Remarkably, both became firefighters.

Here are some more astonishing similarities:

- Both were named James by their adoptive parents.
- Both were married twice—their first wives were both named Linda, and their second wives were both named Betty.
- Both had children—one had a son named James Alan, while the other had a son named James Allan.
- Both owned dogs named Toy.
- Both drove Chevys.
- Both enjoyed vacations on the beach in Florida.
- Both had similar habits, like leaving love notes to their wives, smoking Salem cigarettes and drinking Miller Lite.

Their uncanny similarities were discovered when they were reunited at age 39. They were part of a study conducted by psychologist Dr. Thomas Bouchard of the University of Minnesota, who was researching the nature versus nurture debate. The twins' parallel lives provided significant evidence supporting the argument for nature's role in shaping individuals. Their lives serve as a fascinating case study of identical twins separated at birth who, against all odds, lived eerily similar lives.

I also learned early on of the phenomenon known as spontaneous human combustion (SHC), a term that describes cases where a human body is burned without an apparent external source of ignition. It is a subject of much debate and speculation, often regarded with skepticism by the scientific community because of the lack of comprehensive evidence.

The case of Mary Hardy Reeser in 1951 is one of the most cited instances related to SHC. Reeser, a 67-year-old woman living in St. Petersburg, Florida, was reduced to ashes in her apartment, with only part of her left foot remaining unburned. The chair she was sitting in was also destroyed, but the room in which she was found showed little fire damage.

The investigation considered various theories as to the cause of the fire, including a dropped cigarette, but no conclusive evidence was ever found to explain the intense heat required to cremate the body without extensively damaging the apartment. This case has often been pointed to as an example of SHC, but alternative explanations, such as the wick effect, where clothing or another fabric can act as a wick and body fat as a combustible substance, have also been suggested. Despite many theories, the cause of the fire has never been confirmed, and the case remains a classic in SHC discussions.

SHC remains a topic of fascination, with several books and articles exploring cases like Reeser's. However, scientific validation of SHC as a real phenomenon is lacking, and many proposed cases of SHC can be explained by overlooked conventional fire sources or other natural circumstances.

Another topic that has drawn me in is the phenomenon known as the Bermuda Triangle. The Bermuda Triangle, also known as the Devil's Triangle, is a loosely defined region in the western part of the North Atlantic Ocean where numerous ships and airplanes are said to have disappeared under mysterious circumstances. Miami, Bermuda and Puerto Rico roughly bound the area. Despite its notoriety, the Bermuda Triangle is not recognized by the US government as a real geographic area, and the US Board on Geographic Names does not have it listed as an official region.

Disappearances in the Bermuda Triangle have fuelled speculation ranging from paranormal explanations, such as alien abductions and other dimensional portals, to natural phenomena like methane hydrates that could theoretically sink ships by reducing water density. However, most scientists dismiss these theories, attributing the disappearances to human error, piracy and natural disasters, among other explainable causes. They argue that the area does not have a significantly higher number of incidents compared with other heavily travelled regions of the world.

Similar places with reputations for mysterious disappearances include the Dragon's Triangle (or Devil's Sea) near Japan, characterized by similar lore of unexplained vanishings of ships and aircraft. The Dragon's Triangle is located in a region of the Pacific around Miyake Island, about 160 kilometres (100 miles) south of Tokyo. As with the Bermuda Triangle, explanations for the purported occurrences in the Dragon's Triangle range from environmental factors to paranormal activity, though evidence supporting such claims is sparse.

I always presumed my weird obsessions would lead to something, but I was unsure what. The universe has seen fit to help me parlay my odd hobby of collecting weird facts and strange stories into a fascinating and successful career, after years of joe jobs.

I've become known as the voice behind the acclaimed podcast *Dark Poutine* and as the co-host of *Supernatural Circumstances*, with Morgan Knudsen. In these roles, I've explored the mysterious and the unexplained, ventured into the great ocean of the unknown and surfaced with tales that blur the lines between plausible and perplexing.

Taking a page from the life and philosophy of Charles Fort, who made it his life's mission to catalogue and investigate phenomena that challenge our understanding, I've developed a profound respect for Fortean tales—those bizarre happenings and occurrences that resist categorization. The existence of the unexplained, unyielding even in the face of skepticism, offers a tantalizing hint of the wondrous complexity of our world.

As a connoisseur of the strange, the peculiar and the incredible, I'm thrilled to present you with my newest anthology, *Strange, Spooky and Supernatural: Curious Tales of Fascinating People, Places and Things*. This book is a tribute to the extraordinary, a voyage into the mysterious realms that border the everyday, and an acknowledgement of the numerous enigmas that make our world so mesmerizing.

While researching, it intrigued me to find several familiar names, such as H.P. Blavatsky and Sir Arthur Conan Doyle, repeatedly linked to some of these stories. So keep your eyes open for their recurring appearances.

In this brief expedition, we'll traverse the enigmatic and the uncanny, aiming to quench our innate human curiosity. These stories help us gain insights about ourselves, our surrounding world and the subtle border that differentiates the mundane from the spectacular. Immerse yourself in the strange, the spooky and the supernatural as we examine some of the most intriguing, puzzling and unaccounted-for people, locations and phenomena.

A wise person once told me I should write the stories I want to read. I have done that here.

Part 1

PEOPLE

THIS FIRST SECTION posed a challenging task because of the myriad fascinating individuals whose lives intersect with the strange and supernatural. Distilling this extensive pool to only six selections was complex, with each fascinating and compelling story clamouring for inclusion. The subjects I've chosen to profile are but a few of my many favourites.

The first chapter in this section is about a long-time personal hero of mine. "Harry Houdini: Escape Artist, Illusionist and Debunker" provides an intriguing exploration of Houdini's multi-faceted career. It traces his rise to global fame as an escape artist, unpacks his mesmerizing illusions and underscores his unexpected role as a debunker of spiritualism. The chapter presents a balanced view of Houdini, highlighting his talent for theatricality and his determined efforts to expose deception and champion scientific understanding.

Throughout history, there have been scores of stories about enigmatic people who arrive unannounced and cannot explain who they are, where they came from or why they're there.

Kaspar Hauser, a German youth, appeared in Nuremberg in 1828 with a letter, claiming he had been isolated in a dark cell since birth. Despite efforts to educate him and uncover his origins, his background remained unclear. He was taken in by a Nuremberg scholar but was fatally stabbed in 1833 at age 21, leaving his life and death shrouded in mystery. His case highlighted debates on nature versus nurture and the effects of extreme childhood isolation.

"Jerome, the Legless Man of Sandy Cove," also known as "the Mystery Man of Sandy Cove," was found on a Nova Scotia beach in 1863 with both legs amputated and unable to communicate clearly. His true identity and how he came to be in such a condition remain unsolved, leading to widespread speculation about his origins—ranging from an Italian nobleman to an injured lumberjack. Cared for by local families until he died in 1912, Jerome lived in near silence, becoming a local curiosity and a symbol of intrigue. Despite numerous theories, his life story blends fact and folklore, leaving a legacy of mystery in Canadian history.

"The Mysterious Brother XII and His Missing Treasure" unveils the peculiar saga of Edward Arthur Wilson, also known as "Brother XII." The chapter delves into his creation of a spiritual commune in the 1920s, detailing his cult's fascinating and often disturbing practices. Central to the narrative is Brother XII's purported hoard of gold, accumulated through donations, which vanished under mysterious circumstances. The chapter presents a thrilling investigation into Brother XII's life, the eerie allure of his teachings and the enduring enigma of his lost fortune.

"Giants, a.k.a. the Exceptionally Tall: Myths and Reality" explores the captivating realm of giants. It combines tales of fantastical beings from folklore and literature with accounts of actual giants, such as Robert Wadlow and Angus MacAskill, examining our enduring fascination with size and its influence on stories, history and our perception of the world.

Finally, "Wannabe Spaceman: The Disappearance of Granger Taylor" presents the tragic tale of a UFO-obsessed Canadian who built a life-sized UFO replica, complete with a 1970s-styled interior, using reclaimed materials. Granger's obsessions escalated as he increasingly experimented with LSD, asserting that it enabled alien communication. His escalating drug use, coinciding with his absorption in the extraterrestrial, raised questions about his mental health. His life story interweaves creativity, engineering genius and a potentially perilous engagement with UFOs and hallucinogens that ends tragically—or does it?

CHAPTER I

Harry Houdini: Escape Artist, Illusionist and Debunker

Since my childhood, Harry Houdini has been a hero of mine. His daring escapes, illusionist tricks and relentless pursuit of truth captivated me, filling me with a deep curiosity about magic and human potential. His unique combination of showmanship and dedication has left a lasting impression, making him a timeless figure of mystery and enchantment that deeply influenced my formative years. Harry Houdini is a big reason why this book exists.

Houdini's early life began in Budapest, Hungary. Erik Weisz was born to Rabbi Mayer Samuel Weisz and Cecilia (Steiner) Weisz on March 24, 1874. The family lived modestly in a single-room dwelling. Houdini was one of seven children. His older siblings included Herman M. (born in 1863), his half-brother from Rabbi Weisz's first marriage, Nathan J. (born in 1870) and Gottfried William (born in 1872). His brother Theodore was born in 1876.

After Theodore's birth and a series of antisemitic pogroms in Hungary, Erik's father, a newly minted lawyer, sought the promise of a better life in America for his family. Harry's dad moved to the United States first to get established. In 1878, the rest of the family joined him in America. Houdini's younger siblings were born in the United States—Leopold D. in 1879 and Carrie Gladys, who was almost blinded after a childhood accident, in 1882.

Upon arriving in New York, Erik's mother didn't speak English and could interact with the immigration officials only in German. This led to changes in their surname, and *Weisz* became *Weiss*.

The Weiss family eventually settled in Appleton, Wisconsin, where Rabbi Weiss established the city's first temple, thanks to a benevolent Jewish businessman. This relocation was crucial for the family, especially for young Houdini (now Eric), who quickly took to sports. He enjoyed running races and cycling with his friends.

When Eric first visited a circus, it was a life-changing experience for him. Amid clowns, animal trainers and acrobats, tightrope walker Jean Weitzman's dangerous balancing act enchanted Eric. Inspired, he taught himself to walk a tightrope he rigged between two trees. Eric's fascination with Weitzman's performance, and other bold feats he had seen performed by famous stunt performers, would ultimately guide him toward a career in illusion and magic. When he attempted to replicate a stunt that involved hanging by the teeth, he lost a couple of his baby teeth because he didn't realize that a mouthpiece was required for the feat.

When Eric was eight, his father, Rabbi Weiss, lost his job because his conservative ways clashed with his more progressive congregation. The family then moved to New York after a brief stay in Milwaukee. To help make ends meet, Eric sold newspapers and shined shoes on the street. At the age of nine, he performed professionally for the first time as a trapeze artist, contortionist and acrobat in a local circus. He gradually mastered complex stunts, such as dislocating joints, which later aided in his escape performances.

Eric developed an interest in locksmithing during an apprenticeship in Appleton and earned local fame by unlocking all the doors to every shop on one street. He used his skill for good, even assisting a sheriff to free a prisoner when a handcuff key broke in the lock.

Though fascinated by locks, Eric's real passion was performing. He loved magic shows and often attended them with his father. Soon he became obsessed with magic and taught himself as much as possible about the art of magic and illusion.

Harry Houdini was largely self-taught. He developed his interest in magic at a young age and began his career performing card tricks before moving on to escape acts. Houdini's early exposure to magic came through his fascination with the performances of magicians he saw as a child and through books on magic. He devoted himself to learning the craft by practising, experimenting and studying available literature on magic and escapology. While he did have some mentors and influences in his career, much of Houdini's knowledge and skill resulted from his efforts to master the art of illusion and escape.

When his brother Herman passed away (his cause of death is unclear), Eric used the money he earned from odd jobs and shows to pay for the funeral. Despite the hardship, he continued performing and incorporated gymnastics, amateur boxing and magic tricks into his show. Soon he began billing himself as "Eric the Great."

At 17, Eric Weiss was inspired by a book called *Memoirs of Robert-Houdin, Ambassador, Author, and Conjurer*. He connected with Robert-Houdin, who was a man deeply interested in feats of magic. Eric decided to honour his hero by changing his name to Harry Houdini and embarked on his own career in magic. He spent some time with the Welsh Brothers circus and even tried managing a burlesque show, but performing was Harry's real passion.

As a youth, Houdini performed as many as 20 magic shows daily at a dime museum. Harry's father passed away at 63 of complications from surgery for tongue cancer. Attending his father's deathbed, he made a promise to take care of his family in any way he could. After a brief collaboration with his friend Jacob Hyman, Houdini started performing with his brother Theo, whose stage name became Dash Hardeen. The brothers made a name for themselves at the Columbian Exposition in Chicago in 1893 with their magic performances on the street.

One of Harry's go-to stunts was the metamorphosis act. The metamorphosis, or substitution trunk, Houdini's first major illusion, debuted with his early partners Jacob Hyman and brother Theo. The act involved Houdini being tied, sacked and locked in a trunk, after which his performance partner would exchange places with Harry, who then emerged free while the partner would be found locked inside.

During one of these performances, an older showman named Rysie challenged Houdini, claiming he could perform the same trick. However, Rysie was unsuccessful and had to be rescued from the trunk. Houdini had found his true calling: escapology.

During this time, Houdini met and fell in love with an 18-year-old singer and dancer named Wilhelmina Beatrice Rahner, later known by her stage name, Beatrice (Bess) Raymond. Bess came into the world on January 23, 1876, in the bustling city of Brooklyn, New York. She was a member of a large family of German-speaking immigrants and was drawn to the entertainment industry in her early teens. Bess was showcasing her talents at Coney Island as part of a song and dance group known as the Floral Sisters when she first caught the eye of Houdini's brother Dash. However, Harry Houdini, the elder of the two brothers, won her heart and became her husband on June 22, 1894.

Bess and Harry collaborated, performing as the Houdinis for several years. Despite his new-found fame, they occasionally revisited their metamorphosis act. Bess was also responsible for their pets, was an avid doll collector and crafted costumes for Houdini's grand evening performances. She made sure her frequently forgetful spouse was always well groomed and presentable. Bess was known for her tenacity and vibrant personality, but unlike her clean-living husband, she liked to drink and smoke.

Besides his ability to escape from a locked trunk, Houdini could also free himself from any pair of handcuffs. This talent caught the public's eye, and he began performing this trick regularly at his travelling show, where he would challenge local police to present him with their strongest set of handcuffs. Harry Houdini was not tall or heavy. He was just 166 centimetres (5 feet, 5 inches) tall and weighed around 52 kilograms (115 pounds). Despite his small physical stature, he had an outsized personality and used his diminutive size and agility to his advantage throughout his career.

Harry's reputation soared after he escaped from a combination of handcuffs and leg irons presented by the police department in Saint John, New Brunswick, which led to him being called "the Handcuff King." Houdini next taught himself to escape from a straitjacket, another crowd-pleasing stunt.

In 1897, Houdini and Bess introduced clairvoyance to their shows, but they later stopped once Harry realized the seriousness of spiritualism. Houdini continued performing his escape shows around the United States and Canada, challenging anyone to present a pair of handcuffs he couldn't escape from for a $100 reward.

Houdini became a household name when a picture of him in shackles appeared on the front page of the *Chicago Journal*. His feats were lauded as miraculous, leading to the creation of a full show of escape stunts, which usually ended with a death-defying act.

By 1900, Houdini was famous in North America and made a significant weekly income from his show. He and Bess then took the show to Europe, where they performed for five years. There is some speculation that Houdini was a spy for the US government during this time, although this remains unconfirmed.

Upon returning to the United States in 1906, Houdini published *The Right Way to Do Wrong: An Exposé of Successful Criminals*, based on his interviews with criminals and police. The book drew from Houdini's expertise as a magician and escapologist and offered an insightful examination of various criminal behaviours and scams popular during the era. Intended to educate the public and guard against deceit, the book was a fascinating look into the tactics and operations of con artists and thieves. Sometimes his audience was made up exclusively of law enforcement officers and officials, who watched in fascination as Houdini proved that no jail, or set of handcuffs, was invincible given the right escapee.

As his popularity continued to surge, Houdini sought to elevate the risk and spectacle of his performances. He began jumping off bridges while hog-tied and manacled, only to resurface moments later, free of his restraints. And he continued to ratchet up the drama of his act: He escaped from straitjackets while suspended upside down from cranes and bridges. In another act, he was manacled, put into a wooden crate and lowered into the water; 57 seconds later, he emerged, leaving the crate intact with his restraints still inside. In 1908, Houdini introduced the milk can escape to his act. In this trick, he was shackled and sealed into an industrial-sized milk can filled with water. He would ask the audience to hold their breath as long as his escape took, increasing the suspense and involvement of the spectators. The audience members would have long had to take a breath when, just over two minutes after the stunt began, Harry emerged from the cabinet, soaking wet and gasping for air.

In 1909, Harry ventured into aviation: He learned to fly and purchased a French Voisin biplane. He was only the 25th person in the world to ever fly a plane. He even taught soldiers to fly in Germany. Later, in Australia, he made the country's first controlled flight, on March 18, 1910. Despite his planning a transatlantic flight, in 1920, the feat never happened. Houdini hoped his aviation accomplishments would outlive his fame in magic, but sadly, aviation is just a fascinating footnote in the famous man's life.

Though known primarily as an illusionist—which is essentially an occupation as a professional liar—Houdini was always interested in seeking the truth. As well as being an escape artist, he had a long and storied career as a debunker. This branch of his life's work began in earnest in 1908, when Harry wrote and published *The Unmasking of Robert-Houdin*. In the book, Houdini turned his ever-critical eye toward the man from whom he had taken his famous stage name. Houdini had begun questioning Robert-Houdin's acclaimed contributions to the field of magic, prompting him to pen this contentious exposé.

Houdini meticulously scrutinized and demystified Robert-Houdin's magic tricks and illusions. He asserted that much of Robert-Houdin's repertoire consisted of adaptations or slight improvements of traditional magic tricks or tricks invented by his contemporaries rather than original creations, suggesting that Robert-Houdin deliberately usurped credit for the inventions of others. This depiction sharply contradicts the widely held view of Robert-Houdin as a respected gentleman of magic and stirred considerable controversy within the magic fraternity. Harry Houdini's book effectively laid bare his hero's character flaws for all to see.

The allegations against Robert-Houdin have been challenged by several magic historians, who believe that Houdini's feelings of resentment skewed his perspectives. Controversy aside, the book has had a considerable impact on discussions of the history of magic and is worth a read for magic buffs.

Many believe that Harry's skepticism of spiritualism and mediums was born from his deep love for his mother, Cecilia Weiss. The story goes that after her death from a catastrophic stroke in July 1913, Houdini was desperate to communicate with her and, along with Bess, turned to spiritualism, hoping it could provide a clear bridge to the afterlife. However, his experiences with mediums left him disillusioned and angry, as he realized that many were frauds exploiting people's grief. A later interview given to the *Dayton Daily News* indicated that Harry's doubt about mediums had started even earlier than that.

He'd gone to his first seance at 11 after the death of his brother, but it was after Rabbi Weiss passed that Houdini had what would be a transformative experience. Harry said that after his father died when he was 17, he and his mother sought the help of several mediums to communicate with his father's spirit. Harry had to sell his watch to afford the sittings. All the mediums claimed contact, but the alleged messages conveyed to Cecilia and young Harry struck him as odd as the language and tone were nowhere close to his father's. Harry had also briefly been a fraud medium himself, but the ease with which he could take people in disturbed him, so he abandoned the practice out of conscience, determined to reveal fraudulent mediums but, at the same time, always seeking the real thing. But it would be a decade before Harry truly set about debunking fakes. Until then, he had more spectacular illusions to perform.

Houdini introduced the Chinese water torture cell into his act, in which he was lowered headfirst into a glass case filled with water, suspended by his ankles, and would escape behind a curtain. Finally, in 1915, he performed a "buried alive" stunt where he was placed in a hole 1.8 metres (6 feet) deep and covered with dirt. Houdini nearly died during the act, dramatically losing consciousness after clawing his way out.

Many of Harry's stunts were tremendously dangerous, especially the buried alive stunt, and escape artists who have attempted to replicate it have proven so, with at least one dying in an attempt to recreate the feat.

At a festival in West Yorkshire, escape artist Antony Britton nearly died while attempting a buried alive stunt, aiming to outdo Harry Houdini by escaping unaided from a six-foot-deep grave with his hands shackled. After nine minutes without signs of activity, his team rescued the unconscious Britton. The event left onlookers at Slaithwaite Spa horrified as medical professionals had to administer oxygen to Britton, who later reported a near-death experience. Britton, who had attempted this classic escape trick without a casket and had his lungs collapse under the weight of compacted soil, was ultimately unearthed by his crew using a mechanical digger and frantic human diggers using shovels to uncover the performer.

British escape artist Alan Alan similarly required a rescue during his attempt in 1940. The stunt took a deadly turn in 1992 when

American magician Joe Burrus succumbed to fatal injuries as the weight of soil and concrete caused his Plexiglas casket to cave in.

By 1918, Houdini owned his own movie studio and starred in a film called *The Master of Mystery*. He played a Justice Department agent and did many of his own stunts in the film. In his second movie, *The Grim Game*, he was filmed transitioning from one biplane to another mid-flight. His movies, however, were not as successful as his live shows, and his last film, released in 1923, received mixed reviews. As Harry's popularity began to flag, his revenue streams began to diminish.

In a purely financial move in early 1924, Houdini collaborated with author H.P. Lovecraft on a short story, "Imprisoned with the Pharaohs," published in *Weird Tales* magazine. The story, which sold a lot of magazines, told a fictional tale of Houdini being kidnapped and then escaping, only to encounter bizarre creatures.

Throughout the 1920s, Houdini continued his efforts to debunk fraudulent mediums and spiritualists, earning him many enemies. He gave talks nationwide exposing frauds and their methods and then began writing a book about the subject.

Houdini released the book *A Magician Among the Spirits* in 1924. In the book's introduction, he detailed his extensive investigation, including those of his childhood, into spiritualism and mediums over the span of 30 years. This included a trip in 1919 where he attended over a hundred seances across England and France. Throughout his years of study and research, he encountered many of the era's most famous mediums and subjected himself to their conditions in the hopes of finding genuine proof of spirits.

Despite his exhaustive research and the vast library he amassed on topics like spiritualism, magic, witchcraft, demonology and evil spirits (some of which dated back to 1489), Houdini remained unconvinced of their veracity. He found no incident that he deemed truly authentic or that couldn't be reproduced by earthly, non-supernatural means. He concluded that all the spiritualistic phenomena he encountered were the result of either delusion or a fervent willingness to believe rather than any evidence of the supernatural.

While open to spiritualism, Houdini criticized its inability to substantiate its claims and its reliance on deceptive practices. He notes in the book that people from all backgrounds have fallen prey to such deceptions because of their emotional desire to connect with departed loved ones. Despite his skepticism, he affirmed his belief in an afterlife, longing for credible evidence that would allow him to communicate with his deceased mother.

Houdini even made agreements with 14 individuals, including his wife Bess, that whoever among them passed away first would attempt to communicate with the others from the afterlife if possible. Despite these agreements, Houdini revealed he had not received any form of communication from those who had passed away, further bolstering his skepticism and criticism of the spiritualist practices prevalent during his time.

In the first chapter of his book, Harry tells the story of the Fox sisters from Hydesville, New York. On March 31, 1848, the Fox family began hearing unexplained rapping noises within their household, which they interpreted as spiritual communication.

The two youngest daughters of the family, Margaretta and Kate, devised a method to interact with the rapping sounds, using them to symbolize "yes" and "no." Later, their elder brother, David, refined their communication system by using the alphabet to spell out words and asking the spirit to mimic the snaps of their fingers or respond with a certain number of raps. This enabled them to tap out full sentences. The spirit called himself "Mr. Splitfoot" and told them he was a murdered peddler who was interred beneath the house.

The unearthing of human remains from under the house appeared to verify this claim, leading to widespread news about the rapping. When Margaretta and Kate visited their elder sister, Leah Fish, in Rochester, they found they could establish communication with spirits, irrespective of their location, causing them to conclude they were mediums.

By the close of 1848, the three Fox sisters had established themselves as professional mediums, and spiritualism was on the rise. Despite accusations of deceit, the sisters' popularity increased exponentially, with many others claiming paranormal abilities. By 1851, spiritualism had proliferated nationwide, triggering a wave of fascination. Spiritualist societies emerged, and self-professed mediums started delivering lectures. Bookstores were filled with new volumes on the subject. During the US Civil War, the practice exploded in popularity.

However, in the concluding pages of the first chapter of *A Magician Among the Spirits*, Houdini discussed Margaretta Fox's public confession of fraud. Margaretta, one of the famous Fox Sisters who played a significant role in the creation of spiritualism, admitted to producing mysterious sounds during seances by manipulating her toe joint.

This confession left her socially and financially destitute and ruined her credibility. Despite her admission, some spiritualists continued to believe in her and the practice of spiritualism, attributing her admission of deceit to the influence of evil spirits. Houdini also shared the story of a Boston woman who expressed forgiveness toward Fox despite losing thousands of dollars on fraudulent mediumistic messages. Even after Fox's clear demonstration of how the sounds were produced, the most stubborn spiritualist fanatics refused to accept her confession.

In the same year he released *A Magician Among the Spirits*, Houdini wrote and published a shorter, more controversial essay detailing his experiences with Mina Crandon, a Canadian-born medium known popularly as Margery. Although she impressed others with her abilities, including Sherlock Holmes author Sir Arthur Conan Doyle, Harry was suspicious that Margery was a fraud.

Born in 1888 in Princeton, Ontario, Mina Stinson was the youngest of six children. After completing secondary education, she moved to Boston to work as a church secretary and performed in the church orchestra as a cellist. Her life took significant turns through two marriages—first to Earl Rand, a grocer, and later to Le Roi Goddard Crandon, a surgeon and Harvard Medical School professor.

Crandon introduced Mina, now called Margery, to the world of spiritualism, and they held seances at their home, during which Mina emerged as a medium. An encounter with a medium facilitating communication with her deceased brother Walter fuelled Mina's interest, and further development, in mediumship.

Starting in 1923, her abilities as a medium were put to the test by various investigators, including a significant investigation by *Scientific American* magazine. Margery apparently demonstrated remarkable abilities, such as levitating a table, during sessions with experienced investigators of physical mediumship in Europe.

Margery accepted a challenge issued by *Scientific American*, which had put up a prize of $2,500 for any medium who could successfully demonstrate their psychic abilities and convince a panel of investigators of their authenticity.

The investigating committee comprised respected personalities such as psychologist and parapsychologist William McDougall, physicist and MIT professor Daniel F. Comstock, psychical researcher

Walter Franklin Prince, investigator of psychic phenomena Hereward Carrington and Houdini himself, who was well known for his skepticism toward spiritualism and mediumship.

During one of the seances that were part of the investigation, Houdini was seated next to Margery, holding her hand and maintaining physical contact with her via his calf. In this setting, Margery reportedly rang an electric bell that was enclosed within a box. However, Houdini claimed that he felt Margery manipulate the box with her foot to ring the bell, implying that the act was a fraud.

In a subsequent sitting, an incident of table levitation was reported. Houdini, however, attributed the event to Margery using her head to lift the table, once again suggesting that she was committing fraud.

Houdini persuaded Margery to sit in a specially designed cabinet during a seance to investigate her abilities further. After the seance, a collapsible ruler was found within the cabinet. Houdini claimed that Margery had used this ruler to operate the bell box, insinuating a case of deliberate deceit. However, Margery counter-accused Houdini, stating that he had planted the ruler in the cabinet, leading to a contentious dispute between the two.

Sir Arthur Conan Doyle, who had been a friend of Harry's for years, became disenchanted with what he saw as Harry's closed-minded unwillingness to believe. Doyle also gave an alternative version of events surrounding the exposure of medium Margery, implying that Houdini, with his dexterity, was responsible for sabotaging the seance rather than the medium having manipulated it.

Thus, the investigation into Margery's mediumship abilities became a complex and controversial case in the annals of psychical research. Houdini later added her methods to his performances to show exactly how Margery deceived people.

In the autumn of 1925, Harry Houdini launched his tour of an extensive full-evening show. However, this was not merely another showcase of his iconic tricks and illusions. This new performance was centred on the theme of debunking psychics and mediums, revealing the deceptive practices and tricks they often used to convince people of their alleged supernatural abilities.

Houdini boldly offered a reward of $10,000, a whopping sum for the time, to anyone who could present any form of supernatural phenomena that he, with all his magician's expertise, could not mimic or explain. This audacious challenge gripped the nation's imagination, leading to sold-out performances everywhere his tour took him.

Houdini's exposure of spirit medium Mina Crandon (Margery) gained national attention during contentious seances in July 1924. Many pointed to Houdini's efforts as key to her not winning the *Scientific American* prize for mediumship. In 1925, newspapers circulated an item likely disseminated by Houdini, mentioning a "curse" predicted by Margery's spirit guide, implying Houdini would die within a year. Margery denied ever making the claim. Harry made it through 1925 unscathed but would not survive the next year.

Following a successful performance season, Houdini returned to his home in New York in the spring of 1926. The plan was to spend the summer months unwinding from the whirlwind tour, enjoying some well-deserved relaxation and replenishing his creative energies. He also intended to invent new magic tricks and illusions for his forthcoming fall season, keeping his act fresh and exciting for his loyal audiences. This was Houdini in his element, constantly pushing the boundaries of his art and craft while questioning and debunking the ostensible mysteries of the spiritualist world.

In early October 1926, Harry and Bess ran into some adversity. Bess fell ill from ptomaine poisoning. *Ptomaine poisoning* is an out-dated term that historically referred to foodborne illness caused by consuming bacteria-contaminated food, resulting in symptoms similar to those of food poisoning. To add to their troubles, Houdini broke his ankle during a water torture cell act.

On October 22, 1926, while in his dressing room at the Princess Theatre in Montreal, Houdini was visited by Concordia University students Sam Smiley, Jacques Price and, later, J. Gordon Whitehead, who had borrowed a book from Houdini. Whitehead asked Houdini unusual questions about miracles in the Bible and his ability to withstand hard blows to his stomach. Houdini agreed to allow the young man to test his ability to take a punch. Before Harry was fully prepared, with all his might, Whitehead hit Houdini's right side below the belt, causing him significant discomfort.

Houdini performed in Toronto and Detroit despite having a fever of 40°C (104°F) and the broken ankle acquired from the water torture cell act mentioned previously. Harry abandoned the Detroit show during the third act because he felt too ill to continue. He was admitted to Detroit's Grace Hospital on October 25, where an operation revealed a ruptured appendix, which likely caused poison to spread throughout his system. Despite initial signs of improvement, Houdini passed away on October 31, 1926.

The cause of death was peritonitis and gangrene. However, many believe the abrupt blows by Whitehead in Houdini's dressing room led to his death. There was speculation that Whitehead, a Concordia student and alleged amateur boxer, was an assassin hired by resentful spiritualists.

After Houdini's death, Sir Arthur Conan Doyle publicly stated he did not believe that the punch delivered by Whitehead had killed Houdini. Doyle was skeptical that a punch could cause appendiceal gangrene, noting this would imply many boxers had died similarly. While agreeing that Houdini died as doctors reported, he disputed the gangrene's cause. He also mentioned prophecies from mediums, particularly the supposed curse by Mina Crandon, who asserted that Houdini's denouncements of their work had enraged spirits, foretelling his "doom."

In the wake of Harry Houdini's death, his wife held on to the promise they'd made to each other about trying to communicate from the afterlife. Bess held a seance every Halloween for a decade, engaging top mediums of the day and even offering $10,000 to anyone who could provide proof of contact with Houdini.

In 1928, prominent medium Arthur Ford claimed to have received a message from Harry Houdini's mother saying "forgive," which Houdini's widow recognized as significant. The following year, Ford alleged he received a coded message from Houdini that had been pre-arranged between Bess and her husband before his death. Although Bess initially confirmed the code as authentic, she later retracted, accusing Ford of a hoax. Some speculated that Bess didn't want to pay the $10,000 reward promised to anyone who could prove communication with the spirit world.

Regardless of all the speculation, Bess continued holding seances on Halloween every year. The final one occurred on the 10th anniversary of Harry's passing, October 31, 1936. According to an audio recording of the 1936 affair, Bess claimed that, a few days before he died in Detroit, Houdini said, "Bess, darling, I'll come back to you, if it is possible, even if I have to go through hell to do it."

Besides Bess Houdini, significant attendees at that last seance included Dr. Edward Saint, Charles Fricke and two journalists. The gathering also included a former president of the California Spiritualist Organization, paranormal investigator Hereward Carrington, Caryl Fleming and magician William Larsen Sr. An impassioned plea was made to the spirit world, particularly aimed at contacting Houdini, using a trumpet as a conduit. Everyone present was asked to lend their spiritual strength to enable Houdini's spirit to communicate.

Yet despite the earnest invocations, prayers and pooling of spiritual energy, no contact with Houdini's spirit was established. As the gathering ended, Bess Houdini said that after a decade-long belief in the potential of spiritual communication, she had concluded that the ability of spirits to interact from the afterlife does not exist. The 10-year vigil for her husband came to a definitive end when Bess solemnly extinguished the light at the Houdini shrine. A sudden thundershower occurred right after her declaration, prompting some people to speculate that it was a sign from the late escape artist.

Despite differing opinions regarding the facts of Houdini's death, his legacy as a historical and almost mythological figure in magic persists to this day. Houdini inspired many of today's famous magicians, such as David Copperfield, Penn & Teller and David Blaine.

There are people who continue to explore the veracity of mediumship and the possibility of life after death. Through my work on the *Supernatural Circumstances* podcast, I learned about the Windbridge Research Center. Established in July 2017 in Tucson, Arizona, by husband and wife Mark Boccuzzi and Julie Beischel, PhD, the centre continues the Windbridge Institute's work of life-after-death studies, further augmenting it with public outreach and educational activities. According to its website, the Windbridge Institute is "dedicated to conducting world-class research on unexplained phenomena within traditional scientific frameworks."

The site is a great resource for healthy skeptics seeking a much more scientific approach to afterlife research and mediumship. One interesting article on the site asks "Are All Mediums Frauds?" The article states it is a misconception that all mediums are fraudulent and are solely interested in making money from their clients. While some mediums use deceptive tactics, not all do. The article highlights that around 30 percent of mediums in the United States offer free readings and that their mental state during communication with the deceased is unique, as per EEG findings. (An EEG, or electroencephalogram, is a test that measures electrical activity in the brain.)

The centre uses rigorous testing protocols to evaluate mediums, finding evidence of anomalous information reception (AIR), where mediums accurately report specific information about deceased individuals without prior knowledge.

The article clarifies that mediums receive, not retrieve, information and cannot force the deceased to communicate. The purpose of mediumship is to share messages from the deceased, not to prove anything.

Finally, the article notes the lack of official regulation for mediumship in the United States, urging consumers to check references and understand refund policies. The centre is hard at work developing further educational materials to help consumers avoid fraud.

Check it out!

CHAPTER 2

Kaspar Hauser: The Nuremberg Stranger

On May 28, 1828, between 4:00 and 5:00 p.m., a resident of Nuremberg, Germany, noticed what appeared to be a wobbly legged, possibly drunken stranger near the town's public square. The curious resident, a local shoemaker named Weickmann, and another of the townsfolk approached the stranger and discovered he was a young male, most likely in his mid-teens. He was small in stature and hunched over. He had a blank look on his face when they questioned him, appearing not to comprehend what was being said. Without answering, the odd little fellow held out a note.

The note was addressed to "his honor the Captain of the 4th Esgataron of the Shwolishay regiment. Nuremberg."

The first page of the note began:

From a place, near the Bavarian frontier which shall be nameless, 1828. HIGH AND WELL BORN CAPTAIN! I send you a boy who wishes faithfully to serve his king. This boy was left in my house the 7th day of October, 1812; and I am myself a poor day labourer, who have also ten children and have enough to do to maintain my own family [TRANSLATION BY HENNING GOTTFRIED LINBERG; FROM THE AMERICAN EDITION OF VON FEUERBACH'S *CASPAR HAUSER* (BOSTON, 1832)]

The note continued that the writer had raised this abandoned boy in secret, never reporting him to authorities. He educated the boy at home, keeping his existence hidden. The boy wished to join the horse regiment like his unidentified father and could have been scholarly under different circumstances. The labourer sent the boy to Nuremberg to enlist, intending to fetch him later, under threat of personal risk. The note advised the captain that the boy knew nothing of his past or home, and the labourer chose to remain anonymous for fear of punishment. The writer left the boy's fate to the captain's discretion, mentioning the boy had no money.

Another page requested the recipient to name and educate a baptized child, born April 30, 1812, again mentioning that his father was a member of the Chevaux-légers, the horse regiment of the armed forces. The writer said the youngster should be sent to the sixth Chevaux-légers regiment in Nuremberg at age 17, where his deceased father had served. The child's care was entrusted to the recipient by his mother, described as a poor girl unable to support him.

Another sheaf of paper in the small bundle identified the youngster only as Hauser and left any details about the letter's author blank. It read:

Hauser will be able to tell you quite precisely how I look and from where I am. To save Hauser the effort, I want to tell you myself from where I come __ __ . I come from __ __ __ the

Bavarian border __ __ On the river __ __ __ __ __ I even want to tell you the name: M. L. Ö.

The youth seemed unable to move without pain and difficulty, as though walking was new to him—he required assistance to make it any distance. He had shaggy brown hair and pale skin. He was dressed in peasant rags and looked malnourished and dehydrated. Following the note's directions, Weickmann took the boy to the home of Captain von Wessenig of the local horse regiment. There, they attempted to feed the youngster. He spat out the cooked beef and vegetables he was given and drank only a few drops of beer. However, when given bread and water, he wolfed it down hungrily.

The police were called and attended the captain's home to investigate. Again, the young man was questioned about his identity. The police asked who he was, where he was from and why he was there. The youth seemed puzzled by the simple questions and responded tearfully with "Don't know." He had several strange outbursts during questioning, saying, "Horse! Horse!" and "I want to be a cavalryman, as my father was."

He was handed a pen, ink and a blank piece of paper on which he wrote "Kaspar Hauser," which would become his name from that point forward. Not knowing what else to do with him, the police arrested him for vagrancy and took him to the city's holding cells.

A doctor examined him and found that his legs had developed in a way that suggested he'd rarely walked or even stood for long periods during his short life. When seated on the floor, his posture was unusual and indicated to the doctor that the youngster had spent most of his life in that position. He had a single mark on him, a large bruise on one arm.

During his time in jail, young Kaspar displayed even more peculiar behaviours. His movements and reactions to people who interacted with him were odd. The aroma of cooked food seemed to frighten him. He'd sniff at the proffered meal, screwing up his face as though he didn't understand what it was, and refused to eat. Coffee and milk were also not to his taste. Both made him quite sick to his stomach. It took some time to get him used to eating any food besides bread and water, which is what he preferred to eat.

When someone gave him a hand mirror, he was shocked and bewildered. Then he became fascinated, waving his hand before it and making odd faces. At first, he didn't seem to understand that he was looking at his own reflection and looked around the room for the person he saw staring back at him.

Eventually his jailer, Andreas Hiltel, grew fond of the boy. Feeling sorry for him and recognizing a certain innocence in the stranger, he made the compassionate decision to bring him into his home, where he would reside with the rest of his family. Kaspar and Hiltel's son quickly became close, and the other boy patiently taught Kaspar how to speak more than the few odd phrases he already knew.

Word of the odd boy made its way around the city. In Nuremberg society, socialites and those of higher positions were fascinated by Kaspar's story, and many came to visit and ogle him. One persistent visitor was Nuremberg mayor Burgermeister Binder. Although Kaspar was still refining his language skills, over several weeks, the mayor gradually pieced together fragments of the boy's tragic origin story.

Kaspar could not recall exactly where he had come from before arriving in Nuremberg but could relate stories of his previous life. He said he lived in a dark hole in the ground, perhaps a basement, which he referred to as a cage. He had no clue how long he had been there. He was dressed only in a shirt and underwear.

He'd not seen sunlight, the stars or the change from day to night until his trip to Nuremberg. In his cage, he was always in near-complete darkness. Kaspar never heard any sounds and lived in silence.

The only possessions he recalled were two small wooden horses and some ribbons. He played with those objects to pass the time.

When he was tired of playing, he would fall into a deep sleep and wake up to find fresh bread and water next to him. Sometimes, when he awoke, he'd find himself wearing a clean shirt or notice that his fingernails had been clipped. He never saw the face of the man feeding and caring for him. Kaspar had always known to look away from the man for as long as he could recall. The thought of doing otherwise filled him with dread. The man only said, over and over, "I want to be a cavalryman, as my father was." This is where Kaspar had learned the phrase.

He claimed the man never hurt him, except for once, shortly before he arrived in Nuremberg. Kaspar had been noisily playing with his horses, and the man struck him on the arm with a piece of wood, creating the mark the doctor discovered on his initial examination.

Anselm von Feuerbach's 1832 book, *Caspar Hauser: An Account*, translated from German, describes a man who entered Hauser's prison and placed a table over Hauser's feet with a sheet of white paper on it. The man then guided Hauser's hand, holding a lead pencil, to make marks on the paper without Hauser seeing him. Initially unaware of what he was doing, Hauser was delighted to see the black marks he made on the white paper. After the man left and Hauser realized he could move his hand freely, he became so engrossed in repeating this drawing activity that it nearly made him neglect his toy horses, even though he did not understand the meaning of the characters. The man continued to visit and repeat this process several times.

He also forced Kaspar to his feet and taught the foundling to stand and walk. The man would stand behind Kaspar, grab him around the chest and pull him up; then the man placed Kaspar's feet on top of his to simulate walking. This process was repeated a few times until Kaspar seemed to be able to do it on his own, albeit shakily.

When Kaspar was removed from his cage, the man first carried Kaspar over his shoulder. The man also forced boots onto Kaspar's feet, which hurt him, and dressed him in the peasant clothing Kaspar was later discovered wearing. The man made the bewildered youngster stand and forced him to walk forward. Kaspar kept his gaze down, watching his feet as they walked. It was a long journey, and they stopped to eat bread and water and slept on the ground several times when the sky darkened. As they trudged along, the man continued repeating the phrase "I want to be a cavalryman, as my father was."

When they arrived in Nuremberg, the man placed the notes into Kaspar's hand and vanished. The abandoned boy was discovered soon after.

An investigation into the case was initiated by Paul Johann Anselm Ritter von Feuerbach, who served as the president of the Bavarian Court of Appeals. Recognizing the significance of Hauser's story, von Feuerbach took on the task of delving deeper into the young man's life.

As the investigation progressed, the town of Nuremberg formally adopted Hauser, providing him with support and stability. Generous donations were also made to ensure his future well-being and education. The community was dedicated to his care and development.

After two months of living with the Hiltel family, a local schoolteacher, Georg Friedrich Daumer, took Kaspar in to provide him with more intensive schooling. Daumer hoped he could help Kaspar achieve the level of education shared by his peers.

Under Daumer's tutelage, Kaspar learned quickly. The teacher noted Kaspar's uncanny ability to read and to distinguish colours in complete darkness. His sense of smell was also extraordinary. Daumer claimed that Kaspar could distinguish one type of berry from another by smell alone at one hundred paces. He also noted that Kaspar could not walk near or through a graveyard because the stench of rotting flesh coming from the graves, a smell imperceptible to anyone else, made him ill.

The story of the extraordinary "lost boy" captured the attention of news editors and their readers across Europe.

By October of 1829, Kaspar had advanced so far in his writing that he began penning his autobiography.

As Kaspar was writing at his desk in his room at Daumer's home, an intruder entered and struck Kaspar on the forehead with an axe. As the black-haired man swung the weapon at Kaspar, he yelled, "You must die before you get away from Nuremberg!" Thinking he had killed the boy, the man fled.

Kaspar survived a superficial but large wound and sported a scar on his forehead for the rest of his life. No one was ever arrested for the attack, nor did anyone claim responsibility.

Around the same time, the first news stories were published that called young Kaspar a fraudster. Skeptics questioned Hauser's account of the attack. They believed he deliberately caused the wound on his forehead using a razor. It is suggested that Daumer, having developed doubts about Hauser's honesty, may have confronted him about his tendency to fabricate stories in the hours before the attack.

Death threats began arriving at the Daumer home, so Kaspar briefly moved in with another family named Biberbach. While living in that home, another odd incident occurred.

On April 3, 1830, a gunshot was heard from within Hauser's room. Mr. Biberbach rushed into the room and discovered him bleeding from a wound on the right side of his head. After regaining consciousness, Hauser explained that he had been attempting to reach some books by standing on a chair. However, the chair toppled, and in his attempt to find support, he inadvertently dislodged a pistol hanging on the wall, causing it to discharge.

However, doubts soon arose about whether the superficial wound was the result of a gunshot.

Some people speculate that this incident, like the previous one, was connected to an accusation that he had been lying. Like the phantom axe attack, Hauser fabricated or exaggerated the circumstances surrounding the discharge of the gun.

This incident led to Kaspar moving house once again. In May 1830, he moved in with a man named Baron von Tucher, who became his legal guardian. But that relationship also went south, and the baron claimed Kaspar was a vain young man and an inveterate liar.

Hauser's credibility was questioned for various reasons, including inconsistencies in his narrative, absence of corroborative evidence, unexpectedly advanced skills for someone claiming to have been isolated and behaviour suggesting a desire for attention. Investigations found no proof of his alleged lifelong captivity, and his understanding of social norms was suspiciously sophisticated for his claimed upbringing. Additionally, forensic analysis hinted that he might have written the mysterious letters associated with his case. These factors, alongside potential psychological explanations for his conduct, led to a widespread belief that he was not truthful about his past.

Lord Stanhope, also known as Philip Henry Stanhope, was a British politician, diplomat and scholar who took a keen interest in the Kaspar Hauser case. Since first learning of Kaspar's story, Stanhope was intrigued by Hauser's mysterious background and the circumstances surrounding his appearance in Nuremberg.

Stanhope closely followed the developments and investigations surrounding Hauser, even going so far as to correspond with individuals involved in the case. He exchanged letters with Johann Georg Meyer, a magistrate who played a significant role in Hauser's early years in Nuremberg. Stanhope expressed his curiosity about Hauser's origin and the motivations behind his alleged captivity.

Stanhope gained custody of the troubled young man in 1831 and sought to gather more information by contacting various German authorities, scholars and witnesses connected to Hauser's story. He was dedicated to shedding light on the puzzle of Kaspar Hauser.

Hauser exhibited a curious ability to recall certain Hungarian words, leading him to proclaim that a Hungarian countess named Maytheny was his mother. This declaration hinted that he had a possible connection to Hungary and added to the intrigue surrounding his origins. Stanhope took Kaspar to Hungary twice, hoping something would trigger his memories, but Kaspar failed to recognize anything there.

Stanhope, too, began to wonder if Kaspar Hauser was a liar and left him under the care of Johann Georg Meyer in the Bavarian town of Ansbach in early 1832. Although he continued to pay for Kaspar's upkeep, he rarely visited after leaving him there. After Kaspar's death, Stanhope wrote a book about their time together and claimed the young man had thoroughly fleeced him.

Having mastered reading and writing, Kaspar began work as a copyist at a local law office, but he remained consistently troubled.

Kaspar's relationship with Meyer was strained, and the patient educator soon became frustrated with him and began to think, like all his other previous guardians, that he was lying. Even Hauser's original benefactor, Anselm von Feuerbach, doubted Kaspar's stories. Before von Feuerbach died in 1833, he wrote, "Kaspar Hauser is a smart scheming codger, a rogue, a good-for-nothing that ought to be killed."

In early December 1833, Meyer and Kaspar had a falling out. Days later, Kaspar came stumbling back to Meyer's home, bleeding profusely from a deep stab wound on the left side of his chest. Before losing consciousness, Kaspar claimed a stranger had lured him to the Ansbach Court Garden, handed him a small bag and stabbed him. Kaspar said he had dropped the bag in the garden before leaving.

A police officer later found the bag. It was a small purple velvet purse, and inside was a note in mirrored writing. The note was exactly the same as one of the notes found in Kaspar's hand on the day he'd been discovered in Nuremberg.

The note in the purple bag read:

Hauser will be able to tell you quite precisely how I look and from where I am. To save Hauser the effort, I want to tell you myself from where I come __ __ . I come from __ __ __ the Bavarian border __ __ On the river __ __ __ __ __ I even want to tell you the name: M. L. Ö.

Kaspar Hauser died of the stab wound on December 17, 1833. He was laid to rest in the city cemetery in Ansbach, and his tombstone bears the following inscription in Latin: "Here lies Kaspar Hauser, riddle of his time. His birth was unknown, his death mysterious. 1833." This memorial captures the enigmatic nature of his life. A monument was erected in the Court Garden and features the inscription "Hic occultus occulto occisus est," which translates to "Here lies a mysterious one who was killed in a mysterious manner." A statue, later erected in the old city centre in Ansbach, depicts the Nuremberg discovery of the oddly postured Kaspar Hauser, hat in one hand, notes in the other.

The circumstances surrounding his death remain unclear and are still the subject of much speculation and debate. The note, for example, appeared to have been written in a hand similar to that of Kaspar Hauser. The note had also been folded in a specific way that Hauser was known for. Some believe he was murdered, while others think he may have inflicted the wound himself in an attempt to die by suicide.

The tale of Kaspar Hauser has continued to captivate the public imagination and has inspired many works of fiction, including plays, novels, poems and a film by director Werner Herzog. However, the exact details of Hauser's life have never been determined. Despite extensive investigations, including the use of forensic DNA technology, no one has been able to determine who he was or where he came from. Some believe he was a member of a noble family who had been kidnapped as a child and held captive, while others suspect he was simply a liar or a madman who fabricated the entire story.

CHAPTER 3

Jerome, the Legless Man of Sandy Cove

The enigma of Jerome of Sandy Cove ranks as one of the oldest and most compelling unresolved mysteries in the annals of Canadian history. I was not aware of this story during the time I lived in Nova Scotia and only learned of it more recently.

In the 1860s, Sandy Cove was a small community on Digby Neck focused mainly on fishing but with a smattering of farms. Digby Neck is a thin peninsula 45 kilometres (28 miles) long but only 5 kilometres (3 miles) wide, located in the Bay of Fundy in Digby County, Nova Scotia, extending from the North Mountain range, which emerges from the Annapolis Valley and consists of two thick lava flows. The peninsula is separated from the eastern portion of the North Mountain by a deep tidal channel known as the Digby Gut. Alongside Long Island and Brier Island, Digby Neck forms the northwest shore of St. Mary's Bay.

Sandy Cove, 27 kilometres (17 miles) from the town of Digby, is known for its scenic beauty, beaches and coastal cliffs that mark the region. The picturesque setting and quiet atmosphere make it a pleasant location for visitors looking to enjoy the natural beauty of the Bay of Fundy.

Just after sunrise on the morning of September 8, 1863, George Colin (Collie) Albright, 8, and his 10-year-old brother William saw something they believed at first to be driftwood left by the tide or maybe a seal. On closer investigation, the boys determined they were looking at the body of a man lying near the beach's high-water mark. At first, they assumed the person, who lay still and had a pallid complexion, was dead. Earlier misidentification and this presumption could have come from the fact that the man was missing both legs.

The boys thought he might have been a victim of a shipwreck caused by recent stormy weather or a fisherman thrown overboard in rough seas. They poked at the body with a stick, and they were shocked when the man moaned weakly.

Startled, the Albright boys ran for adult help. Their father, Colin Albright Sr., the first adult they approached, thought the boys were lying and shooed them away. After that, they split up. William went to find their paternal grandmother, and Collie ran toward two local farmers named Bishop and Eldridge.

After some convincing, all three adults agreed to attend, if only to humour the boys, adamant about what they had seen. It was Grandma Albright and William who arrived first. When she saw the blue-eyed, blond-haired legless young man in his late teens, she scrambled up the beach toward her son Colin's house to get assistance for the stranger.

When the adults, Bishop, Eldridge and Colin Albright Sr., approached the stranger with the boys following, he was spooked. Even in his disabled state, he tried to escape, dragging himself toward the water. It wasn't clear where he planned to go. The young man did not respond verbally to calls to stop and assurances that the men meant no harm. Possibly driven initially by a burst of adrenalin, he soon tired and could not continue his flight.

When they caught up to him, the young farmers and Mr. Albright signalled to the man that he had nothing to fear, and he seemed to understand, responding only with unintelligible grunts. Exhausted, the stranger collapsed into the arms of Eldridge and Bishop, who then carried him first to the Albright home.

The young man's condition was alarming. He was cold, wet, suffering from exposure and coughing incessantly. Considering his state, he may not have survived if he had lain out in the weather much longer. Upon closer examination, it was found that both his legs had been amputated above the knees. The wounds appeared professionally treated and relatively fresh, indicating the procedure had been performed not long before his discovery. Blood still seeped from bandages covering the stumps. However, the circumstances leading to this amputation were unclear.

There had been no word of any men missing from boats in the region. However, several residents later recalled seeing an unfamiliar vessel off the coast of Digby Neck in St. Mary's Bay the previous evening. Unlike any other previously observed in the area, this unique ship drew the locals' curiosity because it dropped anchor not far from the shore. Even though no one disembarked, and the community kept a close watch on the mysterious ship into the night, its purpose for being there remained a mystery. When dawn arrived, the ship had disappeared. Perhaps someone had rowed ashore and dropped off the stranger in the dark of night, but why? Since the man's legs had been amputated, it was inconceivable to understand the rationale behind such a barbaric act.

The man was stripped of his drenched clothing, which appeared to be of finer quality and perhaps belonged to a naval officer of some unknown country. His body bore no tattoos or other identifying marks. His pockets were empty save for a small water flask and a hunk of bread. He carried no identifying documents.

When the local Baptist priest and doctor came that evening, they found the stranger sullen and agitated. The doctor concurred with the previous assessment that the man's amputations had been recently professionally dressed by a skilled medic. The reasons for the double amputation were not apparent. The doctor considered a few options known to require such serious intervention, including accidents, frostbite, wounds resulting from battle or a response to gangrene or some other infection that threatened the patient's life.

Over the next few days, the man became a subject of discussion and curiosity in the village, and many locals visited to get a look at him as he recuperated on a cot near the warmth of the Albrights' fireplace. Some of the villagers who spoke other languages attempted to communicate with him—as well as English and French, they tried speaking to him in Spanish, Italian, Gaelic, German and Latin. The man responded only with frustrated grunts or bewildered looks. He spoke a few words, but not in a language that any of the villagers understood.

The moody stranger's silence led the villagers toward fantastic speculations regarding his origins. Was he someone of noble birth, perhaps an illegitimate heir to an unknown regent considered a threat to an official bloodline? The remote shores of Nova Scotia in Victorian times were, perhaps, an attractive place to be rid of a person deemed problematic. Another consideration was the possibility the man was a criminal of some kind, maybe even a murderer, left to fend for himself as his sentence for an offence. There were also speculations that he may have been a crew member of a pirate vessel, who, after his injuries, became a burden to the rest of his crewmates and was cruelly left behind. Some even proposed he might have been an unfortunate victim of the American Civil War, surreptitiously sent north to escape conscription or as punishment for desertion.

Caring for the man soon became a hardship for the Albright family, who were not well off. After several weeks, locals noted that the Albrights could no longer afford to feed and clothe him, so another, more prosperous farming family in nearby Mink Cove with the surname Gidney volunteered to take over his care. Even in the Gidney home's more comfortable surroundings, the stranger continued his silence, mostly unresponsive to questions or invitations to verbal communication.

In 1864, he was moved again to another family before being shipped to the family home of a man in Meteghan, Jean Nicola, also known as "the Russian." He was actually Corsican, speaking French and Italian.

There were more attempts to engage the young man in conversation in multiple languages and dialects, but he remained almost entirely mute, offering only frustrated grunts or emitting a sound resembling "Jerome" when asked his name. This is how he gained the moniker by which people knew him, but whether he was saying this or a similar-sounding word in a language other than English is unclear. He exhibited signs that he understood French and English but seemed unable to read any material given to him or to write in any way. His other mumblings were indecipherable, and as his native language was unknown, they could have meant many different things.

Most of the time, Jerome seemed sullen and grumpy. He often avoided interacting with the family, taking his meals alone.

Jerome had exceptional upper body strength and moved about bumping along on his bottom, using his arms to swing his body forward. As his amputations healed, he learned to walk using his stumps alone.

Jerome stayed with the Nicola family for the next seven years. Because of his disabilities, the Nova Scotia government voted to provide Jerome with a weekly stipend of two dollars to help pay his keep.

Following his wife's passing, Jean Nicola relocated back to Europe, leading Jerome to move in with Dedier and Zabeth Comeau in Saint Alphonse de Clare, close to Meteghan. This would be his final place of lodging. Over the years, the Comeau family, especially Zabeth, provided Jerome care by offering him shelter, food, clothing and medical attention. Gradually, even with his reticence and detachment, Jerome integrated into the family, witnessing the growth and development of the Comeau children.

According to a *Nanaimo Free Press* article on September 28, 1905, a visitor described Jerome. To summarize:

He presented an image of age and wisdom, with his white hair neatly swept back from a prominent, thoughtful brow. His facial hair consisted of a neatly trimmed white moustache and a pointed beard in a style seen mainly in France, accentuating his mature appearance. His demeanour exuded a sense of sophistication, intellect and a palpable sensitivity that rendered it challenging for onlookers to merely view him as an object of pity due to his plight.

Jerome had chosen not to leave his room for over 15 years. He spent his days seated by the stove, breaking the routine with only a short rest after his midday meal. At night, he could occasionally be heard muttering to himself. However, his acute awareness of sound allowed him to detect the slightest footsteps of someone approaching, causing him to cease speaking.

During his 37-year tenure in that household, he had not engaged in conversation with anyone, including the household members, although it's believed he comprehended everything spoken to him.

A theological student related to the family noted that four decades of silence had likely erased most aspects of his identity.

"You can see that he is a man of intelligence and refinement beyond the average," said the young student, "and whatever is the cause of his silence, it is not likely that it is inability to communicate himself. He would have learned our language before this. He is silent because he wishes to be silent, and no one can break down a will such as his."

The mystery man spent approximately 49 years under the care of Nova Scotians, remaining a reticent and enigmatic figure until his passing on April 15, 1912. Despite the enduring curiosity of the local population and subsequent investigations by historians and genealogists, Jerome's true identity and story have remained entirely elusive until recently.

Historian and folklorist Lise Robichaud's 2022 interview with SaltWire news revealed her research into the link between Jerome, whom she became aware of in her teens, and another figure named "Gamby." Collaborating with researcher Caroline-Isabelle Caron and supported by the University of Victoria, Robichaud found similarities suggesting that Gamby might be Jerome.

According to her research, a man was found in Chipman, New Brunswick, in 1859 with severe frostbite, which led to his mental and physical deterioration and the eventual amputation of his legs in 1861.

The decision to transport him from New Brunswick to Nova Scotia was made when his care became too burdensome for the Chipman residents. This research raises questions about Jerome's and Gamby's origins, their identities and whether they were the same individual or two different people discarded in Atlantic Canada within five years.

Jerome's resting place in the Meteghan region can still be visited today, marked by a humble gravestone bearing only the name "Jerome." I'll visit him the next time I go home.

CHAPTER 4

The Mysterious Brother XII
and His Missing Treasure

I have lived in British Columbia for more than 30 years and have taken an interest in the region's legends, folklore and history. One of the most compelling stories encompasses several of my favourite elements. The story of Brother XII has crime, intrigue, a religious cult—complete with a charismatic leader—and a rich treasure yet to be found.

Between 1791 and 1795, British Royal Navy officer Captain George Vancouver undertook a significant expedition to explore and chart North America's northwestern Pacific Coast regions. This included present-day Alaska, Washington, Oregon and British Columbia. His work was meticulous, leading to the first comprehensive maps of the region, particularly of the intricate waters of Puget Sound. Besides mapping, he also engaged diplomatically with Indigenous communities and Spanish explorers in the area. Despite the expedition's hardships, Vancouver's charts proved foundational for later Pacific Northwest explorations and settlements.

In 1792, in what is now called the Strait of Georgia, between Vancouver Island and the mainland of British Columbia, Captain Vancouver made his first sightings of a vast archipelago of 200 diverse islands called the Gulf Islands, a part of the traditional territory of several Coast Salish peoples. The distance from Saturna Island, at the southeastern end of the archipelago, to Quadra Island, at the northwestern end, is approximately 200 kilometres (about 125 miles) if travelling by water.

The main islands, including Salt Spring, Galiano, Mayne, Pender, Saturna and Gabriola, each offer unique landscapes, and the region is rich in biodiversity, including arbutus and Garry oak forests, rare wildflowers and various marine species.

One of the smaller islands in the Gulf Islands archipelago is De Courcy Island, nestled between Valdez, Mudge and Ruxton Islands and covering an area of around 185 hectares (460 acres). Situated in the Northumberland Channel off the east coast of central Vancouver Island, De Courcy Island received its name from Michael De Courcy, who served as the captain of the HMS *Pylades* while mapping these waters from 1859 to 1861.

Historically home to the Coast Salish Indigenous peoples, the Gulf Islands are accessible by BC Ferries, private boats, float planes and some small airlines. The islands are culturally vibrant, showcasing local arts, crafts, organic farming and wineries; lifestyles on the islands range from luxurious to rustic.

In addition to its natural attractions, De Courcy Island holds a unique place in Canadian history. In the late 1920s and early 1930s, it was home to a controversial cult, the Aquarian Foundation, led by Brother XII. Some considered Brother XII a true mystical prophet like Cagliostro or Paracelsus, but others say he was "downright evil."

Brother XII was born Edward Arthur Wilson in Birmingham, England, on July 25, 1878. His parents, Thomas Wilson and Sarah Ellen Pearsall, were pillars of their community, and his father was a prominent figure in Birmingham's flourishing metal and brass bedstead industry. He eventually established his own manufacturing company, which brought prosperity to the family. They resided in the district of Ladywood before moving to Edgbaston, where Wilson and his two sisters were brought up in a household characterized by strict religious adherence.

The Wilson family were dedicated followers of the Catholic Apostolic Church, also known as Irvingites. The Irvingites were named after a Scottish preacher named Edward Irving. Although followers did not favour the term *Irvingites*—they considered him to be more a forerunner than a founder—Irving's charismatic preaching and unique theological beliefs marked the movement. Initially a successful clergyman in the Church of Scotland, Irving's doctrine diverged when he claimed he possessed spiritual gifts, including speaking in tongues, foreseeing prophecies and healing (his powers supposedly extended to raising the dead).

The Irvingites firmly believed in the physical existence of angels as a crucial part of their religious doctrine and spiritual practices. In their theology, angels weren't simply spiritual beings but could appear in the physical realm, serving as crucial connectors between the divine and human worlds. Although many Christian denominations regard angels as heavenly messengers and servants, the Irvingites emphasized angelic interactions and manifestations in the physical world more significantly.

The church was governed by 12 apostles who were believed to have been appointed by God. Each local church was headed by a bishop, also called an angel or pastor, assisted by 24 priests and seven deacons.

So young Edward Wilson's childhood was filled with a healthy dose of apocalyptic religious fervour, with individuals considered divine beings in the flesh at the top of the heap in their church. According to Brother XII's own account, he claimed to have had encounters with "super-physical" entities and highly developed beings from his early childhood. These visitations provided him with assistance, comfort and instruction. Initially, he believed these beings to be angels, but as he grew older and received teachings, he learned about the existence of "the Masters" and their work for humanity.

Wilson claimed that the Masters were enlightened beings or ascended masters such as Jesus, Confucius and Gautama Buddha. Brother XII said these entities provided him with spiritual guidance and esoteric wisdom. He said the Masters were part of the Great White Brotherhood, a theosophical concept referring to spiritually advanced beings who secretly guide the evolution of life on Earth.

Because of the lack of support for such blasphemous experiences in his home environment, Brother XII kept his contact with these entities to himself, and his communication with them continued intermittently throughout his life. It wasn't until later that he claimed to understand the purpose behind these experiences and the teachings they conveyed.

In his early adulthood, Wilson found employment as a sailor, which became a significant source of income for him. His affinity for the sea was evident from a young age, as he learned to sail on a Royal Navy windjammer training ship during his boyhood. In 1902, while in port in Wellington, New Zealand, he met Margery Clark, whom he married that Christmas Eve at Wellington's Catholic Apostolic Church on Webb Street.

The couple soon started a family with the birth of their two children, a son and a daughter. To support his growing family, Wilson took on various roles around Wellington. He worked as a draftsman, surveyor and electrician and even tried his hand at farming.

In 1907, craving further adventures, the Wilson family relocated to Victoria, British Columbia, where Edward initially worked as a baggage clerk for the Dominion Express Company.

Although he was upwardly mobile in his career at the company, the sea continued to sing to him and eventually beckoned Wilson once more. He quit his landlocked job and embarked on a new venture as a pilot on lumber schooners, sailing between San Francisco and Alaska. Victoria served as an ideal home, even though his work often kept him away at sea for weeks at a time.

Although he loved his family, he felt an inner calling toward a higher purpose. He never truly felt settled in his domestic life, sensing that something more awaited him. In 1912, Wilson chose to leave his wife and children behind and set off on a voyage to the Orient. This abandonment left his family in a challenging financial situation. Margery was unable to make ends meet in Canada. Eventually, with the support of relatives, Wilson's wife and children managed to return to New Zealand.

According to his writings, Wilson underwent what he called a "Ceremony of Dedication" at some point that year. What the ceremony actually consisted of has never been explained. Whether Wilson was involved in a physical occult ritual or the entire affair took place internally, in his own mind, is unknown. However, it appears he experienced a spiritual awakening of sorts.

According to Wilson, he suddenly understood that he had a purpose to fulfill, although he was unaware of the specifics regarding its nature or timing. Following this realization, he embarked on 12 years of experimentation and wandered across different parts of the world. Despite facing outward failure in his endeavours, Wilson believed that an inner preparation process was quietly unfolding within him. These years of exploration, and his apparent lack of success, were integral to his personal and spiritual development.

During his travels, Wilson sailed around Cape Horn and explored the coasts of Africa, South America and various Pacific islands. He also served as a navigator in the First World War. His journeys took him to Egypt, India, China and Mexico, where he explored temples, shrines and other sacred sites. His travels allowed him to delve into the world's religions and investigate various occult doctrines. After reading some of Helena Petrovna Blavatsky's writings, Wilson joined the American branch of the Theosophical Society, co-founded by the Russian mystic.

Known more commonly as Madame Blavatsky, Helena is a fascinating character in her own right. In the summer of 2022, while in Cambridge, UK, I went to the Cambridge University Library, where my friends, who worked at the university, aided me in sorting through some letters by Blavatsky's contemporaries and other related writings held there as part of the archives belonging to the Society for Psychical Research, of which I am a member.

H. P. Blavatsky (1831–1891) was a Russian author and occultist influential in the New Age movement. She wrote extensively about her spiritualist philosophy in works like *The Secret Doctrine* and *Isis Unveiled*. Born into an aristocratic Russian-German family, she claimed to have studied esoteric wisdom with masters in Tibet and other parts of the world. After moving to New York City in 1873, she met Henry Steel Olcott, and together they established the Theosophical Society in 1875.

The society aimed to promote a universal brotherhood of humanity; explore ancient religions, philosophies and sciences; and investigate the laws of nature and the divine powers in humans. Madame Blavatsky is often recognized for bringing Eastern and esoteric ideas to the West. However, her life and work have been controversial, with accusations of fraud and plagiarism levelled against her. Despite these controversies, her impact on spiritual and philosophical movements remains significant.

At the outset, at least, E.A. Wilson's philosophies owe much to Madame Blavatsky and the theosophists.

According to the website theosophy.org, theosophy is a philosophical doctrine that delves into the potential of human beings and seeks to answer fundamental existential questions. This body of knowledge, also known as the Ancient Wisdom, the perennial philosophy or the wisdom tradition, aims to help individuals transcend the constraints of ordinary life and attain enhanced happiness, wisdom and peace. The goal of theosophy, a term derived from the Greek for "divine wisdom," is to offer insight into human existence and the nature of the world. While aligning itself with many scientific theories, theosophy extends beyond them to discuss unseen realities, as well as puzzling experiences and unusual phenomena. It addresses essential questions, including the purpose of existence, the concept of a higher power, the presence of evil and injustice in the world, and the quest for a purposeful and meaningful life.

In southern France on the evening of October 19, 1924, Wilson had the first of a series of spiritual epiphanies over three days. The first he called "the Vision."

He was in bed, feeling unwell, and had just lit a candle to get some milk. Upon lighting the candle, he saw the symbol of tau (an Egyptian cross) floating in mid-air at the end of his bed, around 2.5 metres (8 feet) high. He closed his eyes, thinking it was an illusion caused by the sudden light of the match he'd struck. But when he opened his eyes, the tau symbol was even more distinct and glowed like a soft, golden fire. He also noticed a five-pointed star slightly above and to the right of the tau.

Closing and opening his eyes did not change the vision, which seemed to radiate fire before gradually dimming and fading from his sight. Wilson interpreted the tau as a confirmation of his path to spiritual initiation via the Egyptian tradition, while the star symbolized his striving toward becoming a spiritual adept.

The next day, Wilson claimed that his spiritual guide had provided him with "the Password." His guide suggested that the tau and the star represented the ancient mysteries of Egypt, which were about to be resurrected. Wilson was told he was tasked with preparing for the restoration of these mysteries to the world. The message, Brother XII claimed, coincided with the astrological shift from the Piscean age to the Aquarian age, marking a new era of enlightenment.

Two days later, again in bed and feeling unwell, Wilson was addressed by a divine voice, ringing loud and clear in the silent darkness of his bedroom. The words echoed the same significance as the vision he had experienced—the star of the mysteries was about to rise again, shedding light on the darkness of the modern world. He called this experience "the Voice." His bed shook, a cool wind blew, and Wilson saw before him what he called "an immense vista of Time, a roofless corridor flanked with thousands and thousands of pillars. I seemed to be looking into both Time and Space at once."

Wilson was compelled to write down what he'd just heard as the voice subsided. The words, from what he perceived to be his Master, had come from somewhere far away, and the voice said:

Thou who has worn the double crown of upper and lower Egypt, of the high knowledge and the low; humble thyself. Prepare thy heart, for the mighty ones have need of thee. Thou shalt re-build, thou shalt restore. Therefore, prepare thy mind for that which shall illumine thee.

He began calling himself Brother XII after the Voice, which told Wilson it was "the Brother of the Twelfth Degree." Theosophists believed it was part of a spiritual assembly called "the Great White Brotherhood," who were a group of beings that acted as guardians of humanity's spiritual and evolutionary journey.

Brother XII embraced three fundamental truths from theosophist Mabel Collins's 1924 book *The Idyll of the White Lotus*. First, that the human soul is immortal and its future is limitless in growth and splendour; second, that the principle that gives life is omnipresent, undying, eternally beneficent and perceivable by those who seek understanding; and third, each person is their own ultimate arbiter, bestowing either glory or gloom upon themselves and determining their life's path. He concluded that these profound truths are as essential as life itself and as uncomplicated as the human mind. In the conclusion of her book, Collins encouraged her readers to share these truths widely.

Brother XII added his own thoughts in a booklet called "The Three Truths: A Simple Statement of the Fundamental Philosophy of Life." He then penned a manifesto entitled "A Message from the Masters of the Wisdom." In this compelling document, he expounded upon the extraordinary work being carried out by the Great White Brotherhood and their divine mission to guide humanity. Within the manifesto, Wilson passionately expressed his commitment to constructing an "Ark of Refuge," which would be a sacred sanctuary where individuals could seek solace and spiritual enlightenment and prepare themselves for the imminent "Age of Aquarius," a prophesied period of great spiritual awakening and transformation.

Wilson's writings reflected his deep understanding of theosophical principles, his dedication to the Masters' teachings and his fervent belief in the importance of spiritual refuge and preparation for the approaching era. Through these works, he aimed to inspire others to embark on a profound journey of self-discovery, enlightenment and spiritual growth. He believed he was on a mission and began collecting followers, who were mostly theosophists in the early days.

On April 27, 1926, Brother XII reported receiving a divine message known as the Invocation of Light, which he said came to him through time from the era of the renowned pharaoh Akhenaten. He guided his followers to say a prayer twice a day to a being he described as the source of dawn and eternal light, to ask for more wisdom, power and a deeper connection with the mysterious light.

The invocation required significant dedication to recite regularly, and not everyone would be willing or able to commit to such a routine. Some of his followers found it challenging to memorize, and regularly chant, the invocation amid their daily schedules.

Brother XII also strongly believed that a mystical emissary would arrive on Earth in 1975 (or possibly be born in 1975) to bring about positive changes in the world.

Wilson referred to the period around 1975 and the expected arrival of this envoy as "a ship of refuge," a term he discussed openly with anyone willing to engage in conversation. He wrote about this in his essay "A Message from the Masters of the Wisdom."

Brother XII believed he was destined to create a spiritual movement named the Aquarian Foundation, which would be a hub for spiritual energy and knowledge for the entire world in the foreseeable future. The chosen location for this spiritual centre was Cedar-by-the-Sea, a small community about 8 kilometres (5 miles) southeast of Nanaimo and, as previously mentioned, eventually De Courcy Island, just off the coast.

In 1927, Brother XII did actually found the Aquarian Foundation. The intent of the organization was to create a haven for individuals seeking spiritual enlightenment and a deeper understanding of theosophical teachings. The foundation aimed to cultivate a community living in unity and harmony with nature, drawing upon the wisdom of the Great White Brotherhood.

On July 25, 1927, Brother XII celebrated his 49th birthday by holding the first general meeting of the rapidly growing Aquarian Foundation, which was attended by numerous followers and sponsors. The foundation continued to expand as people were drawn to Brother XII's promise of true liberation. The group ran ads in magazines, like *The Occult Review*, published by Rider and Co. out of London. For a fee, those responding to the ad were sent several of Brother XII's writings, including "The Three Truths," "Foundation Letters and Teachings" and the Aquarian Foundation booklet, along with other pamphlets and articles and a biannual newsletter.

Living with Brother XII and his followers at Cedar-by-the-Sea was not required to become a member. However, prospective members had to commit to sending a monthly financial contribution to the Aquarian Foundation's post office box in Nanaimo, British Columbia, after which they would receive membership in Brother XII's group.

Many individuals were prepared to make more significant sacrifices, relocating to join Brother XII. Whole families from across the United States and Canada, including those with multiple children, uprooted their lives and relinquished all their possessions to Brother XII, believing they contributed to the overall community's betterment. Brother XII, however, was holding the funds, converting them to gold coins. While it might be frustrating to hear about people giving up everything to follow a questionable leader, it's important to remember that these followers were manipulated victims.

Brother XII was not entirely truthful in his narratives, falsely claiming he was the child of an Indian princess and that he had never been to British Columbia before, suggesting that spiritual entities had guided him there. Yet as we know, he had resided in Victoria in the early 1920s.

In an intriguing development, Brother XII, with the support of his followers and key members of the Ku Klux Klan in the United States, formed a third party to challenge the Republicans and Democrats in the US election in 1928. They backed a notorious racist senator from Alabama, James Thomas Heflin. Despite their efforts, Herbert Hoover won the election, with Heflin failing to secure a single Electoral College vote. While the candidate may have lost, Brother XII's involvement in the election reveals that his influence beyond his own community was significant.

However, Brother XII's support for Heflin contradicted his previous statements against judging race or gender, revealing significant discrepancies in his professed ideals. Unfazed by the election outcome, Brother XII continued his travels across North America, seeking new members for his spiritual community, primarily among the wealthy. He convinced many that an unseen empire of malevolence was causing distress and misery worldwide, and that only by following him could they escape this evil.

Brother XII often identified the Jewish community and the Roman Catholic Church as critical participants in the supposed evil empire, adding to the long history of victimization of Jewish people. According to John Oliphant's book *Brother XII*, Brother XII's disciples believed that as a member of the Great White Lodge, their leader had the power to leave his physical body at will, travel in his spirit body anywhere in the world, penetrate locked rooms, overhear secret discussions, read sealed documents and wield potent occult forces against the "brothers of shadow," or the Black Adepts, who were allegedly leading humanity astray. These beliefs bear a resemblance to the modern conspiracy concepts of the Illuminati or New World Order.

These assertions about his supernatural powers were really manipulative strategies to gain control of his followers, to make them believe he was all-seeing and omnipresent and thus capable of detecting any deviation from the group's core beliefs or his commands.

It's important to note that anyone can fall victim to such a scam, especially those who are seeking knowledge or guidance in their lives. There's not necessarily a specific type of individual who falls prey to this kind of manipulation. Sometimes, just being in the wrong place at the wrong time or feeling lonely and lost is enough for someone to fall victim to a conniving figure.

With the devastating experiences of the First World War fresh in their minds, and after witnessing the excesses of the 1920s, many conservative people feared society was facing moral decay. Capitalizing on these sentiments, Brother XII warned that humanity was heading toward a horrifying conflict, possibly another world war, a battle between the forces of darkness and light, which he called Armageddon. Apocalyptic predictions are a common theme in many religions and cults. Followers are often told that the end of days is imminent and that they will be saved by adhering to the group's doctrine.

Before relocating to De Courcy Island for more isolation, Brother XII resided in what he termed "the house of mystery," perched on a cliff above the existing boat ramp on Nelson Road. In this house, it is believed that Brother XII began abusing his authority over his female followers. He exploited them for his sexual pleasure under the guise of engaging in spiritual endeavours. Interestingly, sexual exploitation is often another aspect of control in cults. But when Brother XII enticed a married follower from New York, Myrtle Wells Baumgartner, to share his bed, it caused a scandal and aroused the first signs of skepticism among his followers.

Brother XII tried to downplay this situation as a "personal matter," later asserting that he and Myrtle had shared a past life in ancient Egypt. He said they were soulmates and he intended to father a successor for the group with her. However, after two miscarriages and emotional distress, Myrtle departed in disgrace, and her husband eventually secured a divorce on the grounds of adultery.

In the meantime, the leaders within the organization began to worry that Brother XII was losing his grip. Some speculated that the Black Adepts had overpowered Brother XII's vessel, compelling him to act rashly. Denying any external influence, Brother XII once again resorted to spiritual excuses to justify his actions.

Some of those opposing Brother XII decided to take legal action to seize control of the foundation and its funds. Even though he deposited some of the money in local banks, a large portion, primarily gold, had been concealed, and the location was known only to him.

In 1929, Brother XII and a faction of his followers split from the main group. At the same time, he obtained a significant donation that enabled him to buy property on De Courcy Island. This is where he felt he and his faithful disciples could reside without the influence of non-believers.

Brother XII continued to amass considerable wealth through donations. A wealthy *Mayflower* family heiress donated at least $25,000 after just a three-hour meeting with him, while the so-called poultry king of Florida, Roger Painter, gave Brother XII $90,000 after visiting Cedar-by-the-Sea. This was in addition to numerous other significant donations from followers. Although only a small group of devotees, numbering in the dozens, journeyed to British Columbia, financial contributions for the De Courcy settlement that Brother XII's followers called their Ark of Refuge poured in from more than 8,000 backers scattered across the world.

Those who chose to live in the colony were expected to cut all ties with their previous lives and convert all their possessions into gold coins, which they surrendered upon arrival at Brother XII's centre. Brother XII stored these contributions in sealed mason jars inside wooden chests. He defended this practice by claiming that true discipleship required complete self-dedication and the surrender of all personal possessions. This served as both a safeguard and a test of commitment, another tactic to exert control over his followers by making them entirely dependent on him.

The demand to surrender personal possessions is a major red flag in any spiritual or religious group. If someone asks you to sacrifice all your worldly belongings for your so-called spiritual well-being, it's safe to assume they're conducting a dubious operation and do not have your best interests at heart.

In a quest for further control, Brother XII assigned the formerly high-ranking members of society menial tasks such as cooking, washing dishes, cleaning floors, chopping wood and farming. These tasks were executed under the direction of Brother XII and his new partner, a stern English woman named Mabel Skottowe, referred to by the group as Madame Zed. Any grumbles about the demanding tasks were met with Brother XII's assertion that these were merely tests, and they would later reap the rewards upon passing the seemingly never-ending initiation.

Madame Zed ruled over the group on De Courcy Island with strict control, keeping Brother XII informed of any gossip or potential disloyalty within the group. Troublemakers were sent back to Cedar-by-the-Sea. Madame Zed also catered to Brother XII's sexual needs and gave him time to write and work on other projects around the compound. During this period, followers began to flee the compound. Even the most devoted adherents began to drift back to Vancouver Island, and many abandoned the organization altogether.

In 1930, Brother XII performed a non–legally binding ceremony declaring he and Madame Zed married. They then departed for England, spending most of the year abroad. Upon his return, Brother XII revealed a new plan for the colony, which entailed more work for everyone. Failure to comply, he warned, would lead to expulsion and a loss of salvation.

Brother XII soon grew more paranoid, suspecting even the most loyal followers of betrayal. He became increasingly ruthless in response to perceived threats to his power. When the police were called after someone alleged that a girl had been kidnapped, Brother XII insisted the group acquire rifles and ammunition to defend against future threats to the group's liberty.

As people started to leave the island and new recruits dried up, those who remained were forced to work from two in the morning until 10 at night. Even injuries were viewed as a hindrance, with group members compelled to continue working regardless of pain or bleeding. One follower described this time as a "Brotherhood of hell" rather than the promised "Brotherhood of love."

Under Brother XII's orders, strangers who dared to set foot on the island were intimidated and driven away. In 1932, things came to a climax. After an incident involving the maltreatment of Sarah Puckett, a 78-year-old retired schoolteacher who was told to drown herself by Madame Zed, the remaining senior members of his entourage sent a letter to Brother XII announcing they were done with him. They declared their independence and called for a meeting to end his now despotic reign once and for all.

Instead of addressing the dissent, Brother XII ran off the detractors, forcing them back to Cedar-by-the-Sea in his dilapidated tugboat. The abandoned group formed a coalition to continue their commune without their leader. Fearing Brother XII might be spying on them, the group sought legal assistance, demanded their money back and sued him. The followers were still in thrall to Brother XII, and some believed he was psychically attacking them. One man even alleged that Brother XII had temporarily paralyzed him using his mental powers.

In court, Roger Painter explained how Brother XII controlled people through fear and intimidation. He also claimed that Brother XII could kill someone with his mind. While the former followers began winning their court cases, their efforts were ultimately futile, as Madame Zed and Brother XII disappeared along with some of the wealth.

Brother XII sank his precious sailboat and demolished the De Courcy compound before he fled to England. Records suggest he died in Europe, but some speculate he faked his death after it was noticed that his death certificate was signed by a follower who happened to be a doctor.

While some structures from that period remain on the De Courcy property, Brother XII's enormous gold stash has never been accounted for. It's believed that Brother XII and Madame Zed fled with minimal baggage, suggesting there's still gold to be discovered. Followers reported that Brother XII would often venture alone into the forest, possibly to bury gold in as-yet undiscovered spots around the island.

Some believe a large cache might still be awaiting discovery. For years, treasure hunters have rummaged through De Courcy and other areas around Nanaimo in search of jars allegedly filled with gold collected from supporters and followers and secreted away by Brother XII. The 40 cases of $20 gold coins, each weighing roughly an ounce, were valued at $500,000 in 1932, a staggering amount. Given today's gold price of approximately $2,000 per ounce, the unfound treasure would be worth nearly $40 million today.

But people can't go digging around anymore since most of the island is now privately owned. From 1943 to 1957, it was under the stewardship of a Swiss sibling duo, Paul and Anna Wyff. They cultivated the island with a handful of others, leading a modest, self-reliant life based on communal farming. De Courcy Island Estates acquired the land in 1965 and split it into roughly 160 parcels. De Courcy currently boasts about 40 homes primarily used as weekend getaways or summer residences.

CHAPTER 5

Giants, a.k.a. the Exceptionally Tall: Myths and Reality

Being a little shorter than average, I have always wondered what it would be like to tower over my peers. As a result, I have always had a fascination with giants.

The word *giant* often evokes memories of childhood fiction, folk-lore and fables. Across generations, cultures and continents, giants have played a part in tales and legends. They are symbolic characters embodying various aspects of humanity, such as power, ambition and struggle, that also impart moral lessons in the stories in which they appear.

In fairy tales, giants spark a mix of fear and intrigue among readers. In "Jack and the Beanstalk" and Charles Perrault's "Little Thumb," giants symbolize malevolent forces. These narratives often depict the triumph of minor yet intelligent characters over the large and brutish antagonists, underscoring the virtues of wit and bravery.

One of the most well-known stories involving a human and a giant is the Biblical tale of David and Goliath. This is a classic underdog story, powerfully showcasing the triumph of faith and courage over raw strength and intimidation. Goliath, the giant Philistine warrior, symbolizes immense strength and power and is a seemingly unbeatable adversary. However, David, a simple shepherd boy armed only with a slingshot and unwavering faith, dares to confront Goliath, eventually defeating him in an unexpected victory.

Goliath is not the only giant mentioned in the Bible. The Nephilim are giant beings in the books of Genesis and Numbers and are an enigmatic part of the Biblical narrative. According to Genesis 6:4, the Nephilim are the offspring of the "sons of God" and human women. The interpretation of "sons of God" in this reference is controversial among scholars, with some suggesting that the Nephilim might be fallen angels, similar to the demigods in Greek mythology.

The Bible describes Nephilim as formidable and awe-inspiring entities capable of invoking fear and respect from others. They were renowned as heroes, suggesting they wielded substantial influence and were potentially revered or admired. The ultimate destiny of the Nephilim remains ambiguous owing to a lack of clarity in Biblical texts. Did the great Flood eradicate them? Or did they continue to exist? The story of the Nephilim continues to be an intriguing and mysterious aspect of Biblical mythology.

Numerous cultures worldwide have fascinating stories of giants as a part of their mythologies and history. In Norse mythology, the Jötunn live in a place called Jötunheim. They are known for their strength and connection with the natural world. Although often shown as huge, scary monsters, the Jötunn were also considered wise and devious. Interestingly, the stories of the Jötunn intersect with stories of the Norse gods. Some gods, like Loki, are Jötunns. The Jötunn are an essential part of Norse mythology, representing the wild, chaotic side of the universe, while the gods represent order.

Bulgarian mythology also incorporates the concept of giants through the stories of the Ispolini, a name derived from the Bulgarian word for *giant*. The Ispolini are represented in vast stone figures in Bulgaria's Rhodope Mountains.

Bulgarian legend says that before humans existed, there were the Ispolini, giant beings who lived on rugged mountain peaks, ate a diet of raw meat and often found themselves in epic fights with dragons. But despite their terrifying power, the Ispolini were scared of blackberries. They thought the vines were dangerous and might intentionally trip and seriously hurt them. To avoid this, they would give offerings to the blackberry plants as a sign of respect, and to keep the plants happy.

The ancient stone structures depicting the Ispolini are believed to have been carved by the Thracians, who lived in the area thousands of years ago. The Thracian people used these megaliths for unknown religious or ceremonial purposes. One of the best known of the Ispolini stone structures in the remote Bulgarian mountains can be found near Buzovgrad. This stone figure is about 7 metres (23 feet) tall, in a location sometimes referred to as "the Bulgarian Stonehenge."

The Native tribes of the Atlantic region of North America, specifically the Mi'kmaq, Maliseet, Passamaquoddy, Penobscot and Abenaki, have a legend about a giant named Glooscap. This giant is said to have made the world into a place where humans could live. In these ancient stories, the Earth was initially just a big ball of water. The Sky-world was home to many magical beings, including twin brothers—Glooscap, who represented goodness, and Malsum, who represented evil. These beings came to Earth in a massive stone canoe that turned into the land now known as Cape Breton. Glooscap created all the birds and animals from the soil and conquered Malsum to control the Earth.

After this, Glooscap began to create humans. From four arrows shot into four different white ash trees, the Passamaquoddy, Penobscot, Maliseet and Mi'kmaq tribes were born. He taught these new beings about food, telling them what to gather and eat. When it was time for him to leave Earth, Glooscap gave a final message before heading off toward the sunset. He told his people they could find him if they kept looking.

A fascinating collection of stories and legends in Chile and South America also includes giants. The Mapuche people, who are native to the area, tell stories of a creature named Peuchen. This creature is scary because it can change its form into different animals. One of the forms it takes is a gigantic flying snake that can paralyze its victims just by looking at them. If there's a Peuchen around, you'll need a *machi*, a witch doctor, to get rid of it.

Antonio Pigafetta, an Italian explorer who travelled the world with the Ferdinand Magellan expedition from 1519 to 1522, wrote about meeting giants in Patagonia, a region in South America that covers parts of Argentina and Chile.

Pigafetta described meeting native people who were so tall that members of Magellan's crew only reached their waists. Pigafetta's writings are some of the earliest accounts of the Indigenous people of Patagonia, and his stories have been debated and interpreted in many ways over the years. Some people think the "giants" Pigafetta referred to were part of the Tehuelche tribe, who were taller than Europeans at the time but not as tall as Pigafetta described. The name *Patagonia* might even come from Pigafetta's stories, with *Patagón* possibly meaning "big foot" in an old Spanish dialect, but this is not certain. Pigafetta's tales about the giants of Patagonia have had a significant impact over the years, feeding into European myths about giant people living in far-off lands.

In Asia, giants are usually shown as symbols of ancient knowledge or divine power. Sometimes they're considered creators of the world, like the giant Daidarabotchi from Japanese legends, who is said to have formed mountains and rivers. The towns of Daita in Tokyo and Daitakubo in Saitama, Japan, are named after Daidarabotchi because the people there believe the giant created these communities. In the city of Ishioka, there's a famous story about Mount Tsukuba. The legend says that Daidarabotchi was comparing the weights of Mount Tsukuba and Mount Fuji when he accidentally dropped Mount Tsukuba, causing it to split in two, which is why it has two peaks today.

In real life, we also have true giants. These are people who are significantly taller than the average person. Although they might not have the magical abilities or scary traits of fairy tale giants, their stories are still pretty interesting.

In medical terms, the word *giant* doesn't have a specific height attached to it, but it's often used to describe exceptionally tall people. A person might be considered a giant if they're 213 centimetres (7 feet) or taller. For example, in North America, the average height for an adult male is about 175 centimetres (5 feet, 9 inches), while the average height for an adult female is about 163 centimetres (5 feet, 4 inches), so a person who is 7 feet tall would definitely stand out in society.

Some very tall people don't have any medical conditions that make them tall—they just naturally grow to an exceptional height. However, there are other people who grow very tall because of a medical condition called gigantism. Gigantism occurs when a person's body makes too much growth hormone during childhood or adolescence, which causes their bones to grow larger and taller than average.

In people with gigantism, the excess growth hormone leads to rapid growth of muscles, bones and connective tissues, causing them to grow abnormally tall and experience changes in their soft tissues. If not treated, people with gigantism can grow to over 244 centimetres (8 feet) tall, so it's crucial to catch this medical condition early.

Gigantism and a condition called acromegaly are both caused by too much growth hormone, but they affect people at different ages. Gigantism happens in kids and teens before their bones have finished growing, while acromegaly occurs in adults after their bones have stopped growing. Even though acromegaly doesn't cause people to grow taller, it can change the shape of their bones and the size of their organs and affect other aspects of their health. Although acromegaly is rare, gigantism is even rarer. The United States has documented about 100 cases.

People with gigantism usually grow significantly taller or larger than others their age and often have certain physical traits. For example, they might have a large forehead and jaw, wide gaps between their teeth and prominent facial features. Their hands and feet are also unusually large, and their fingers and toes may be thick.

There are also characteristics of gigantism that aren't physical. People with this condition often have large internal organs, especially the heart, and they may sweat more than average, which is known as hyperhidrosis. They might have problems with their vision, like seeing double or having trouble seeing out of the corners of their eyes, and they might get headaches or have joint pain. Other signs of gigantism can include delayed puberty, irregular periods, trouble sleeping and muscle weakness.

According to Guinness World Records, Robert Wadlow was the tallest person in history. Before he passed away at just 22 years old, he had grown to an incredible height of 272 centimetres (8 feet, 11.1 inches) and weighed 199 kilograms (439 pounds). His shoe size was a whopping US 37AA (UK size 36; EU size 75), equivalent to 47 centimetres (18.5 inches) long, meaning he had the largest feet ever recorded in a person.

Robert, or Bob as his family and friends called him, was the first of five kids born to Harold and Addie May Wadlow on February 22, 1918, in Alton, Illinois. Despite Robert's exceptional height, all his siblings—two sisters named Helen and Betty and two brothers named Eugene and Harold Jr.—were of average height and weight.

Robert was a normal-sized baby at 51 centimetres (20 inches) long and weighing 3.8 kilograms (8 pounds, 5 ounces). But it quickly became clear that Robert was not an ordinary child. By the time he was six months old, he was already as tall as the average two-year-old and weighed 14 kilograms (30 pounds). When Robert started walking at 11 months, he was over 106 centimetres (3 feet, 6 inches) tall and weighed just over 20 kilograms (45 pounds)—the size of an average five-year-old.

By the time he was in kindergarten at age five, Robert was almost 170 centimetres (5 feet, 7 inches) tall. At age eight, he had outgrown his dad, reaching a height of 183 centimetres (6 feet). In less than a year, he had grown another 6 centimetres (2.5 inches) and was strong enough to carry his father, seated in a chair, up the stairs. He needed special furniture at school and at home because of his size. Despite his height, Robert wanted to be like his friends. He even joined the Boy Scouts at age 13, with a uniform, tent and sleeping bag all tailor-made for him.

Robert's remarkable growth did cause some health issues. His extreme height and weight caused foot problems, and he visited Barnes Hospital in St. Louis, Missouri, several times. At age 14, he broke two of his foot bones while playing and needed an ankle brace.

At 17, a pad in his shoe caused an infection that required an eight-week hospital stay. Eight men were required to take him to the hospital on a specially made stretcher. Because of decreased feeling in his legs and feet, Robert had to wear leg braces but refused to use a wheelchair.

After graduating high school, Robert, then 17, was 254 centimetres (8 feet, 4 inches) tall, beating the previous record held by an Irishman who had died in 1877 and becoming the tallest person ever. In addition to being incredibly tall, he weighed 173 kilograms (382 pounds) and was still growing, as his body continued making too much growth hormone. He required a massive 8,000 calories a day, and he needed custom-made shoes, which cost $100 a pair (more than $2,000 in today's money), to fit his world's largest feet.

Robert had once said he would never join a circus, but the financial strain of the 1930s Depression led him to join the Ringling Bros. and Barnum & Bailey circus after high school. Although this job brought in money, his parents worried he was being laughed at and exploited.

When a reporter asked him how he dealt with always standing out, Robert replied, "I've gotten used to being stared at. Getting upset would only make others and myself unhappy. Some people say unkind things, but I decided a long time ago to ignore them."

Robert's family wanted him to have a more dignified job and found one with the International Shoe Company, which made his custom shoes. He became a spokesperson for their craftsmanship and toured the country, promoting the brand. With his dad, who had quit his job, Robert travelled over 485,000 kilometres (300,000 miles) and visited more than 800 towns across 41 states for the company.

Robert also used his fame for good deeds. In 1938, he helped raise money for a new pipe organ for his church. The congregation appreciated his effort and dedicated a plaque to him on the organ, which they affectionately called the Robert Wadlow organ.

Robert continued to grow for the rest of his life, but this also meant his health problems related to his growth didn't stop. In July 1940, a blister on his foot turned into a deadly infection while he was in Manistee, Michigan. Because the local hospital didn't have the right facilities, Robert had to stay in a hotel bed. Even after emergency surgery and blood transfusions, his infection didn't improve, and his temperature kept rising. Sadly, on July 15, Robert passed away in his sleep.

His body was returned to his hometown, Alton, Illinois, for the funeral. His 450-kilogram (1,000 pound) casket required 12 pallbearers and an additional eight men to carry it. To honour Robert, whom they called "the Gentle Giant," all local businesses closed during his funeral. Over 40,000 people signed the guest register. His tombstone carries a simple message: "At Rest." People remember Robert as a kind and quiet young man who bravely dealt with his unique challenges, leaving a positive impression on everyone who knew him.

In 1984, a group of citizens decided to create a lasting tribute to Robert. The next year, they put up a bronze statue of him on the Southern Illinois University School of Dental Medicine campus. After Robert died in 1940, his family destroyed most of his belongings to prevent them from becoming collectors' items or "freak" memorabilia. The few things that remain are displayed at the Alton Museum of History and Art with dignity and respect, in line with the family's wish to honour Robert's memory respectfully.

If Robert had been born today, medical advancements might have stopped his extreme growth with surgeries and medications. Given how far medicine has come, we'll probably never see someone grow to Robert's height because of a similar medical condition. His record as the tallest person is expected to stand for a very long time.

According to Guinness World Records, the tallest person alive today is Sultan Kösen. Sultan was born into a Kurdish farming family on December 10, 1982, in the city of Mardin, Turkey. He wasn't extraordinarily tall as a child, but as he got older, a tumour in his pituitary gland caused his body to produce too much growth hormone, and he started to grow very tall.

Sultan's life drastically changed when he had a significant growth spurt at age 10. By the time he was an adult, he had grown to over 244 centimetres (8 feet) tall. His rapid growth made everyday activities challenging, like walking (for which he needed crutches) and finding clothes and shoes that fit him.

Despite these challenges, Sultan manages to live a relatively normal life. He works as a farmer, caring for animals and doing general farm work. But this work is physically demanding because of his enormous height and the size of his hands and feet.

In 2009, Sultan was measured at 251 centimetres (8 feet, 2.8 inches) tall, earning him the record for being the tallest living person and having the biggest hands of any living person. Each of his hands measures 28.5 centimetres (11.2 inches) from the wrist to the tip of the middle finger.

Things got better for Sultan in 2010 when he was treated for his pituitary tumour at the University of Virginia Medical School in the United States using a surgical technique called Gamma Knife treatment. This treatment successfully stopped his growth.

Sultan married a Syrian woman named Merve Dibo in October 2013, despite a significant height difference—Merve is about two-thirds Sultan's height. They filed for divorce in 2021.

Sultan's height eventually provided him new opportunities beyond farming. He began travelling worldwide and appeared in documentaries and TV shows. On Guinness World Records Day, November 13, 2014, Sultan met the shortest man in history, Chandra Bahadur Dangi, who was only 54.6 centimetres (1 foot, 9.5 inches) tall, at an event in London. Sultan joined the Magic Circus of Samoa that same year and participated in shows worldwide. When he turned 40 on December 10, 2022, he celebrated early by visiting Ripley's Believe It or Not! Museum in Orlando, Florida. There, he stood next to a life-sized statue of Robert Wadlow.

Sultan still lives in Turkey but often travels for events and appearances. You can follow his public appearances and daily life on TikTok and Instagram. His story inspires people everywhere because it shows how diverse and resilient we can be.

The most extreme example of variation in height in a single human being is the fascinating case of Adam Rainer. Rainer, an Austrian man born in 1899, is unique because he went from extremely short to incredibly tall. During the First World War, he wasn't allowed to join the army because he was only 137 centimetres (4 feet, 6 inches) tall. Even though Adam had very large hands and feet, he wasn't quite short enough to be classified as a dwarf. However, when he was 21 years old, he started growing very rapidly for the next 10 years, reaching a height of 216 centimetres (7 feet, 1 inch). This sudden growth, caused by a tumour in his pituitary gland, resulted in severe spinal curvature. Doctors tried surgery to stop his growth but only managed to slow it down. Unfortunately, his health became worse over time. He lost sight in one eye, he lost his hearing, and his spine became so deformed that he could no longer leave his bed. When he died at 51, he was 234 centimetres (7 feet, 8 inches).

Another example of unusual height is Angus MacAskill, a true natural giant. Angus was born in Scotland in 1825 and moved to Nova Scotia, Canada, with his family when he was six. Unlike most people who are incredibly tall and suffer from poor health, Angus was very healthy. His height of 236 centimetres (7 feet, 9 inches) didn't come from any known medical condition, and it didn't hold him back in life. His size was proportional, meaning his strength matched his size, allowing him to do things that amazed people.

As a kid, Angus was much bigger than his friends and siblings, which gave him an advantage in fights and wrestling matches. But even though he was strong, he didn't like to fight. By age 14, he had nicknames like "St. Ann's Big Boy" and "Gille Mòr" (which translates to "Big Boy" in Scottish Gaelic) because of his size and occasional clumsiness.

By his early 20s, MacAskill was over 213 centimetres (7 feet) tall. But his height wasn't the only thing that made him special. His shoulders were 112 centimetres (44 inches) across, and his hands were so big that he could cup a man's head entirely. He was also incredibly strong, able to lift a ship's anchor that weighed 1,270 kilograms (2,800 pounds) to his chest and carry barrels weighing over 160 kilograms (350 pounds) under each arm.

Just like Robert Wadlow, Angus MacAskill was known as "the Gentle Giant" because he was calm and kind. He was well liked and respected in his community, where he worked as a farmer and occasional fisherman. He was always willing to use his strength to help others, like assisting in the raising of barns or clearing land, or performing heavy lifting and other tasks that would be impossible for regular-sized people.

News of MacAskill's size and strength spread beyond his community, and he was asked to tour as an attraction in P.T. Barnum's circus. He travelled a lot and amazed audiences with his feats of strength. He even met Queen Victoria, who was so impressed that she called him "the tallest, stoutest and strongest man to ever enter the palace" and gave him two gold rings.

Despite his fame, MacAskill preferred a quiet life and eventually returned to his hometown, where he and his brother opened a store. The store quickly became popular because locals and tourists wanted to meet the famous giant. Stories about his size, strength and character continued to spread throughout his life, making him even more of a legend.

Eventually, MacAskill's health began to decline, and he died peacefully in 1863 at age 38.

Angus MacAskill's marble headstone reads as follows:

In loving memory
of
Angus McAskill
the Nova Scotian giant
who died at his home
in St. Ann's
August 8, 1863
Aged 38 Years
Height 7 ft. 9 in.
Girth 80 in.
Weight 425 lbs.
A dutiful son,

a loving brother,
a true friend,
a loyal subject,
a humble Christian.

Angus MacAskill is still remembered as one of the most fascinating people in Nova Scotia's history. Today, you can learn about his extraordinary life at the Giant MacAskill Museum in both Dunvegan, Scotland, and Englishtown, Cape Breton, where he is buried. The museums display items like his bed, the doorframes of his house and the chair he sat in, all built extra large to suit his incredible size.

Understanding the lives of real giants like Angus MacAskill, Robert Wadlow and Sultan Kösen has always been difficult, because people usually only hear about giants in stories or as sideshow attractions. But thanks to modern science and medicine, we can learn more about conditions like gigantism and understand the physical and emotional struggles real-life giants face.

CHAPTER 6

Wannabe Spaceman:
The Disappearance of Granger Taylor

O n a stormy winter's night, November 29, 1980, a perplexing
event occurred in Duncan, British Columbia. Granger Taylor,
a skilled and inventive 32-year-old mechanic, vanished into thin air,
leaving many bewildered. In the rustic farmhouse where he lived, his
perplexed mother, Grace, and stepfather, Jim, found a cryptic message
attached to a bedroom door after his disappearance.

The enigmatic note, written in capital letters, bore Granger's sig-
nature and was dated the same day. It read:

DEAR MOTHER AND FATHER,
I HAVE GONE AWAY TO WALK ABOARD AN ALIEN
SPACE SHIP. AS REOCCURRING DREAMS ASSURED A
42-MONTH
INTERSTELLAR VOYAGE TO EXPLORE THE VAST
UNIVERSE, THEN RETURN.
I AM LEAVING BEHIND ALL MY POSSESSIONS TO YOU AS I

WILL NO LONGER REQUIRE THE USE OF ANY.
PLEASE USE THE INSTRUCTIONS IN MY WILL AS A GUIDE
TO HELP.
LOVE GRANGER

On the reverse side of the note, Granger's family discovered a hastily drawn map of Waterloo Lake. This lake was approximately a 48-minute drive south of their residence near Somenos Lake. They also found that Granger had amended his will. The original phrase "In the event of my death" had been replaced with the intriguing phrase "In the event of my departure."

Some notable items were also missing from the house, including Granger's trusty 1972 Datsun pickup truck and a quantity of dynamite he intended to use to remove stubborn tree stumps. However, he left all his personal possessions, including $10,000 in cash and his passport. That same night, a violent windstorm ravaged the area, resulting in uprooted trees, property damage and widespread power outages across Vancouver Island.

The last sighting of Granger occurred at Bob's Grill at 6:30 p.m. that evening. This establishment was a familiar haunt of his. Witnesses reported no peculiar behaviour on his part. A Bob's Grill employee, Linda Baron, remembered seeing Granger clad in his typical attire: a brown zip-front knitted sweater, a black T-shirt, jeans and rugged logger boots. However, his customary winter coat was noticeably absent. Curiously, Granger's stepfather found the coat several days later in the doghouse he had constructed for their loyal Newfoundland dog, Lady.

Neighbour Hilda Degraaf made a striking revelation to the Royal Canadian Mounted Police (RCMP) after Granger disappeared. She informed law enforcement that on the stormy night of his disappearance, she heard a jarring noise shortly after his last known sighting. Hilda and her husband were aware of Granger's plans to voyage among the stars. In the 2019 documentary *Spaceman*, Hilda recounted how her husband turned to her after hearing the loud bang and uttered the profound words "There goes Granger."

Upon learning of Granger's sudden vanishing, the local RCMP searched extensively, meticulously combing hospitals, roadways, ferries, logging routes and nearby forests around Duncan. Regrettably, their efforts bore no results. Although rumours circulated, concrete evidence of his whereabouts remained elusive.

As the days turned into months, Granger's family still held on to a glimmer of hope that he would one day return.

It was not until 1986, a full six years after the disappearance, that forestry workers chanced upon the site of an explosion near Mount Prevost, a mere 26 kilometres (16 miles) north of the family's homestead. The RCMP's investigation revealed fragments of a Datsun vehicle and bone shards, shedding light on the grim reality of the situation.

In a time before DNA testing became commonplace, a BC coroner's inquest made the startling conclusion that the remains were indeed those of the vanished Granger Taylor. The report also inferred that an explosion had taken place, likely triggered by the dynamite known to be in the truck. Granger's mother identified pieces of clothing found at the blast site, which provided a bit of clarity to the mysterious discovery. However, whether the explosion was accidental or intentional remained unanswered.

The entire narrative of Granger's disappearance was fascinating and complex, and it raised many questions. For instance, how could they confirm the bones were Granger's without the benefit of DNA testing? The coroner based the identification on Granger's mother's recognition of some clothing items, which, while remarkable, is not an infallible method of identifying people.

Granger's life was not without tragedy, even before he went missing. A significant loss marked his early life in the town of Duncan, on Vancouver Island; his father disappeared and was later found to have accidentally drowned while fishing near their cabin along Horne Lake, west of the Qualicum Beach community.

Inherently shy, young Granger deeply missed his father. However, life moved on, and his mother eventually remarried a kind man named Jim, who already had children, and together, they formed a blended family. Going to school was never Granger's favourite activity, and he dropped out in the eighth grade. His lack of formal education did not, however, reflect his intellectual abilities. Granger was bright and possessed a curious streak. He loved dissecting objects to understand their workings, and he had a natural talent for anything mechanical.

At 14, Granger built a single-cylinder car from various parts he had collected and some he had crafted himself. This impressive achievement was recognized when local curators displayed his creation in Duncan's Forestry Museum.

After leaving school, Granger began an apprenticeship at a local auto repair shop. The arrangement, however, lasted only about a year. Granger's independent, rebellious spirit was better suited to self-employment, and he spent the rest of his life taking on various independent projects and fixing things for people. He was self-taught in auto and heavy machinery mechanics and welding, and he had an unquenchable thirst for challenging mechanical projects.

Many believed that Granger's exceptional skills could have led him to a successful career as a mechanical engineer if he had pursued a formal education. Some people even referred to him as an eccentric genius. However, he wasn't interested in titles or degrees. He found pleasure in his work, tinkering with machinery and solving mechanical puzzles.

Physically, Granger grew into a formidable figure. Standing 191 centimetres (6 feet, 3 inches) and weighing approximately 110 kilograms (240 pounds), he was as large in life as his ambitions and accomplishments. Despite his size, Granger, who enjoyed engaging in playful wrestling matches with his smaller friends, was known for his kind-hearted and easygoing nature, which earned him the affectionate nickname "Gentle Giant." In the late 1960s, friends sometimes called him "Gentle Ben," inspired by the TV series of the same name starring Clint Howard, the younger brother of actor Ron Howard.

In 1969, Granger discovered an abandoned locomotive left to decay in the woods at some point during the Great Depression. Unfazed by the challenge, he worked tirelessly to extract the steam engine from its overgrown resting place and transported it to the 21-acre farm he shared with his parents. The property, which had transformed into a makeshift junkyard housing Granger's various projects, became the restoration site for the old, rusted train.

After two years of relentless effort, Granger restored the locomotive to its former glory. The province of British Columbia purchased the revived steam engine from him in 1973. After a brief tour around the province, the train found its permanent home at the BC Forest Discovery Centre in Duncan.

Granger's curiosity wasn't limited to land-based vehicles though; he also developed a fascination with aviation. He bought the remnants of a Second World War-era Kitty Hawk warplane, which was essentially just a rusted fuselage. Once again, he demonstrated his talent by meticulously restoring the plane. After Granger's disappearance, his family sold the aircraft for a considerable sum.

Granger's intriguing projects and warm nature attracted local kids and young people who enjoyed spending time with him and his "large toys," as they called his machinery. While they sometimes indulged in drinking and occasional marijuana use—mostly harmless socializing—Granger and a few others occasionally used LSD. Despite his friendly demeanour, Granger had few romantic relationships, primarily as a result of his shy and eccentric nature. His sister later suggested that he may have been a bit lonely because he was so different from others.

During the mid to late 20th century, the Duncan area of Vancouver Island was known for its numerous reported UFO sightings. One such sighting occurred outside a hospital in the early hours of New Year's Day in 1970. This particular sighting would significantly influence Granger's later obsessions.

Henry McKay, the first director of MUFON Canada (Mutual UFO Network Canada—a prominent non-profit organization dedicated to investigating and researching reports of unidentified flying objects and related phenomena) and a Canadian ufologist who specialized in investigating physical traces of UFOs, recorded an account of the hospital UFO sighting.

In the recording, McKay tells the story of an anonymous nurse working in an intensive care ward at the district hospital in Cowichan on Vancouver Island. She noticed an intense light coming from a patient's room into the hallway. Assuming someone had accidentally left the lights on, she entered the room to turn them off, only to find the light coming from the window.

She approached the window to close the drapes and saw a UFO hovering at her level, just 24 metres (80 feet) from the building. The

UFO hovered between the main building and the children's wing of the hospital. She reported seeing two creatures in the UFO, one behind the other. The one at the back slowly turned and looked directly at her, then reached forward and touched the creature in front, who moved a lever.

When asked for more details, the nurse reported that she could see the interior of the craft, which became more visible when the being inside moved the lever. She described a control panel inside and the two humanoid figures perched on tall stools. After this, the craft began to slowly drift away.

Realizing she needed to get the attention of other potential witnesses, the nurse started yelling. The other nurses on duty responded to her call and rushed down the corridor. Unfortunately, when the others arrived, they only briefly saw the light moving away into the distance. Other staff and patients also confirmed that they saw something flying away. Despite the challenges of reporting such an incident, especially for a medical professional, this is one of several similar UFO cases reported across Canada.

Patient Joan Hieta vividly recalls seeing the UFO from her hospital room on New Year's Day in 1970, just after giving birth. Awakened by a nurse's excitement, she joined others in witnessing what seemed to be an otherworldly craft, complete with instrument panels and shadowy figures, hovering near the window before moving away. This encounter has been immortalized on a new $20 silver coin from the Royal Canadian Mint's series on unexplained phenomena. However, local resident Dan Hughes suggests the UFO was actually a clever New Year's prank by a couple using a candle-lit, hot-air-filled plastic bag. Despite this rational explanation, Hieta remains convinced of the UFO's authenticity.

Granger Taylor, a fervent enthusiast of the unknown and a dedicated follower of UFO phenomena, was deeply drawn to this intriguing local tale. The release of iconic films like *Close Encounters of the Third Kind* and *Star Wars* further fuelled his fascination with UFOs and the infinite expanse of space. He tirelessly sought everything he could find about extraterrestrial encounters, from local to global sightings.

Granger spent countless nights immersed in his exploration of UFOs, and he read extensively about other extraterrestrial subjects, including outer space, black holes and comprehensive analyses of the reality behind flying saucers. His collection included notable works such as *Flying Saucers: Here and Now!* by the well-known American writer and broadcaster Frank Edwards.

Edwards's book, published in 1967, aimed to shed light on the UFO phenomenon, focusing on American encounters. Using a journalistic approach, he meticulously documented and investigated people's numerous sightings of and encounters with unidentified flying objects. The book, which includes reports from credible sources such as pilots, military personnel and scientists, sought to legitimize the study of UFOs, challenging the prevailing skepticism of the time.

While the most famous UFO stories often focus on events in the United States, particularly the 1947 incident in Roswell, New Mexico, and the rumoured activities at Area 51 in the Nevada desert, such tales are not unique to America. There have been countless reports of UFO sightings worldwide, dating back to the earliest written records. Some even believe that the Biblical story of Ezekiel includes a sighting of UFOs, where he described four large wheels moving across the sky, each guided by an alien entity:

Wherever the spirit would go, they would go, and the wheels would rise along with them because the spirit of the living creatures was in the wheels. When the creatures moved, they also moved; when the creatures stood still, they also stood still; and when the creatures rose from the ground, the wheels rose along with them because the spirit of the living creatures was in the wheels.

—EZEKIEL 1:20-21

The first documented UFO sighting in Canada, as per the book *The Canadian UFO Report*, by Chris Rutkowski and Geoff Dittman, dates back to 1663, when Jesuit missionaries reported seeing a fireball in the sky that resembled "fiery serpents." Other early sightings include "a globe of fire" observed in the sky in 1791 and a supposed fleet of ships seen above in 1796 that were documented by Simeon Perkins, a diarist and politician from Nova Scotia. While some sightings could be meteorites, the true nature of these phenomena remains a mystery.

Throughout the 18th and 19th centuries, reports of unidentified objects in Canadian skies continued. However, it wasn't until 1947, the year of the infamous Roswell incident, that the Canadian government began to take these reports more seriously. Various governmental departments began accepting voluntary submissions of sightings, witness statements and credibility assessments.

Canada's interest in the potential technology behind UFOs led to the creation of Project Magnet in 1950, which was led by Wilbert Brockhouse Smith, a senior radio engineer for Transport Canada. The project aimed to study UFOs and related physical principles, especially magnetic phenomena, as a way of discovering new and valuable technologies.

Three of the most famous physical UFO sightings in Canadian history took place in 1967, a busy year for reported UFO phenomena.

The Falcon Lake incident: In May of 1967, Stefan Michalak, an amateur prospector near Falcon Lake, Manitoba, claimed he saw two UFOs, one of which burned him severely and allegedly gave him radiation poisoning. He stated that after he spotted the two vessels, one took off and the other landed near him. When the landed craft took off again, it blew hot air from an exhaust panel that set Michalak's shirt on fire and left a burn mark on his chest. Authorities were skeptical until Michalak showed them the site where he claimed the craft had also burned vegetation. Michalak reported suffering from a chest burn with a strange pattern, which intermittently reappeared for years.

The Duhamel crop circles: In August 1967, six crop circles appeared mysteriously in a farmer's field in Duhamel, Alberta. An investigating scientist found some tread marks within the circles that seemed as if from a tire, but these marks covered only small portions of the circles. Soil samples tested were inconclusive for radiation. Ultimately, the scientist admitted that the marks might have been made by a hovering aircraft, but the investigation remained inconclusive.

The Shag Harbour crash: In October 1967, the local RCMP detachment in Shag Harbour, Nova Scotia, received several calls about a craft down in the harbour. Witnesses reported that the craft made a whistling sound and then flashed as it hit the water. It then floated on the water's surface for a few minutes, surrounded by glittering yellow foam. However, before a boat could reach the site, the craft sank, and a subsequent dive team could not find any wreckage. Like the Duhamel and Falcon Lake reports, the Shag Harbour case remains unsolved. Locals have embraced the sighting and have created the Shag Harbour Incident Interpretive Centre. The Shag Harbour UFO

XPO, held in the fall, is a yearly gathering that unites UFO specialists and witnesses to discuss their experiences along with the most recent hypotheses and investigations concerning unidentified flying objects. The XPO typically incorporates one or more presentations focused on the events and lasting impact of the 1967 Shag Harbour incident.

Unlike most people, who are merely intrigued by UFOs, Granger Taylor put his fascination into action. He pondered how real UFOs might be powered, with the ultimate goal of building a functioning spacecraft. He started his project by building a life-sized UFO model.

Using salvaged junk, he began constructing his replica of a space-ship in his backyard with the help of his young pals, many of whom were local kids who loved to watch him work on his other projects. The makeshift spacecraft was approximately 6 metres (20 feet) across and mounted on stilts. A porthole-like window adorned the side of the silver vessel along with a big, red painted lightning bolt. How-ever, it wasn't just an exterior model of Granger's interpretation of a spacecraft; he also went to great lengths to create a detailed interior.

Inside the makeshift UFO, he used various materials to create a very 1970s interpretation of what the interior of a flying saucer might look like. Granger furnished the ship with a television, stove and seating, making it a habitable place. He would often party with his friends, primarily local youth, in his backyard UFO, drinking, smoking weed and dropping acid, all while discussing their dreams of cosmic exploration.

In the summer before his disappearance, Granger's usage of LSD became more regular. He believed the substance unlocked communi-cation channels that were typically inaccessible to human perception, asserting that, while on LSD, he engaged in frequent dialogues with extraterrestrial beings.

Granger claimed these exchanges occurred while he was in bed and on the verge of falling asleep. He described the communication as a mental connection, as if the aliens directly addressed his thoughts. He often inquired about the propulsion technology of their spacecraft, and while the visitors offered little information, they hinted that it involved magnetism in some manner.

In an interview with *Vice* reporter Tyler Hooper, Granger's sister, Grace Anne "Gay" Young Reynolds, disclosed that Granger had been ingesting LSD multiple times daily in the months preceding his disappearance. Such consistent usage undoubtedly had a profound impact on his perception of the truth. Speculation arose that Granger may have become detached from reality owing to the hallucinogenic effects of the drugs.

LSD profoundly affects a person's perception and cognition. It can induce a state resembling drug-induced psychosis, where an individual's ability to think, communicate and process reality becomes significantly distorted. Visual hallucinations are a hallmark of LSD use, where individuals may perceive vivid and intricate patterns, colours or even objects that are not physically present. Distorted perceptions of movements, sounds, body image and touch are common, leading to a profound alteration in sensory experiences. The perception of time may become distorted, with minutes feeling like hours or vice versa. Depth perception can also be affected, making objects appear closer or farther away than they are. Delusions—fixed false beliefs—can arise during an LSD trip, contributing to an altered sense of reality and a departure from rational thinking. Euphoria, or intense feelings of happiness and well-being, may be experienced as well, accompanied by a sense of heightened self-identity and interconnectedness with the world.

However, it is essential to note that the effects of LSD are not solely limited to the acute period of intoxication. The substance can have long-term risks, although they are relatively rare. One such risk is persistent psychosis, where individuals may continue to experience visual disturbances, mood changes and psychotic symptoms even after the immediate effects of LSD have subsided. Hallucinogen-persisting perception disorder (HPPD) can occur in users, causing individuals to experience recurring visual disturbances and flashbacks, even a year or more following the last use of LSD.

In some cases, LSD can intensify underlying psychotic disorders in susceptible individuals, meaning that individuals who are already prone to conditions like schizophrenia may experience a worsening of their symptoms under the influence of LSD. Furthermore, negative experiences, commonly called "bad trips," can induce profound anxiety and despair. During a bad trip, individuals may be overwhelmed by intense emotions and frightening hallucinations. They may develop a deep sense of fear, sometimes accompanied by thoughts of insanity, death or losing control.

As his drug use escalated, Granger's conversation topics increasingly revolved around an upcoming 42-month journey across the stars he planned to embark on with his alien friends. About a week before his disappearance, he even threw a farewell party for himself. Some of his friends wanted to believe his stories; others assumed he was just joking or thought his claims were outlandish.

Granger shared a heartfelt moment with his stepfather the evening before his disappearance, expressing gratitude for his kindness and acceptance. The following day, Granger vanished. His parents thought it strange that he had left his wallet and identification behind when he left. But more telling, Granger left his beloved dog at home. It was exceptionally rare that Granger went anywhere without his loyal pooch.

RCMP corporal Mike Demchuk told the *Times Colonist* newspaper in February of 1984, "We have no idea whatsoever [what happened]. Everybody who knows Granger says he does not tell a lie, and he'll show up in 42 months." Granger's promised timeline set his return sometime in May of 1984.

But May 1984 came and went with no sign of Granger Taylor.

By the end of the month, Granger's family, however, still clung to the hope that he would make his promised return after his 42-month stint aboard an alien spacecraft. They expected he would walk through the door any day with stories of his fantastic voyage.

Some people thought he had just left town for some reason, while others still hoped for his return. There was also unfounded speculation that Taylor had moved to Colombia or had been seized and detained by the US government. There were also rumours that his deserted pickup truck had been found by locals in an overgrown area in the thick forests of Mount Prevost.

In 1986, when a work crew discovered a blast site featuring fragments of a truck and what was possibly the remains of Granger Taylor, Taylor's friends and family had to contend with some uncomfortable questions. Did Granger cause his own demise? Was the blast accidental or intentional? If so, what could his motives have been? His loved ones insisted that Granger was far from suicidal, despite his claims of alien contact.

Another theory was that Granger might have staged his death to escape his life. Still, this scenario seemed unlikely to those who knew him. Some even speculated that aliens may have picked Granger up and detonated his truck upon their departure.

His friend Robert Keller did not believe that Granger had a death wish, nor that he was crazy. Keller was only 15 when Granger disappeared, but the two had been close. Robert had helped Granger build his backyard UFO.

Keller told the *Times Colonist*'s Mike Devlin, "Granger was the most intelligent, down-to-earth, wise man that I've ever met in my life. He wasn't a nut. He was a very, very intelligent guy who carried on with his life normally. But after you say 'spaceman,' then all of a sudden, he becomes a nut."

There were suggestions that Granger might have had schizophrenia. Still, this mental disorder typically manifests earlier in life, and apart from his belief in alien communication, he showed no other signs of psychosis. Again, it is plausible that his frequent use of psychedelic substances could have influenced his experiences.

After an article by Tyler Hooper was published on *Vice News*, a documentary was made about Granger's disappearance.

In 2019, Jennifer Horvath, executive producer at Alibi Entertainment, spoke to me on the *Dark Poutine* podcast about her involvement in making the film, titled *Spaceman*. There were some challenges, she said. Foremost was gaining the trust of Granger Taylor's family.

Horvath told me that Taylor's family was understandably concerned that the filmmakers wouldn't approach the story with the seriousness they would like. They opened up once they got to know the crew and understood that they weren't there to prove one theory over another. Jennifer told the family they just wanted to hear Granger's story from start to finish. These are some of the details the documentary uncovered.

On the night Granger Taylor disappeared, some people in the area reported hearing a loud sound. However, it's unclear if it was a UFO leaving Earth, a pickup truck exploding or thunder from the severe storm that was happening that night. Taylor had mentioned to Keller that aliens would likely arrive during bad weather for cover. While Taylor had experience with explosives and was known to possess dynamite, Keller argues against the likelihood of an accident, citing his friend's expertise and prioritization of safety.

During the filming of *Spaceman*, the crew failed to locate the reported blast site. Doubts were also raised about the evidence found, as Keller pointed out discrepancies between the reported colour of Taylor's truck and the one found at the scene. His truck was pink, and the one found was blue, according to police. The police report indicated, however, that the vehicle identification number matched the vehicle registered to Granger Taylor, which is why police believed the truck was his.

According to Keller, he is uncertain whether the remains found at the site were Taylor's. The members of Granger's family who participated in the documentary have accepted that he is dead.

Robert Keller admits to feeling sad not knowing his friend's fate but finds it equally distressing to accept that Taylor might have taken his own life. Despite extensive research and interviews conducted for *Spaceman*, for many, the true nature of Granger's disappearance remains inconclusive.

Part 2

PLACES

In this section, we embark on a journey around the world, touching down in locations cloaked in mystery and steeped in spine-chilling stories of hauntings, unexplained deaths, lost civilizations and other darker topics.

We begin with "Was Borley Rectory England's Most Haunted Property?" and investigate the reportedly very haunted manor in Borley, Essex, England. You will learn about the various sightings of apparitions, inexplicable noises and other paranormal phenomena that have been reported at the house and meet the cast of colourful characters who originally labelled it "the most haunted house in England."

The next chapter explores the eerie legends surrounding Nahanni National Park in the Northwest Territories, known as "the Valley of the Headless Men" because of numerous tales of unexplained disappearances and the discovery of decapitated bodies. The story delves into the area's chilling lore and attempts to decipher the mysterious occurrences.

"Eerie Occurrences at Old MacDonald's Farm" recounts the mysterious happenings at the MacDonald family farm in Nova Scotia, which were particularly focused on the teenager Esther Cox. The chapter details the alleged paranormal events that Esther experienced, including mysterious fires, object levitations and spectral assaults.

"Suicide Forest: The Sea of Trees" dives into the melancholic allure of Japan's Aokigahara Jukai, also known as "the Suicide Forest." We unravel the reasons why this forest has tragically become a destination for individuals to take their own lives and discuss the cultural and societal factors contributing to this phenomenon.

We close this section with "A Brief History of Lost Civilizations: Atlantis and Others," which explores the tantalizing mystery of lost civilizations, primarily focusing on Atlantis. This chapter scrutinizes various theories surrounding these mythical cities' possible existence and locations, examining one of history's most enduring puzzles.

CHAPTER 7

Was Borley Rectory England's Most Haunted Property? (Borley, Essex, England)

Constructed in 1863, Borley Rectory had a somewhat short existence, as it was decimated by fire in February 1939, only 76 years after it was built, and then demolished. However, during this brief span, thanks mainly to the investigation by Harry Price of the Society for Psychical Research in London, it gained a notorious and perhaps dubious reputation as the most haunted house in England. But was it?

Borley Rectory has captivated the imaginations of ghost hunters and skeptics alike. I looked into the investigation when I visited the Society for Psychical Research archives in the Cambridge University library in the summer of 2022. It is a fascinating tale. Witnesses claimed to have seen spectral apparitions roaming the grounds, including nuns, headless figures and phantom coaches pulled by ghostly horse teams. There were many reports of unexplained footsteps, objects moved or smashed by unseen hands and mysterious messages that appeared on walls.

The infamous house once stood across the road from Borley Church on the Essex side of the border between Essex and Suffolk beside the River Stour. The church's graveyard lay between the two structures. The rectory was constructed in 1863 under the supervision of the Rev. Henry Dawson Ellis Bull (1833–1892), the first rector of Borley. The two-storey red-brick structure consisted of 23 rooms and featured three staircases. It was situated on extensive grounds that spanned almost 1.6 hectares (4 acres). Adjacent to the rectory were additional structures, including a cottage that formed part of the original stable block and various smaller outbuildings.

Borley is a tiny hamlet that falls within the jurisdiction of the Braintree Council District, which encompasses the Stour Valley conservation area. Humans have inhabited the area since the Neolithic period. According to the 1836 book *The History and Topography of Essex*, Borley is compounded by the Saxon words *bár*, meaning "boar," and *lea*, meaning "pasture," thus Boar's Pasture. So its beginnings may have had to do with hogs. However, the Braintree Council's research states that the etymology of the name *Borley* possibly originates from the Celtic term *bore*, meaning "summer meadows," which continue to be a notable characteristic of the region.

The property on which the Borley Church still sits has a known history that dates back to the 11th century, to a survey of England ordered by William the Conqueror at Christmas 1085 and undertaken beginning in 1086. The survey, later called the *Domesday Book*, listed the property as Borley Manor. At the time, the property was held by Adelaide, Countess of Aumale, the half-sister of William the Conqueror himself.

The Extent of the Manor of Borley, a survey conducted in 1308 during the reign of Edward II, provides a comprehensive glimpse into the medieval community. Historians consider this document crucial for understanding the medieval period in England. It depicts a well-constructed manor house that included a water mill with a fish pond in the mill dam, 300 acres of arable land, 29 acres of mowing meadow and 28 acres of pasture where cows and oxen grazed.

The origins of Borley Church can be traced back to the Saxon period, with remnants of the pre-conquest structure still visible in the nave. Substantial expansions took place during the 15th and 16th centuries, and in the 19th century, external rendering was added to both the nave and chancel. It's worth noting that Borley Church holds the prestigious Grade 1 listing, acknowledging its historical and architectural significance.

In England, when a building or structure receives a Grade 1 listing, it signifies the utmost architectural and historical importance. Typically, these buildings hold national significance and are crucial to the nation's heritage. The purpose of such listings is to provide legal safeguards that ensure the preservation and maintenance of these significant structures for future generations.

In 1362, King Edward III granted Borley Manor to the Benedictine monks, specifically the prior and community of Christ Church in Canterbury. This transaction marked a noteworthy historical event, highlighting the exchange of property and privileges between the monarchy and religious institutions during King Edward III's reign.

The first bit of history led to one of the property's most enduring ghost stories, which is supposed to have occurred around this time. However, it's important to note that this is a local tale without historical documentation to confirm it. The story goes like this:

In the 13th century, when it was home to the Benedictine monastery, there was a small convent nearby. A monk from the monastery and a nun from the nearby convent allegedly fell deeply in love and a romance began between them. Their affair defied the religious vows they had taken to live a life of chastity, so they had to keep their relationship a secret.

They planned to run away and start a new life together, away from their religious duties. They attempted to elope in a black coach driven by a pair of horses, but their plan was tragically discovered before they could escape, and they were captured. Ecclesiastical authorities of the time were relentless in their punishment for such religious violations. The monk received a death sentence and was to be hung in a public execution, likely designed to deter other potential rule breakers.

The nun faced a similarly grim fate. As her punishment, she was sealed alive within the walls of her convent, a horrifying and cruel death. The story suggests that she was put into a small space in the walls and left to die, bricked up with no hope of escape. It was an action intended not just to punish her but also to warn others of the dire consequences of breaking their vows.

The spirits of these star-crossed lovers were said to have lingered at the site, with the most frequently reported apparition being that of the nun. Dubbed "the Borley Nun," her ghostly figure was allegedly seen numerous times, walking mournfully between the site of the rectory and the church's ruins, especially at twilight. Sometimes a dark, ghostly coach drawn by black horses was seen, with the pair of ethereal spectres huddled inside.

A convent did exist approximately 13 kilometres (8 miles) away from Borley in Bures. However, there needs to be more substantiating evidence to support the veracity of this story. For example, the invention of coaches was still two centuries away from the time when the story allegedly occurred. There are also no records of nuns, or anyone else, being bricked up inside the walls of local nunneries.

True or not, many witnesses claim to have seen the nun and the coach over the years, with undocumented sightings beginning in 1843, two decades before Borley Rectory's initial construction.

Ghosts are not the only historical drama to surround Borley. When King Henry VIII established the Church of England in 1534 during the English Reformation, he outlawed Catholicism in England. A year before Henry VIII died, he presented Borley Manor to Sir Edward Waldegrave. However, five years later in 1551, young King Edward VI's men arrested Sir Edward at Borley Hall. Sir Edward faced accusations of conducting an illicit Catholic Mass at the home of Princess Mary, who later became Mary I, also known as "Bloody Mary." Following a thorough search of the hall and surrounding premises, authorities discovered a priest, a nun and various religious books used during a Mass. Sir Edward was arrested and locked up in the Tower of London.

When Mary I came to power after Edward VI died in 1553, her old friend, Sir Edward, was released and elected as Chancellor of the Duchy of Lancaster. He also received a manor in Cobham, Kent. However, following Queen Mary's death in 1558, he was removed from all his positions and imprisoned again in the tower, this time by Queen Elizabeth I. His arrest was again for allegedly celebrating Catholic Mass within his residence. He died in the Tower of London in 1561. Both Sir Edward and his wife were buried in a tomb in the Borley graveyard, and the family later erected a large monument to celebrate them.

Laws suppressed Catholicism during the reigns of Henry VIII's successors, particularly Edward VI, Elizabeth I and the early years of James I. They enacted laws to enforce the practice of Protestantism over any other religion. These statutes, known as the Penal Laws, restricted Catholic worship, imposed fines and penalties on Catholics, and prohibited their involvement in public and political life. Catholicism regained limited legal recognition and tolerance with the Roman Catholic Relief Act of 1829, which granted certain rights to Catholics in England.

The Rev. Henry Dawson Ellis Bull, a relative of the Waldegraves, became the rector of Borley in 1862. Bull came from a lineage of the clergy, including his father, the Rev. Edward Bull, who served as the rector of Pentlow. He promptly planned the construction of the rectory on the site of the former monastery situated opposite the church, where a previous rectory had burned down in 1841. The new structure featured high gabled walls and a peculiar-looking tower above the front entrance. As the reverend's family grew—Bull and his wife had 14 children—he made hasty but necessary additions to the building with little thought given to aesthetics. In 1875, a completely new wing was added to accommodate their needs. After Bull died in 1892, his son, the Rev. Henry Foyster Bull (also known as Harry Bull), succeeded his father as the rector. Interestingly, the second-storey room where his father passed away, called "the Blue Room," later became the site of numerous alleged paranormal events, including more sightings of the spectral nun.

An early account claims a spectral nun had been seen on the rectory grounds by a Mr. P. Shaw Jeffrey, a respected Colchester Royal Grammar School headmaster, who was a frequent visitor to Borley Rectory. During his visits in 1885 and 1886, he said he had encountered the phantasm of "the nun" numerous times, had seen the ghostly coach and had witnessed phantom pebbles falling from out of nowhere and other household items moving on their own. Jeffrey stuck to his accounts until his dying day. The Rev. Harry Bull later revealed that he, too, had witnessed the apparition of the nun multiple times before and after his father died.

One of the most compelling sightings of the spectral nun was made on the afternoon of July 28, 1900, in broad daylight. Three of Harry Bull's sisters, Ethel, Freda and Mabel, were returning from an afternoon tea party at a friend's home. As they entered the gate and were nearing the house, they saw a black-clad figure with her head bowed moving along a pathway, later known infamously as the Nun's Walk. The frightened girls ran into the house and brought their older sister, Caroline, outside to show her what they had seen.

When the foursome arrived, the nun was still slowly walking along the path in the yard. The apparition seemed so real that Caroline thought perhaps it was a local nun who had lost her way and needed help. Caroline approached the figure as the other girls, terrified, hung back. The nun vanished in vapour when Caroline was just a few metres away. The young women could not believe what they had seen. They went back inside to tell the rest of the family about it. Not known to be liars, their stories of the event remained consistent over the years, and they spoke about the encounter until the end of their lives.

Ethel had another sighting of the nun with a visiting cousin four months later. There she was again, dressed the same way, head again bowed, in the very same place, treading the same path, headed in the same direction. Similarly, the figure instantly faded from sight when the girls approached.

This kind of ghost sighting is considered a "residual haunting." The encyclopedia at llewellyn.com describes a residual haunting as a phenomenon in which spirits or ghosts perpetually replay specific incidents. These hauntings typically manifest in historical places, as the spirits replay significant life events, such as marriages, births or deaths. Psychic investigators believe these are not conventional ghosts but energy confined to a specific location or object that plays back in a continuous loop.

These kinds of residual hauntings are explained in the paranormal field by the speculative idea known as the Stone Tape theory. This theory suggests that mental impressions during emotional or traumatic events can be imprinted in the form of energy, recorded onto rocks and other items in the environment, and repeated under certain conditions. This theory often explains residual hauntings or ghostly phenomena that involve repetitious patterns or events.

Named after a 1972 BBC horror teleplay that popularized the concept, the Stone Tape theory posits that buildings and places can absorb energy from the living beings that inhabit them, especially during high stress or tension. This energy is then stored and can be released, resulting in a type of haunting that is not an active spirit but rather a playback of a past event.

Harry Bull, who inherited the house after his father's death, was known for his quirky habits. For example, he often lounged on the drawing room floor for extended periods. Moreover, he was a keen cat enthusiast and maintained a household of up to 30 felines, who would join him on his walks around the grounds. Whenever a cat passed away, Bull buried it in a dedicated cat cemetery he created in the garden.

Harry did not marry until age 48, when he fell for a 29-year-old widow who was a shopkeeper from nearby Sudbury. Harry's marriage to his new wife was a match his unwed sisters disapproved of. They were concerned about losing their inheritance and having her take over the estate. The marriage lasted 16 years until Harry died in 1927 in the same Blue Room where his father passed away. The official cause was chronic bronchitis, but rumours suggested his wife might have poisoned him, a story likely fuelled by his sisters' animosity toward their sister-in-law.

Sensing he was going to die, Harry threatened to haunt the rectory and throw mothballs at the relatives who had annoyed him in life. And he made good on his promise. There were reports of Harry's ghost being seen around the building and of mothballs striking unsuspecting people in the house. It was not a surprise that there was no replacement rector for some time.

After 16 months of vacancy, in October 1928, the new rector, the Rev. Guy Eric Smith, and his wife took over residency. Since Harry Bull's death, the building had fallen into disrepair. The Bull family had not been the best caretakers. The building was drafty, with rats and mice running amok, the plumbing was awful, and the roof leaked. Years of garbage lay throughout the building.

Rev. Smith also experienced paranormal events after moving to the house. After reports in national newspapers about the reverend's experiences, renowned paranormal researcher Harry Price paid a visit to Borley Rectory in 1929. Price, who had an early fascination with conjuring, began investigating the techniques used by seance mediums, leading him into psychical research and eventually a membership in the Society for Psychical Research (SPR).

Established in London in 1882, the SPR was the first scientific body dedicated to investigating psychic and paranormal phenomena. The SPR doesn't hold a collective stance on the existence or interpretation of such phenomena; instead, its goal is to gather information and encourage understanding through comprehensive research and education.

The SPR is a registered charity governed by a council of elected members. Various committees supervise activities within the organization. Noteworthy past presidents include philosophers William James and Henri Bergson, scientists William Crookes, John Strutt (Lord Rayleigh) and Charles Richet, and the British conservative prime minister Arthur Balfour.

The membership of the SPR spans a diverse range of academic and professional fields globally. It warmly welcomes both active researchers and volunteer helpers, as well as those who are eager to learn about the subject. I have been one of those enthusiastic members since 2022.

Harry Price was a member of the Magic Circle, a club of magicians, and became its honorary librarian in 1921. He connected with people like Eric Dingwall and Harry Houdini, who shared his interest in magic and psychical research. He was also a member of the Ghost Club, where he rubbed shoulders with Sherlock Holmes author Sir Arthur Conan Doyle.

Price made a significant impact on paranormal research by revealing the fraud committed by well-known "spirit" photographer William Hope. Doyle was a loyal fan of Hope, and the exposé upset the author and led him to write several negative articles about Price.

According to his book *The Most Haunted House in England*, Harry Price put together a ghost-hunting kit. He packed a large suitcase with felt overshoes (for silent movement), a steel measuring tape, sealing tools and basic hand tools like a hammer, a saw, wrenches and screwdrivers. He also packed items for experiments with electricity such as cords, bells, batteries and switches. He included a reflex camera, film packs and flashbulbs for photographic documentation. Sketching materials were brought for documenting floor plans, and a first-aid kit was packed for emergencies. He also took miscellaneous items like a ball of string, chalk, a torch, a candle and a bowl of mercury for detecting tremors. Advanced equipment in his kit included a cinematograph camera, a thermograph for temperature variations and graphite for fingerprint development. He brought infrared filters, lamps and sensitive films for dark photography. He used an electric signalling instrument for special cases to automatically detect object movement or temperature changes from a base room.

On June 12, 1929, Price and his secretary, Lucy Kaye, and *Daily Mirror* reporter Vernon Wall visited the rectory. They interviewed a diverse group, including the Rev. Guy Eric Smith and his wife, Mabel; the rectory maid, Mary Pearson; the Bull family; rectory gardener Edward Cooper and his wife; Fred Cartwright, the carpenter; the Rev. Lionel Foyster and his wife, Marianne; Lady and Dom Richard Whitehouse; the Rev. Alfred Clifford Henning; and locals Charles Browne and Rosemary M. Williams. The group regaled Price with the rectory's history and with stories of their own paranormal experiences.

The Smiths had no idea of Borley's haunted past when Rev. Smith agreed to take over as rector. Only after encountering spectres themselves, as well as other disturbing occurrences, did they realize that something unusual was going on. Shortly after Rev. Smith and his wife moved into the rectory, they began experiencing various strange phenomena. Rev. Smith would often hear unexplainable whisperings overhead when he walked across the landing. On another occasion, he heard a woman's voice moaning and saying, "Don't, Carlos, don't!" Interestingly, "Carlos" was rumoured to be the nickname of the rectory's builder.

Additional incidents they reported to Harry Price included inexplicable bell-ringing, plodding footsteps echoing in the corridors and upper rooms, and apparitions reported by the two maids who worked in the house. Mrs. Smith reported that, after returning home from church one night, she noticed the window in the rectory's schoolroom illuminated, though the maid, upon inspection, had not been in the room at all. Later, church choir members witnessed the same window with the lights on.

Mrs. Smith also reported seeing a shadowy figure leaning over one of the driveway gates one evening. She investigated the area several times but never found anyone there. Various witnesses reported this figure's abrupt appearance and disappearance as well. One maid also claimed to have seen a spectral "coach" on the lawn.

Another maid, brought in from London, stayed only two days after being terrified by a figure in black she saw leaning over the gate. Rev. Smith noticed a higher frequency of strange noises during the winter compared with the summer. Among the odd phenomena were keys that popped out of their locks and were then found a short distance away. A vase, usually on their bedroom mantelpiece, was found shattered at the bottom of the main stairs when the Smiths were in the garden.

Shortly after moving in, Mrs. Smith found a neatly wrapped parcel in a library cupboard that contained the perfectly preserved skull of a young woman. Unable to understand its presence in the house, Rev. Smith respectfully buried the skull in the churchyard, which was witnessed by the churchwarden and Harry Bull's widow.

Price reported many poltergeist activities during his visit, including a glass roof shattering, a red glass candlestick breaking, pebbles thrown by unseen hands and "spirit" raps during a seance held in the Blue Room.

Shortly after Price's visit, after having been in the house only nine months, the Smiths decided to leave. While visiting the SPR archive at Cambridge University's library, I read some of Harry Price's notes, saw maps he'd drawn of the rectory and went over a few transcribed correspondences between the Smiths, Harry Price and his secretary, Lucy Kaye. What follows are the contents of two of the notes sent soon after Price departed from Borley in 1929.

On July 2, Mrs. Smith sent Lucy Kaye a note, just as the Smiths were preparing to leave the rectory.

Mrs. Smith wrote that she had been packing up to leave, undeterred by the possibility of disturbing the resident "spook" rumoured to inhabit the house. Despite experiencing a couple of peaceful nights, the atmosphere had remained unnerving, taking a toll on her health. She had experienced ominous premonitions and had awoken once to the sensation of a presence near her dressing table. According to local tales, Rev. Bull had been known to walk the hallways until the early hours, which could explain the mysterious footsteps. Rumours had also surfaced about a tragic self-drowning in the garden pond. Additionally, the front doorbell had rung intermittently, which Mrs. Smith surmised could be attributed to local children's pranks or the movements of rodents.

On July 9, 1929, a week after Mrs. Smith wrote of the disturbances, the Rev. G.E. Smith recounted to Harry Price another peculiar incident in the Blue Room. The reverend described how a table had been inexplicably thrown from one side of the room to another, causing alarm, especially to his wife. Furthermore, the mysterious ringing of all the house's bells one evening, with no apparent mechanical cause, added to their distress. The lack of explanation for crashes they heard just before the investigators' departure only deepened the mystery.

With the family having moved into quarters usually reserved for the staff, they planned to relocate the following week to escape the unexplained activity. Nevertheless, the reverend assured that they would report any further disturbances to Price.

The Smiths moved into more suitable, less haunted accommodations nearby. Rev. Smith resigned as rector the following year.

Price continued investigating the rectory, conducting more research after the Smiths had gone. The building remained uninhabited for just over a year.

A new reverend named Lionel Foyster became the new rector, and the Foyster family moved into the rectory in October 1930. They immediately started experiencing disturbances reminiscent of poltergeist activity. The intensity of these occurrences grew between 1931 and 1932. During this period, Price documented more than 2,000 unexplained events, including sounds like footsteps and whispers, spontaneous fires and thrown objects; in addition, Marianne Foyster, the reverend's wife, was forcibly thrown out of her bed. Foyster wrote several accounts of the events occurring during his time there. However, some believe his stories to be highly fictionalized.

While Price generally trusted the Foysters' accounts, he voiced some doubts about the phenomena during an event in 1931. The disturbances seemed focused on Marianne. She reported strange occurrences like being locked in her room and wine changing into ink. Some observers presumed that a man with whom Marianne allegedly had an affair was responsible for some of the events. Regardless, other visitors also reported paranormal occurrences like stone-throwing and bell-ringing, which supported the accounts of the Foysters.

In 1932, medium Guy L'Estrange and a group called the Marks Tey Spiritualist Circle performed an exorcism at the rectory, and the disturbances seemed to subside afterward. Lionel's health began to decline, and Marianne could not bear any more attention from the entities, so the Foysters abandoned the rectory in 1935 and moved back to London.

From May 1937 to 1938, Price leased the rectory so he could investigate it with a team of 48 observers, who gathered reports, including seance revelations from a spirit claiming to be French nun Marie Lairre, who had allegedly been murdered at Borley.

After Price left, Captain William Hart Gregson purchased the rectory in 1938, but a fire destroyed the building in 1939 after someone accidentally knocked over an oil lamp in the hallway. Even though the building was gone, paranormal investigations continued in the ruins until its full demolition in 1944. Excavations in 1943, under Price's supervision, led to the discovery of items including a female jaw bone, the origins of which remain in dispute. The demolition in 1944 was attended by Price and captured in photographs by *Life* magazine.

Even after the demolition, Price's interest in Borley endured, and he continued to visit the site until 1947. He died in 1948.

Throughout Harry Price's life, accusations of fraud had been levelled against him following several investigations, including his work at the Borley Rectory. Some said Price was more interested in promoting himself than performing scientific experiments of supernatural and paranormal phenomena. Charles Sutton, who had been at Borley with Price in 1929, made a particularly damning claim the year Price passed away. Sutton had kept his revelations secret, fearing legal repercussions while Price was alive. After a loud noise during a visit to the rectory with Price, Sutton claimed to have found Price's pockets filled with bricks and pebbles. In notes that I read at the SPR archive in Cambridge, Lord Charles Hope, another SPR investigator, claimed that a large half-brick fell downstairs while Price, Lucy Kaye and Sutton were present and that Sutton had accused Price of throwing it. Kaye later came to Harry's defence, theorizing that Price's presence attracted poltergeist disturbances.

The Haunting of Borley Rectory: A Critical Survey of the Evidence by Eric J. Dingwall, Kathleen M. Goldney and Trevor H. Hall (also known as the Borley Report) scrutinized Harry Price's work. Their 1956 document suggested that misperceptions, hallucinations, mundane activities, the residual smell of incense, coincidences, distorted memories and even deliberate deception for entertainment or profit could explain his reported paranormal phenomena. Although they stopped short of accusing Price of being a hoaxer, they found numerous flaws in his research.

Following the demolition of Borley Rectory in 1944, reports of paranormal activity were said to have moved to the adjacent church and persisted through the second half of the 20th century. A man named Rev. Henning and a writer named Philip Paul took an interest in these strange events, with Paul performing archaeological digs on the site in the mid-1950s. Ghostly occurrences allegedly escalated during the 1970s, when investigator Geoffrey Croom-Hollingsworth recorded inexplicable sounds in the church. The site's infamous reputation drew a substantial increase in visitors, and investigations and reports on supernatural phenomena on the property continue today.

Thanks to all the attention brought by Price and others, the village of Borley was thrust into the spotlight and gained a reputation that the locals would prefer to do without. Curious visitors continue to inundate the village church, hoping to glimpse the elusive spectres that allegedly still haunt the property.

However, the hamlet's residents staunchly maintain that these ghostly apparitions are only fabrications or figments of the imagination. The influx of eager sightseers persists despite locals' insistence that the supernatural does not reside within their village. Borley remains a place of fascination and intrigue, forever tied to its unwelcome renown.

Chapter 8

Valley of the Headless Men
(Nahanni National Park,
Northwest Territories, Canada)

My fascination with the unknown and the unseen brings us to a corner of the Canadian wilderness that is as intriguing as it is eerie. Nahanni Valley is a place that has given rise to tales as timeless as the surrounding mountains. Yet a disturbing legend mars its untouched beauty: the Headless Men of Nahanni Valley. The story isn't just a fable but a series of unsolved mysteries associated with unexplained disappearances, Indigenous folklore and chilling ghost stories.

Does the Nahanni Valley, a place of serene beauty, hold a dark secret? How has this macabre tale woven itself into the tapestry of Canada's wilderness lore? A journey into the Nahanni Valley is a journey into the shadows of the Canadian wilderness, where strange things exist unseen in our natural world.

The lower west corner of the Mackenzie Mountains in the Northwest Territories, specifically the region along the South Nahanni River, was a site of numerous inexplicable and disturbing incidents during the first half of the 20th century. Between 1905 and

1945, at least 44 people vanished under mysterious circumstances, and numerous other unexplained events occurred in this remote and rugged area of wilderness.

The most disturbing of these occurrences was the discovery of four decapitated bodies, two found together, associated with three separate incidents. Strangely, no one has recovered the victims' heads, which led to the eerie moniker for the area. Who or what decapitated these people remains unknown, as does the fate of the others who went missing in the same area.

Nahanni National Park was established in 1976 and gained World Heritage status in 1978. In 2009 the park boundaries significantly expanded, adding 2,500,000 hectares (more than 6,000,000 acres) to create the Nahanni National Park Reserve. This expansion increased the protected area to approximately 3 million hectares, ensuring the preservation of the park's geological heritage and the South Nahanni River system.

Within Nahanni, visitors can explore many types of rivers and streams that showcase the park's unique hydrological diversity. The Flat River and the South Nahanni River, older than the surrounding mountains, have carved out impressive canyons that rank among the world's finest north of the 60th parallel. Virginia Falls, one of North America's most awe-inspiring waterfalls, is a testament to the park's natural grandeur. Nahanni's remarkable combination of geological features and stunning natural landscapes makes it an exceptional destination for exploring and appreciating the Earth's geological heritage.

One distinctive and rather odd aspect of the Nahanni Valley is its tropical-like ambience, often referred to as a northern Eden. The valley boasts lush vegetation and abundant wildlife, likely nurtured by the warm waters of the Kraus Hot Springs. Prospectors in 1947 described the area as a vibrant, almost tropical land where the river never froze, even in frigid temperatures. The valley became the subject of exaggerated accounts over the years, with some people describing it as a place where bananas hang from pine trees.

The Dene people have inhabited the region for thousands of years and have stories about it, including the existence of an ancient giant who used the Gahnhthah (Rabbitkettle Hot Springs) to cook his food. These narratives offer a glimpse into the rich cultural heritage and folklore associated with the Nahanni region.

According to author Hammerson Peters in his book *Legends of the Nahanni Valley*, the region was believed to be haunted by malevolent spirits, leading the Dene people to avoid the valley out of fear for their lives. Survivors who ventured into the valley shared terrifying tales with their fellow hunters, describing encounters with an evil spirit whose eerie screams resonated through the canyons on windy nights. Others spoke of a tribe of fierce, hairy giants dwelling in caves that were carved into the canyon walls. Led by a beautiful, pale-skinned chieftess, these primitive mountain dwellers allegedly killed and consumed anyone who trespassed into their territory.

By the early 1900s, the influx of gold seekers in the Klondike had waned, and the population of the Nahanni Valley began to dwindle. However, some people still ventured to the area to pursue their fortunes. Among them were two Métis brothers, Willie and Frank McCleod, who were enticed north to Fort Liard by their younger brother Fred's tales of Indigenous miners discovering sizable gold nuggets there. Believing there was still more gold to be found, the McCleod brothers embarked on a gold-hunting trip to the area.

Willie travelled from Edmonton to Fort Nelson in British Columbia, where Frank joined him. Together, they travelled north to meet their brother Fred at Fort Liard. Their first attempt at gold panning along the Nahanni River in 1904 yielded moderate success. Willie and Frank had some of their gold fashioned into a fine pocket watch, which they presented to Fred. As winter approached, they decided to return south to Edmonton and planned to resume their search for gold in the spring.

Determined to venture deeper into the Nahanni, and aiming to surpass their previous summer's success, they worked for the Hudson's Bay Company to save enough money for their expedition in the spring. Unfortunately, the brothers struggled financially, often squandering their earnings on gambling with the fort's trappers, hunters and other winter residents.

A Scottish man named Robert Weir noticed Fred's gold watch and inquired about its origin. Fred revealed that it came from the gold his brothers had panned the previous year. Intrigued, Weir expressed interest in joining the McCleod brothers on their next journey up the river and even contributed funds for much-needed equipment.

In the spring of 1905, Willie, Frank and their new partner ventured deeper into the Nahanni. They assured everyone before leaving, including their brother Fred, that they would return in late autumn laden with gold.

When the men did not return for the winter, Fred assumed they had found a lucrative gold strike, which was delaying them. Confident in their outdoor skills and wilderness survival abilities, Fred did not immediately worry about their safety.

However, two years passed, and there was still no sign of Willie, Frank or Weir. That's when concern began to grow within the family. Another brother, Charlie, joined by their youngest brother, Danny, travelled to Fort Liard to meet Fred. A search party of six, which included Sergeant Poole Field of the North West Mounted Police, was formed. In May 1908, they embarked in canoes and travelled up the Nahanni River in search of the missing men.

After navigating treacherous rapids and covering several kilometres without any sign of the missing brothers, the group contemplated turning back. However, as they entered a lush valley, they noticed signs of human activity—a clearing with trees cut by axes. Charlie discovered a broken dogsled runner on the riverbank and a message from one of his brothers indicating they had found a promising prospect. Despite not finding Frank and Willie there, the search party continued upstream, cautiously hopeful.

At the valley's northern end, they encountered another clearing and the remnants of what seemed to be a camp. There, they made a grim discovery—the bodies of Frank and Willie McCleod, although not fully intact.

The positioning of the bodies suggested they had been attacked during the night while they slept. One body lay on its back, neatly wrapped in a blanket, as if the person had died peacefully in their sleep. The other body was sprawled on its chest, the blanket haphazardly twisted around it, with one skeletal arm reaching out toward a rusty rifle leaning against a nearby spruce tree. The arrangement of the bodies indicated a nocturnal ambush.

The remains of Frank and Willie McCleod were found without their skulls, which had mysteriously vanished. Their Scottish companion, Robert Weir, was nowhere to be found. Most of the supplies they had brought on the trip were still in their crates at the camp, except for their picks and shovels. Their canoe was also missing.

It seemed that the brothers had succeeded in their search for gold. A crate containing exceptionally vibrant samples of gold-bearing quartz confirmed their discovery. However, investigators suspected foul play in the deaths of Frank and Willie. Some speculated that Weir's greed may have driven him to kill the brothers as they slept. However, the question remained as to why Weir did not take the gold and supplies. There were no sightings of Weir anywhere. When a body was discovered near Fort Simpson it was presumed to be Weir, but the identity of the person was never definitively confirmed.

Rumours circulated regarding Weir's whereabouts, with alleged sightings in various locations in the Northwest Territories and British Columbia. Some rumours claimed he was living a prosperous life in Vancouver, benefiting from the gold he had supposedly stolen from the McCleod brothers. However, none of these reports were ever substantiated.

An investigation by the North West Mounted Police (NWMP) concluded that Frank and Willie had starved to death in the valley after losing their means of transportation. Some suggested illness, such as scurvy or malnutrition, as the cause of death. However, the McCleod family disputed this explanation, asserting that the brothers' health and wilderness survival capabilities made this kind of demise unlikely.

The deaths of Frank and Willie McCleod remain unexplained over a century later. Following the discovery of their bodies, the valley earned new nicknames, such as Deadmen Valley and the infamous Headless Valley. More gossip about what may have happened spread throughout western Canada, as did the belief that the valley held vast gold deposits that were first discovered by the McCleod brothers.

In 1910, a prospector named Martin Jørgensen arrived in the Nahanni Valley to seek his fortune, lured by tales of gold. Jørgensen, an experienced outdoorsman in good health, disappeared shortly after arriving, raising concerns about his fate.

Two years later, in 1913, an Indigenous guide shared a story at a Yukon trading post of an encounter with a sizable Scandinavian man who had paid him in gold to guide him in the Nahanni region. Believing this story to be a sighting of Jørgensen, Sergeant Poole Field of the NWMP assembled a search party to find the Norwegian.

Despite a year-long search, Sergeant Field was unsuccessful in locating Jørgensen. However, on September 28, 1914, deep in the Nahanni Valley, the search party discovered an artificial trail leading into the forest from a creek that flowed into the Flat River. There, they found the remains of a burned-down cabin and the headless skeleton of Martin Jørgensen. The precise details of the discovery of his body vary in differing accounts, the truth lost to the passage of time.

Consequently, the area where Jørgensen's body was found was renamed Murder Creek.

Intriguing claims made by Sergeant Field suggest the Mounties had identified the murderer of Martin Jørgensen. However, no one has corroborated these claims, and the possibility arises that Jørgensen, like the McCleod brothers, may have fallen victim to the same killer. The circumstances surrounding the Norwegian's death, including the absence of his head, indicate that his demise may not have been natural. To this day, the fate of Martin Jørgensen remains unknown.

The Nahanni Valley continued to be associated with strange occurrences over the years, including stories of gold prospectors, hunters and trappers being driven to madness.

In 1926, May Lafferty, a hunting party member, vanished in the Nahanni Valley without a trace. Months later, an Indigenous witness reported seeing a naked figure scaling a steep rock face. The witness believed that an evil forest spirit had possessed the person and refrained from pursuing them. May's fate still remains a mystery.

In 1927, the bones of a man named Yukon Fisher were discovered near Bennett Creek, close to the area where the McCleod brothers had staked their gold claim. Fisher, an outlaw, had been evading the Mounties and had been observed purchasing ammunition using large gold nuggets from an undisclosed location.

The following year, prospector Angus Hall went missing after volunteering to scout ahead for his group. Despite an extensive search that commenced immediately after his disappearance, Hall was never found.

In 1931, a man named Phil Powers met an unexplained death when his charred bones turned up amid the ashes of his cabin on the Flat River. The RCMP investigated and attributed the incident to a faulty stovepipe that caused the shack to catch fire, ultimately cremating Powers. However, many people doubted this explanation.

First, Powers was an experienced prospector who constructed his cabin to ensure ample space for the stovepipe without touching the timbers. Additionally, if the pipe had ignited the roof, causing it to collapse, the poles and dirt would have fallen inside the cabin, potentially helping to extinguish the fire and leaving some charred logs. However, the intensity of the fire that engulfed the cabin was so extreme that only one log was left, along with a small portion of Powers's remains.

Speculation arose that someone standing outside the window had shot Powers while he lay on his bunk, and then set fire to his cabin. The case of Phil Powers remains unresolved, but the evidence suggests foul play rather than an accidental death caused by a faulty stovepipe.

In 1936, Joe Mulholland and Bill Epier went missing, and despite years of searching, their whereabouts remain unknown. Their burned-out cabin, located 160 kilometres (99 miles) above Virginia Falls on Glacier Lake, was found after their disappearance.

Four years later, in 1940, William Gilbertson, an aeronautical engineer exploring the area, was found dead in his cabin near the Nahanni Valley. The same year, a man named Ollie Holmberg, a Scandinavian, went missing and was never seen again.

In 1945, a body was discovered in a sleeping bag with the head missing. There is ongoing debate about the person's identity.

Many more strange deaths and disappearances occurred in the area during that period. Between the deaths of the McCleod brothers and the end of the Second World War, at least 44 people went missing, which added to the enigmatic nature of the region.

Numerous intriguing theories have emerged regarding the mysterious deaths in the Nahanni Valley. Among these theories is the suggestion of an unidentified serial killer operating in the region during the time of the disappearances, although this hypothesis lacks substantial evidence. Another person who has drawn attention is Albert Johnson, known as "the Mad Trapper of Rat River." Johnson's activities, however, occurred hundreds of kilometres from Nahanni, near Fort McPherson, making it unlikely that he was involved in the Nahanni incidents. Some have speculated that the Indigenous population, resentful of colonization and the invaders' exploitation of their sacred lands, may have been responsible for the Europeans' deaths. Still, there is no evidence to back these claims.

Other theories—besides criminal activity or attacks by Indigenous groups—that have been shared as possible explanations for all the mysterious deaths in the Nahanni Valley involve cryptids or supernatural beings.

The Dene legends speak of various supernatural entities and mythical beasts, such as the Waheela, or Saberwolf—an enormous wolf-like creature said to live in the Nahanni Valley. The Waheela is found in folklore of Alaska and the Northwest Territories. It is larger and more robust than a regular wolf and features a broad head, larger feet and long, pure-white fur. Its hind legs are shorter than its front legs, and its widely spaced toes are visible in its tracks. Witnesses estimate its height to be around 1 to 1.2 metres (3.5 to 4 feet) at the shoulder. It is considered a solitary creature that is never seen in packs.

Ivan T. Sanderson, an esteemed zoologist and early investigator of Fortean phenomena, is credited with presenting the concept of the Waheela to a global audience. He is one of the pioneering figures in the realm of cryptozoology, which is the study of legendary or possibly extinct animals whose actual existence is questioned by science. In the year following Sanderson's death, an unprinted piece written by him, "The Dire Wolf," found its way into the pages of *Pursuit* magazine in October 1974. The essay explored the existence of an enormous white wolf in the Nahanni Valley.

Another creature from Indigenous legends some think might be responsible is the Nuk-luk. The Nuk-luk, sometimes referred to as "the Man of the Bush" or "the Bushman," is a cryptid (a creature whose existence or survival is disputed or unsubstantiated) originating from the legends of Indigenous tribes of the Northwest Territories of Canada.

The descriptions of the Nuk-luk vary, but common elements often include the following:

- Short stature: Unlike the Sasquatch or Bigfoot, often depicted as towering figures, the Nuk-luk is relatively short in stature—often around the height of an average human or even smaller.
- Hairy appearance: Much like Bigfoot, the Nuk-luk is typically covered in hair, often brown or reddish in colour.

- Forest dwelling: The Nuk-luk is said to inhabit the forested regions of the Northwest Territories. It is a skilled hunter that uses primitive tools.

In his writings on the Indigenous Dene people of the region, Hammerson Peters discusses a creature known as the Nekedzaltara. This peculiar being could be behind the strange occurrences in the area.

Peters depicts the Nekedzaltara as a shape-shifting entity that sometimes resembles a creature akin to a dragon or a whale. However, more frequently, it transforms into a figure that closely resembles a type of goblin.

Author Algernon Blackwood, who penned a fictitious narrative called "The Valley of the Beasts" in 1921, also suggested that the Wendigo might be responsible for the Nahanni Valley deaths.

For those unfamiliar, the Wendigo is a legendary entity deeply embedded in the mythology and traditions of various Indigenous cultures in North America, especially among tribes who speak Algonquian languages. It's crucial to approach this subject with cultural respect and sensitivity, as the Wendigo carries profound spiritual and cultural meanings within these communities.

Often portrayed as an evil supernatural creature that was once human, the Wendigo is said to engage in cannibalism because of its unquenchable craving for human flesh. Legend posits that extreme hunger, isolation and spiritual decay can trigger a person's transformation into this monstrous entity known as the Wendigo.

Basil Johnston, an Ojibwe teacher and scholar from Ontario, described the Wendigo as a terrifying creature. He claimed the Wendigo appeared extremely thin, almost skeletal, with skin stretched taut over protruding bones. Its grey, deathly complexion, deep-set eyes and frayed, bloodied lips gave it the appearance of having been recently exhumed. Emitting a disturbing scent, the Wendigo was associated with decay, death and the foulness of rotting flesh.

The Wendigo is often depicted as a gigantic entity with matted hair, recessed eyes and a yellowish complexion. Its perpetual hunger and craving for human flesh, which it persistently seeks to satiate, define its existence. Some narratives portray the Wendigo with deer-like features such as antlers, symbolizing its profound bond with the wilderness and the forest spirits.

Frequently linked to the severity of winter conditions, the legend of the Wendigo may be representative of the challenges faced by Indigenous communities in surviving harsh climates. Endowed with supernatural abilities like weather control, mind manipulation and inciting insanity in its victims, the Wendigo is a cautionary figure in folklore, warning against the perils of greed, overindulgence and disrespect for nature. The legend emphasizes the importance of harmony with nature and avoiding destructive urges for individuals and communities.

While many non-Indigenous North Americans may perceive the idea of a creature with an icy heart roaming the North American forests as pure fantasy, Indigenous traditionalists consider the Wendigo very real. They interpret the Wendigo not as a physical entity but as a culturally specific psychological disorder leading the afflicted toward cannibalistic actions.

While not originating from the Nahanni Valley, the heartbreaking story of Swift Runner, arguably the most famous case of Wendigo psychosis, exemplifies this interpretation.

Swift Runner, or Ka-Ki-Si-Kutchin in Cree, was a member of the Cree First Nation residing in Alberta, Canada, in the late 19th century. During the winter of 1878, Swift Runner and his family endured extreme adversity as a result of food shortages and severe weather conditions in their remote Cypress Hills home.

As winter advanced, Swift Runner's family weakened, facing potential starvation. Swift Runner resorted to an unthinkable act—he killed and ate his wife and five children, despite the availability of aid from nearby Indigenous settlements. He concealed his horrific deeds and maintained that his family had died from starvation or suicide.

However, his tale raised doubts among local Indigenous communities, considering the available resources, leading to the authorities' eventual involvement. Evidence of human remains near Swift Runner's camp uncovered his guilt. He confessed to the shocking crimes and guided the authorities to the bodies.

Swift Runner's case drew significant attention because it was the first recorded instance of cannibalism in Canadian criminal history. He was apprehended, prosecuted and ultimately sentenced to death. Swift Runner was hanged in 1879, etching a tragic and horrific episode into Alberta's history.

While these stories are part of local folklore, there is no scientific evidence to back them up. However, some proponents of these theories argue that the beheadings and mysterious disappearances in the area are the work of such creatures.

The most logical non-supernatural explanation is that the people who died in these incidents passed away from misadventures, like a fall. Or they suffered a medical emergency, such as a heart attack or stroke, or succumbed to exposure. The region is rich in boreal forest wildlife, including iconic species like wolves, grizzly bears and other scavengers. After these people died, their heads may have been dragged off by one of these animals.

It's been a long time since the last disappearance in Nahanni. Today it's a popular destination for wilderness junkies looking to escape the hustle and bustle of urban life and disconnect for a while. Many visit the Nahanni Valley annually to go rafting, canoeing, fishing, hunting, hiking and camping, with or without a guide.

CHAPTER 9

Eerie Occurrences at Old MacDonald's Farm (Caledonia Mills, Nova Scotia, Canada)

In the rural hamlet of Caledonia Mills, located in Antigonish County, Nova Scotia, a series of inexplicable fires erupted at a farm in January 1922. The farm belonged to 70-year-old Alexander MacDonald, his 69-year-old wife Janet, and their adopted daughter Mary Ellen, aged 15. The MacDonald family reported that the mysterious fires, totalling 30, ignited quickly in areas far removed from any wood stove.

They were driven from their home by the fires, but there were also other chilling incidents, which they believed were instigated by a malevolent poltergeist intent on wreaking havoc in their lives. Intriguingly, Mary Ellen, the family's young daughter, was the primary focus of the supernatural activity in the house. The bizarre and alarming events unfolding at the farm soon captured the attention of celebrated international investigators specializing in the paranormal.

The narrative surrounding the events in Caledonia Mills bears striking similarities to another notorious tale from Nova Scotia, the Great Amherst Mystery, which occurred in 1878. At the heart of this bizarre incident was an otherwise ordinary 18-year-old girl named Esther Cox, who was subjected to terrifying poltergeist assaults by a malignant entity.

Esther's ordeal started when she had the unsettling sensation of something under her bed. Next she began hearing strange noises, then the phenomena escalated to the point where objects began flying around the room, and spontaneous, unexplained fires began igniting in and around the home.

Although it may not be as well known as the Great Amherst Mystery, the story of the Caledonia Mills occurrences is just as frightening and unexplainable.

To reach Caledonia Mills in Antigonish County, one must venture a 22-minute drive southeast from the nearest town, Antigonish. The MacDonald farm has long since disappeared, and only a handful of farms can still be found in the area. The region remains so isolated that even the Google Maps car has not managed to traverse its terrain, rendering Street View exploration ineffective.

Back in 1922, Caledonia Mills, while small, had its own post office and a little schoolhouse for local children. It also had a grist mill and a sawmill. The residents earned their living and maintained their livelihood by farming and logging their lands, as well as working in various lumber camps or coal mines.

Like many other families in rural Nova Scotia at the time, the MacDonalds lived in their farmhouse without amenities. Water came from a hand-dug well, telephones were still decades away, and electricity was non-existent.

Their house was modest as far as farmhouses go. A small front room, or parlour, served as a gathering spot or for visiting with the occasional guest. In her book *Fire Spook*, author Monica Graham described the MacDonald home. Graham wrote that wallpaper covered the dining room's walls and the parlour ceiling, while the parlour walls and dining room ceiling boasted a brown wooden finish. Roll-up blinds dressed the downstairs windows, and upholstered furniture invited relaxation for the tired. A loft was situated above the kitchen, and a larger bedroom was found on the second floor above the central part of the house, accessible via a staircase from the front parlour. A ladder provided the sole access to the kitchen loft, wholly disconnected from the bedroom on the second floor.

The family used an outhouse behind the home for personal needs. However, they turned to the bedpans stored under each small bed in colder nighttime conditions.

A barn nestled just north of the main dwelling housed the family's livestock—a small herd of cattle, horses, a few sheep and a tiny chicken coop. There were two sheds on the property. One accommodated farm equipment, such as plows for their work animals, and the other was used to store firewood that provided warmth during winter and fuel for cooking throughout the year.

Janet Cameron and Alexander MacDonald, both locals who had grown up nearby, were married in 1873. Janet, one of 11 children, gave birth to their only child, a daughter named Mary, shortly after their wedding. Reflecting the Celtic roots prevalent in the area, the family was bilingual, speaking both Gaelic and English fluently.

Janet MacDonald was a woman of resilience and compassion. After her father, John Cameron, passed away in 1885, Janet witnessed her mother, Mary, deteriorate over the next 14 years, as she succumbed to severe dementia. Unable to handle the situation, Janet's siblings wanted to place Mrs. Cameron in a care home. However, Janet, unable to bear the thought of her mother in such a place, decided to bring her mother to her home to provide care in 1899.

Caring for old Mrs. Cameron proved far more challenging than Janet had imagined. Like many dementia patients, Mrs. Cameron's short-term memory had vanished. She struggled to remember the people around her, including her daughter. She occasionally uttered harsh and hurtful words and frequently called for her deceased husband, requiring constant reminders of his passing.

Mrs. Cameron's propensity to wander became the MacDonalds' most pressing concern. She would roam aimlessly day and night, sometimes venturing into inclement weather inadequately dressed. Janet and Alex locked her in her small bedroom off the dining room for her safety. Yet, somehow, Mrs. Cameron always managed to escape, and she was often found wandering and shouting in the dead of night.

Janet's solution for the escaping senior was a drastic and desperate one. Janet would nail the door closed at night, which limited her distressed mother to ravaging and raving in the confines of her room. Within a few months, to further quiet things down and to prevent Mrs. Cameron from further injury, Janet had begun to secure her mother to the bed using ties.

Between her farm duties and the relentless care needed for her ailing mother, Janet found herself stretched thin. There was no respite for Janet in sight, as her siblings shirked any responsibility for their elderly mother, whom they viewed as nothing more than a burden.

Yet despite her struggles, Janet still enjoyed the company of her neighbours, whom she and Alex regularly invited over for dinner and friendly card games. The first of the inexplicable events transpired in their quaint farmhouse amid one such gathering.

On the evening of April 27, 1900, Mrs. Cameron was noticeably more distressed than usual, and was screaming and ranting in her room. Janet attempted to soothe her mother, but her efforts proved futile. The more comfort she offered, the more violently the older woman reacted. Eventually, the years of accumulated stress frayed Janet's patience, and she lost her temper.

Guests at the card game heard Janet curse her mother and say, "I hope the devil in hell comes and takes you before morning." At this moment, those present observed a large, unkempt black dog with luminescent red eyes stroll through the dining room and into the bedroom where Janet struggled to pacify Mrs. Cameron. The dog did not belong to the MacDonalds or any of the guests.

When Janet exited the room, Alex asked his wife about the dog, but she said she had not seen it. She re-entered the room to search for the animal but found no trace. Alex also inspected the room and found nothing. Alex, Janet and their guests conducted a house-wide search for the strange dog, but all efforts to locate it proved fruitless.

As the evening drew to a close, the guests departed, leaving the MacDonald home with the unnerving vision of the black dog still fresh in their minds. To the contemporary observer, a black dog might not hold particular meaning, but it carried a dark and profound significance for the inhabitants of rural Nova Scotia in the early 1900s.

Some people believed the black dog to be a Black Shuck, a creature entrenched in the folklore of East Anglia and believed to be a harbinger of death, dispatched from hell to carry one's soul away to the underworld. Legend maintains that if one hears the chilling howl of this creature, one should keep their eyes firmly shut to avoid the mark of death.

Following the guests' departure, Mrs. Cameron settled into an uncharacteristic calm that lasted throughout the night, which afforded Alex and Janet a much-needed peaceful night's sleep. When Janet went to wake Mrs. Cameron for breakfast the following morning, she discovered that the older woman had passed away peacefully in her sleep. But Janet worried, uncertain whether her curse had come to pass or if her mother's death was a mere coincidence.

Gossip soon spread among the neighbours about Janet's curse, the black dog and the peculiar timing of Mrs. Cameron's passing. Some even suggested that Janet, driven by desperation and exhaustion, had taken her mother's life because she could no longer endure her burdensome care.

The MacDonald farm fell under a shroud of gloom following Mrs. Cameron's death. Janet was desolate and withdrew from social interactions. She was consumed by a profound sorrow as she mourned the passing of her mother. Her once vibrant personality was never quite the same.

In November 1903, Alex's brother, Andrew, returned to Nova Scotia, flush with earnings from his work in the United States. His arrival injected jarring energy into the subdued atmosphere of the farmhouse. Without ceremony, Andrew sat at the table and began drinking from a bottle he had brought along, boasting and cracking crude jokes, much to the discomfort of Mary and the growing ire of Janet.

Overwhelmed by Andrew's raucous demeanour, Janet exploded, ordering him to leave despite the harsh weather outside. She declared him unwelcome in her home henceforth. Reluctantly, Andrew gathered his belongings and stormed out of the farmhouse. Once outside, he hurled a Gaelic curse back at the house, which translated to "You'll be driven out onto the dung heap on a far worse night than this."

Unfortunately for Andrew, his life took an abrupt downturn, leaving him penniless and confined to the local poorhouse within a few years. He passed away there in 1910, leading many to believe that his curse had backfired and befallen him instead.

Also in 1910, four-year-old Mary Ellen, who would later become the focus of many supernatural events in the farmhouse, came to live at the MacDonald farmstead. Mary Ellen's story was a sad one. Her father, John Peter MacDonald, a relative of Alexander's, had tragically lost his life in an accident at the Drummond coal mine near Waterville when she was just a baby. A heavy coal box had fallen down the mine shaft and crushed him.

John's widow, Annie, a close friend of Janet's, was left with the burden of four children, including the youngest, Mary Ellen, and no source of income. Overwhelmed, Annie was clueless about her next step. Her second-youngest child, Walter, was already in foster care, but securing a placement for Mary Ellen was challenging. Janet, ever the caregiver, was instantly taken by the little girl's charm and decided to adopt her. Alex and Janet promised Annie they'd treat Mary Ellen as their own, and would provide her with education and a nurturing home.

The arrangement seemed perfect for the MacDonalds, as their birth daughter, Mary, would likely get married and leave home soon. Mary Ellen would keep the aging couple company and infuse youthful vitality into their gloomy household.

The farm was an alien landscape for the little girl, who had hitherto lived in the bustling town of Waterville, where she had an abundance of playmates, including her siblings. Even the school was a long 5-kilometre (3 mile) walk from the farm, leaving Mary Ellen to a solitary journey alone each day.

Curiously, Mary Ellen's arrival coincided with an uptick in strange and inexplicable events at the farm. It seemed as though Mary Ellen either attracted some unseen entity or her presence stirred something dormant.

Soon after the young girl's arrival, visitors to the farm reported seeing orbs of fire the size of beach balls floating around the property before vanishing. Some unknown force frequently disrupted the family with noises: an unsettling cacophony of shrieks, creaks, bangs and disturbing sounds resembling deep growls and animal roars. Many outsiders also heard the sounds.

Sometimes during these noise disturbances inside the house, people felt as though they could not breathe, and despite their desperate attempts to escape outside for some fresh air, the door remained stubbornly shut. However, once the mysterious noises ceased, the door would open without resistance, and the suffocating sensation would disappear.

Farm animals mysteriously slipped their secure barns and pens in the dead of night. Precious porcelain dinnerware would inexplicably crash to the floor. Household items disappeared, only to be discovered later buried far from the house or lodged high in the trees around the property.

One afternoon, Alex returned from St. Andrews with a new harness for his workhorse. When he woke up the next day, he was eager to fit the harness and get to work. But when he unlocked his barn, Alex discovered the harness missing. Despite searching his entire property, he couldn't locate it. None of his neighbours had seen it either. He was the only person with a key to the barn, and there was no alternative entrance. The disappearance of the harness, a significantly sized item, from a locked barn perplexed him.

The missing harness resurfaced years later following another peculiar incident. While standing near the woods on his property, Alex heard a cowbell ringing. Assuming one of his animals had slipped through the fence, he followed the sound. The source of the sound always seemed just out of sight, and after a while, Alex, exhausted, took a seat on a stump. To his surprise, he glanced down at his feet and saw a metal buckle attached to a piece of leather sticking out of the ground. He pulled on the leather and was shocked as he unearthed the long-lost harness.

Decades after these eerie events, locals would still occasionally find strange items buried in the ground, within their wells or nestled far up in trees. These mysterious items were thought to be remnants from the MacDonald homestead.

However, the source of these disturbances at the MacDonald farm was not always benign or playful. In one disturbing incident, a lamb Mary Ellen had taken in as her pet turned up on the family's doorstep with its throat brutally slashed. Mary Ellen was devastated.

Eventually, locals were convinced that an evil presence lurked around the MacDonald property. Some speculated it to be a bauchan, a Scottish household hobgoblin known for its mischievous, sometimes aggressive behaviour but also recognized for its occasional helpful tendencies.

There were stories of bauchan encounters in the vicinity and along the road connecting Antigonish and Guysborough. Mary L. Fraser, in her 1930 book *Folklore of Nova Scotia*, recounted a local story that happened at Beech Hill.

Shrouded in the whispers of the supernatural, Beech Hill, a stone's throw from Antigonish, was infamous for its otherworldly sightings and the chilling tale of a vanished peddler from bygone days.

On a bone-chilling winter dusk, the Camerons, bearing no known familial ties to Janet, journeyed back to Antigonish with their young daughter from a visit to South River. A ghostly procession appeared before them as they edged closer to the notorious Beech Hill.

Before their eyes, a pair of colossal oxen laden with burdens too shadowy to discern were ushered by a stooped, withered old man. He toiled with the rope over his shoulders, tethered to the yoke's heart, fighting to hasten the beasts' lumbering tread. Compounding the eeriness, a quartet of women in outlandish attire followed, their headdresses bizarre and their gowns whispering a chilling symphony that terrorized the Camerons' horses.

While the Camerons fought desperately to soothe their spooked horses, these phantom figures slipped by, dissolving into the encroaching night.

The enigma of Beech Hill deepened with further spectral encounters. One such encounter befell a man named Donald, who spied a figure draped in grey ambling ahead on the road. Yearning for companionship, Donald hastened to catch the stranger but was thwarted by an unseen force. He sliced through the woodland to intercept the stranger at the road's curve.

Arriving at a clearing where the grey wanderer should have been, a mournful groan met Donald's ears. Pushing through his dread, he stumbled upon the man sprawled beneath a gnarled tree. One glimpse of the man's ghastly visage sent Donald fleeing in abject horror, not stopping until the woods were but a memory.

Whether caused by a bauchan or not, the strange incidents at the MacDonald farm reached a crescendo beginning on January 7, 1922, and gained the attention of ghost hunters worldwide.

It was a mundane Saturday, and it started, as usual, with Alexander MacDonald going about his daily chores. His initial task was to ignite the fire for the day, to heat the house for the family and warm the stove so Janet could prepare breakfast. As he moved toward the wood stove, Alex spotted burned wood fragments scattered on the floor. Glancing upward, he discovered a kitchen beam marred by deep scorch marks that stretched about a metre (3 feet) long. Alex suspected there had been a chimney fire during the night, but the region around the flue was unscathed. Despite his best efforts, he was puzzled about what could have caused the scorch marks.

That night, after he retired to bed with the mystery still unsolved, Alex was roused by Janet, who claimed she could smell smoke. Initially, Alex assumed the mysterious events of the day had fuelled his wife's paranoia. However, at Janet's insistence, Alex got out of bed to inspect the house. When he opened the kitchen door, he found a fire blazing in the loft above the kitchen. He quickly extinguished it, but just as he had doused one fire, another erupted in another room in the house. In total, five small fires broke out in the house before dawn. Fortunately, Alex managed to quell them all before any significant damage occurred.

Despite thoroughly inspecting the house to determine the cause, Alex could find no explanation for the fires. The following day, despite the biting cold outside, the family let the home fires die in the afternoon, hoping to avoid repeating the previous night's events. They retired around 10:00 p.m., but only minutes later, Alex detected the smell of smoke. He rose from his bed and followed the scent into the kitchen.

Flames danced on an upholstered rocking chair about 3 metres (9 feet) from the stove. Alex swiftly grabbed it, barged through the kitchen door and hurled it into a nearby snowbank. Returning to the kitchen, he discovered a couch aflame on the opposite side of the room. He dragged it to the door and flung it into the snow beside the chair. For the second night in a row, Alex remained vigilant until the early morning hours, but no additional fires sprung up that night, nor were there any more fires on Monday or Tuesday.

However, the following Wednesday proved to be the most challenging yet. Fires began igniting spontaneously throughout the house. As soon as Alex managed to douse one, either Janet or Mary Ellen would raise the alarm about another outbreak. Alex sent Mary Ellen to summon their neighbour, Leo MacGillivray, for assistance. Over the next 24 hours, they successfully battled 38 fires that had erupted in various corners of the MacDonald farmhouse.

They reported that while the flames had charred their hair, the fires were peculiarly calm, silent and, occasionally, a brilliant blue colour. Having worked around electricity, MacGillivray noted that the fires glowed like high-tension wires but far brighter.

Fearful of returning home, the MacDonalds sought refuge at the MacGillivray residence for the next few days. News of the mysterious fires began to spread. Harold Whidden, a journalist in Antigonish, was the first to publish the story in the *Halifax Herald* and the *Halifax Evening Mail*.

Whidden and a police detective named Peachie Carroll spent two nights in the house, during which they both witnessed several strange occurrences. Whidden wrote that he intended to uncover the truths behind the eerie happenings reported there. After a perplexing 48 hours with Detective Carroll, their stay had only thickened the surrounding aura of mystery. On the second evening, an unexpected experience befell them amid the shadowed silence. They were disturbed by unusual, inexplicable sounds emanating from the room above, unlike anything Whidden had previously encountered.

Whidden claimed he was suddenly and unmistakably struck on the upper part of his left arm. The sensation pierced through his protective layers of clothing: two shirts, a light inner coat, a thick woolen sweater and the weighty embrace of a fur-lined overcoat, all beneath the sturdy shelter of a new horse rug.

Convinced that his senses were not betraying him, Whidden recognized that the source of this impact was neither imagined nor self-inflicted. With a journalist's keen instinct for detail and fact, he immediately sought to verify the source of the blow. He turned toward Carroll, inquiring with a mix of urgency and curiosity whether he had been the one to strike him. This question served not so much to accuse as to confirm Whidden's strong belief that the detective was not the source. Carroll, just as bewildered, denied any involvement, and it was evident he hadn't shifted from his initial position, which would have made it impossible for him to reach Whidden without detection.

With this information, Whidden considered Alexander Mac-Donald, who was resting on the floor to his other side. MacDonald, appearing to be on the cusp of sleep, was undisturbed and not the agent of the mysterious blow. He lay in the same posture as Whidden had observed moments before the incident, indicating that he, too, was incapable of such stealthy interference.

Harold Whidden was left with the inescapable conclusion that the forceful contact had been delivered by some unseen entity, an encounter that defied logical explanation. Both Carroll and Mac-Donald were in positions that precluded them from administering the blow without Whidden's notice, solidifying the night's event as an inexplicable chapter in the haunting of the MacDonald homestead.

The story caught on like wildfire. Two local papers, the *Evening*

Mail and the *Herald*, hosted a contest, inviting readers to offer their theories. They promised to publish people's theories and promised a modest cash reward to whoever presented the most compelling explanation.

On January 26, 1922, in answer to the contest, a rather philosophically minded anonymous reader from Halifax wrote a considered explanation about the cause of the eerie goings-on at the MacDonald farm. The letter writer felt that the fires had been outcomes of spiritual events intended to guide those who were becoming overly focused on the material world. This didn't refer to the individuals forced to evacuate their homes in Caledonia Mills but rather to the wider population that was growing increasingly materialistic. It wouldn't have been surprising if there were comparable events in different regions of the country. People needed to smile more, frown less and adopt a more Christian-like demeanour. That was the expectation placed upon them.

Amid the perplexing events at the MacDonald farmhouse in Caledonia Mills, residents initiated a campaign to bring in famed British author Sir Arthur Conan Doyle, known for creating Sherlock Holmes and his interest in the paranormal, to investigate. Despite their hopes that his combined detective skills and spiritualist knowledge would illuminate the mystery, Doyle declined their invitation. His refusal was a setback to the community, leaving the unexplained phenomena at the MacDonalds' home unsolved.

Renowned psychic investigator Dr. Walter Franklin Prince joined the investigation eventually. Prince, a former clergyman, joined the American Society for Psychical Research (ASPR) in 1908. He partook in numerous high-profile inquiries and later served as president of the global Society for Psychical Research from 1930 to 1931.

Prince was known for his skepticism about specific forms of psi and other psychical phenomena but held strong beliefs in telepathy, clairvoyance and precognition. In the study of parapsychology, *psi* refers to the mysterious element responsible for phenomena such as extrasensory perception and psychokinesis, which cannot be accounted for by any existing scientific or biological principles. The word *psi* comes from the 23rd letter of the Greek alphabet and is also associated with the Greek word *psych*, meaning "mind" or "soul."

In 1927, Prince's work was featured in the book *The Case For and Against Psychical Belief*, which was a collection of essays from skeptics and believers of psychical phenomena. He was a close associate of the famed parapsychologist Joseph Banks (J.B.) Rhine and even published and wrote the introduction for Rhine's celebrated book *Extrasensory Perception* in 1934.

Dr. Prince, ever the keen skeptic, endeavoured to uncover the truth. He brought Alex, Janet and Mary Ellen back to the farmhouse to trigger the mysterious events that had previously transpired. Harold Whidden was also present and, at one point, engaged in automatic writing at the MacDonalds' kitchen table. He claimed that he was channelling communications from the spirit inhabiting the farmhouse. Through this session, the unseen entity, using Whidden's hand, confessed to the strange events plaguing the MacDonald home.

Whidden expressed that individuals should recognize that those who have passed on continue to be with us. He affirmed that he believed God embodies mercy, benevolence and fairness. Additionally, he stated that he was confident the deceased do, in fact, return in spirit to visit the Earth.

A subsequent *New York Times* article spotlighted Dr. Prince's conclusions. Prince determined that the mysterious fires in the house were caused not by paranormal activity but by human intervention. He speculated that the MacDonalds' young adopted daughter was involved. Nonetheless, he pointed out that Mary Ellen should not be held mentally accountable, as her psychological maturity was significantly below what would be expected for someone of her age.

Prince suggested that Mary Ellen had experienced altered states of consciousness, and these dream-like states could have led to her involvement in these incidents. He hypothesized that a disembodied intelligence influenced her actions.

While intriguing, the article pointed out that Whidden's automatic writing did not provide a definitive conclusion about what happened in the house. Prince's findings did not close the case of what became known locally as "the Mary Ellen Spook Farm."

Mary Ellen was frustrated by Prince's portrayal of her in the article. Despite the unresolved mystery of what caused the fires, the family moved back to the farm. While more inexplicable fires did ignite from time to time, none matched the intensity of those from January 1922.

The case became so infamous that curious spectators swarmed the property to look at the house. It reached a point where Alex had to publicly declare in a newspaper that visitors were no longer welcome on his land. Mary Ellen also endured public ridicule and bullying for years following the incidents. In October 1922, she was committed to what was then known as the Nova Scotia Insane Asylum after being apprehended while attempting to set fire to a barn.

Mary Ellen was eventually released and faced numerous challenges over the years, including several arrests and incarcerations. She changed her name several times, relocated to Ontario, married and had four children with a man who worked at a Coca-Cola bottling plant. When Mary Ellen passed away in Sudbury, Ontario, in June of

1987, she was known as Helen McGuire. Before her death at 64, she was a popular landlady who managed a local boarding house. There were no more unexplained fires around Mary Ellen.

Over the years, new theories have emerged as fresh minds attempted to decipher the enigma of all the fires at the MacDonald residence in 1922. A factual explanation of the happenings in Caledonia Mills will forever remain a mystery, although these days, most believe that a troubled Mary Ellen was responsible. Perhaps the attention received by creating havoc was the only way she felt seen.

CHAPTER 10

Suicide Forest: The Sea of Trees
(Aokigahara Jukai, Japan)

Content warning: The following chapter references suicide, attempted suicide and suicidal ideation, which could disturb or trigger some readers. Reader discretion is advised.

My enduring love for nature, and the curiosity it sparks, has led me to explore various landscapes, including the paradoxical Aokigahara Jukai. This lush and vibrant forest in Japan, also known as the Sea of Trees, holds a grim reputation as "the Suicide Forest." Despite its natural allure, it's associated not with life's celebration but with a quiet, lonely end.

My interest in Aokigahara Jukai doesn't romanticize its grim reputation; instead, I investigate the intriguing juxtaposition inherent in its character. It is difficult to comprehend how a location so abundant with natural splendour can paradoxically embody desolation and demise. I hope the following exploration offers a journey as hauntingly beautiful as it is illuminating, a narrative woven around the concepts of life and death and the obscure, elusive boundary between them.

Mount Fuji, Japan's tallest peak, holds significant cultural and spiritual significance. It is deeply rooted in myths, folktales and religious ascetic practices, and it has served as a symbol of faith for centuries in Japanese society. The forest called Aokigahara, or Blue Tree Meadow, spans over 35 square kilometres (14 square miles) north of the mountain. This lush forest, comprising a mixture of coniferous and broadleaf trees, is situated on volcanic rock—the hardened remnants of a significant eruption of Mount Fuji in 864. It got its nickname, Jukai, the Sea of Trees, from hikers on Mount Fuji, who view the forest from above. Its uneven terrain undulates much like the waves of a sea, enhancing this impression of the ocean. At the same time, the forest's dense vegetation, vast size and quiet, undisturbed ambience combine to create the illusion of a sea made of trees.

The forest's environment is cool and humid, providing an ideal bryophyte habitat, including vibrant green mosses and lichens. This natural sanctuary is not just for these plant species; it's also home to diverse fauna, such as deer, foxes, wild rabbits and various bird species. Despite this, the forest is often spookily quiet; the sound-absorbing quality of the porous volcanic lava that makes up the forest floor contributes to this unique, tranquil and somewhat disorienting sense of solitude. The forest is so dense that in certain areas it can block out the sunlight completely, reducing visibility and adding to the eeriness of the environment.

Aokigahara forest is also famous for its geological attractions. A network of designated hiking trails weaves through the area, linking three significant lava caves: the Narusawa Ice Cave, the Fugaku Wind Cave and the West Lake Bat Cave. Each cave offers its own unique spectacle and is a fascinating exploration of the forest's subterranean world.

Walking in Aokigahara forest can also be treacherous owing to various environmental factors. The hardened lava of the forest floor creates a very uneven and rocky terrain that can make navigation difficult and potentially hazardous, even for experienced hikers. The forest's floor is riddled with hidden crevices and caves that could also pose dangers for the unprepared.

While it's a misconception that compasses malfunction in the forest because of the magnetic properties of the volcanic soil, compasses do, in fact, behave unpredictably if held too close to the ground, potentially causing confusion for visitors who may rely on them for direction. For this reason, visitors are advised to stick to the designated trails and to not venture off the paths, as getting lost in Aokigahara can be extremely dangerous.

But the reasons behind staying on the trails are about more than navigation or safety issues.

Aokigahara has a darker side and is a complex symbol of natural beauty and human despair. It is infamous worldwide as a common site for suicides, a reputation that has led to a variety of stories, myths and references in popular culture. Efforts have been made by authorities to combat this issue, with signs posted in the forest encouraging visitors to think of their families and contact a suicide prevention hotline if they are feeling despondent.

The forest's reputation as a place to end one's life has a complex history rooted in Japanese mythology and cultural attitudes toward death. Suicide in Japan has deep historical and cultural roots, and understanding it requires acknowledging a complex interplay of societal values, historical practices and individual pressures. The notion of suicide as an "honourable act" hearkens back to the samurai class in feudal Japan. The samurai practised seppuku, a form of ritual suicide by disembowelment, which was carried out to avoid disgrace or as a form of protest and was considered an act of great honour, courage and loyalty. *Hara-kiri* is a more widely recognized term for this practice in the West.

According to Jack Seward's book *Hara-kiri*, seppuku emerged as an honourable method of execution for samurai during the late Ashikaga period. During the Tokugawa period, there was a move toward formalizing all aspects of the social system, which led to the institution of five penalties for the samurai class.

These penalties, progressing in severity, were as follows: hissoku (voluntary, contrite seclusion), which comprised restraint, circumspect prudence and humility; heimon (house arrest), between 50 and 100 days; chikkyo (solitary confinement), encompassing confinement to a single room, temporary suspension from duty and permanent retirement; kai-eki, which was the permanent removal of the offender's name from the samurai roll; and finally, seppuku.

The ceremony of seppuku was highly ritualized, conducted in a precise, formal manner and often witnessed by select high-ranking individuals. In the case of males, the act involved self-infliction of an abdominal wound with a short blade, following which a designated second, trusted individual would perform a ceremonial beheading to hasten death and limit suffering.

Historically, while seppuku was predominantly a male practice, there were instances where females, mainly wives of samurai, performed a variant of the ritual called jigai. This act was considered the female equivalent of seppuku, carried out to avoid disgrace or to avoid falling into enemy hands, particularly during a siege or invasion. The method differed slightly. Instead of the abdominal cut performed in traditional seppuku, jigai involved cutting the neck, traditionally using a short sword known as a tanto. Like seppuku, it was a deeply ritualized act carried out in a very specific manner.

It's essential, however, to tread carefully when linking ancient practices like seppuku to modern suicide rates. Modern Japan is far removed from the samurai era, and the causes of suicide today are primarily related to mental health issues, societal pressures and economic hardships, as they are everywhere else in the world.

While historical and cultural contexts can provide a backdrop to understanding societal attitudes, they should not be seen as justifying or romanticizing the serious and pervasive issue of suicide. It's also crucial to remember that these attitudes are not held universally across Japan, and the country has made significant strides in recent years to raise awareness about mental health and suicide prevention.

That said, every year in Japan, deaths by suicide occur when a person feels a sense of responsibility for an accident or experiences acute embarrassment. According to a *Lancet* article by Nori Takei and Kazuhiko Nakamura in April 2004, there is also a phenomenon known as inseki-jisatsu, or responsibility-driven suicide. This form of suicide often involves individuals in high social positions who feel compelled to take responsibility for something tragic that's happened to another person, and it can even extend to families dealing with members who have committed serious crimes.

A recent example of suspected inseki-jisatsu came on May 17, 2023, when the famous kabuki actor Ichikawa Ennosuke IV, 47, was arrested for allegedly helping his 75-year-old mother die by suicide by giving her sleeping pills. His father, also a kabuki actor, had also died with the same sleeping pills found in his body. Both parents reportedly agreed to a family suicide after Ennosuke informed them about a scandal he was involved in, which was about to be made public.

Ennosuke, who had also ingested the sleeping pills, was found unconscious but survived. He told police that he had dissolved the pills in
water, and he had suffocated his mother with a plastic bag. He is suspected to have also played a part in his father's death. As of this writing,
according to the Tokyo Metropolitan Police, the case remains open.

Japan's rate of suicide is slightly higher than in Canada and the
United States, but overall, it remains about average for countries that
report their suicide rates. In 2022, the suicide rate in Japan was 17.5
per 100,000 people (the United States is around 16 per 100,000, and
Canada is close to 12 per 100,000). This figure signalled a concerning
shift in trends, as Japan had been experiencing a steady decline in
suicide rates over the preceding decade.

However, at the beginning of 2020, there was a reversal of this positive trend, when suicide rates once again began to rise. Many experts
believe this uptick is tied to the hardships and heightened anxieties
associated with the COVID-19 pandemic. The pandemic's effects,
including social isolation, job loss and the overall uncertainty of the
global health crisis, are believed to have significantly contributed to
the increase in suicides, emphasizing the urgent need for enhanced
mental health support and intervention measures during such challenging times.

Attitudes toward suicide in Japan have undergone a significant shift
over the past century. Historically, certain forms of suicide were seen
as honourable acts, particularly in the context of the samurai culture
and during the Second World War. However, in more recent decades,
there has been a growing recognition of suicide as a public health
issue and a preventable tragedy. Efforts have been made to destig-
matize mental health concerns, provide better support services and
raise awareness about the importance of seeking help. Despite these

positive steps, Japan continues to grapple with relatively high suicide rates, and societal attitudes still carry remnants of the past, where suicide was sometimes viewed as a permissible solution to personal or familial problems. Overall, while progress has been made, further work is needed to fully reframe suicide as a preventable loss of life and to foster a more compassionate and supportive environment for those struggling with suicidal thoughts.

With that said, why, if a person has chosen to die, do they choose Aokigahara?

The first recorded suicide in Aokigahara Jukai was in 1340 by a Buddhist monk named Shohkai. The act he committed, however, was known as nyujoh, which was a form of religious ritual rather than a modern form of suicide. Nyujoh, also spelled nyūjō, is a Buddhist practice that translates roughly to "entering into conditions" or "entering the way." In a broader context, it refers to an ascetic practice where Buddhist monks willingly enter a state of meditative serenity after considerable prayer and fasting, essentially awaiting death.

Buddhist monks undertook this practice believing they could save the sinful world and its people through their self-sacrifice. This concept is deeply rooted in Buddhism's focus on transcending the physical world and its inherent suffering. It's important to note that this practice is not synonymous with suicide in the modern sense but instead reflects a complex cultural and religious understanding of life, death and spiritual duty. Over time, nyujoh has become less common and is not widespread in contemporary Buddhist societies.

Aokigahara Forest is also associated with the historical practice of ubasute, a form of euthanasia in which an elderly relative is abandoned in a remote area by their family. *Ubasute* is a term from Japanese folklore that roughly translates to "abandoning the old woman."

It refers to a historical practice where an elderly or infirm family member, often a woman, would be carried into a remote area such as a mountain or a forest and left to die by dehydration, starvation or exposure to the elements; it was often done during times of extreme hardship when a family could not afford to feed its members.

The practice is featured in many Japanese folktales and legends, particularly those set during periods of famine. In these stories, ubasute is depicted as a highly sorrowful yet necessary decision brought about by desperate circumstances.

It's important to note, however, that the historical accuracy of these tales is uncertain. Many historians and scholars believe that while the idea of ubasute makes for a compelling and tragic narrative, it was not likely a common practice, if it even occurred at all. Furthermore, the acceptance of widespread elder abandonment does not align with Confucian values prominent in historical Japanese society, such as filial piety and respect for one's elders.

Regardless of its historical accuracy, the concept of ubasute has left a lasting impression on Japanese culture, influencing literature, film and even the perception of locations like Aokigahara Forest, which is sometimes called "the place of ubasute" in folk legends.

There are also local beliefs that it is nearly impossible for a person to find their way out of the forest once they enter it, leading many, because of their inability to escape, to suicide. This sense of disorientation and the forest's historic association with demons in Japanese mythology also contributes to the forest's foreboding reputation. In Japanese folklore, the forest was thought to be inhabited by yūrei, or ghosts, and was associated with death and the afterlife. Such a reputation could be another reason why some individuals, particularly those seeking to end their lives, might be drawn to this location.

The mid-20th-century popularity of Aokigahara Forest as a place to die by suicide can also be attributed to a romantic novel that was released in the early 1960s by renowned Japanese mystery writer Seicho Matsumoto. The novel, *Nami no Tou*, which translates to *Tower of Waves*, portrays suicide in a positive, idealistic and romantic light. The story follows a love affair between Onogi Takao, a young prosecutor, and Yoriko Yuuki, a woman trapped in a loveless marriage to a man implicated in a political scandal. As their relationship deepens, Onogi is removed from the prosecution team handling Yoriko's husband's case, which leads to his resignation. Meanwhile, Yoriko divorces her husband, but the scandal leaves them both socially ostracized. Seeing no other options, Onogi suggests a double suicide, but Yoriko chooses to die alone in Aokigahara Jukai.

Matsumoto uses a serene natural setting to underscore the calm and peaceful atmosphere of the scene before Yoriko's death. Rather than portraying the gruesome reality of dying alone in a forest, the author ends the story with Yoriko running into the woods, making her death seem romantic and beautiful. The potent imagery of this final scene was so powerful that it cemented the forest's association with suicide in the collective consciousness of Japan. The book's bestseller status significantly amplified Aokigahara's reputation as a place where people go to end their lives, which increased the number of suicides there.

The Complete Manual of Suicide is a controversial book written by Wataru Tsurumi, published in Japan in 1993. It provides detailed descriptions of various methods of suicide, including a guide to Aokigahara Forest. Tsurumi's book refers to Aokigahara as "the perfect place to die," further contributing to its notoriety and popularity. The book notes that the dense forest and its complex pathways make it easy for someone to venture in and never be found, which is tragically attractive for individuals looking to end their lives.

While *The Complete Manual of Suicide* does not solely account for the suicide rate in Aokigahara Forest, its publication has undeniably played a significant role in reinforcing the forest's infamous status. The book, and its contribution to the forest's reputation, continues to be a cause of controversy and concern, particularly from suicide prevention advocates.

A 2010 *Vice* documentary about Aokigahara Forest, called *The Suicide Forest*, features geologist and environmentalist Azusa Hayano, who explains the history of the region and his work to deter individuals from taking their lives there. The documentary covers the forest's history, its infamous reputation as a suicide hot spot and the eerie aura that surrounds it.

Hayano highlights measures undertaken to prevent suicides in the area, such as warning signs at the entrance urging people to consider their loved ones and seek help. He claims that more than 100 bodies are found annually in the forest. During his forays into the woods, he has personally discovered many bodies of people who had died by suicide. Hayano expresses his empathy for the victims and encourages a broader discussion of the importance of face-to-face communication, which he believes is lacking in today's digital age and contributes to people's feelings of isolation.

As part of the documentary, Hayano delves into some dark aspects associated with the forest, such as the rumour of local yakuza (Japanese criminal organizations) exploiting the forest's reputation as a way to hide their murders. He also delves into the belief that angry spirits haunt the area. He mentions that locals do not go there, thinking the forest is evil, and that people from elsewhere are the ones who come there to die. Hayano further describes how victims who are uncertain about their decision often use tape to mark their paths, allowing them a way back should they change their minds. (Although blurred out for YouTube, the video on *Vice*'s site shows graphic photographs and footage of deceased people in varying states of decomposition, so viewers beware.)

The documentary ends on a hopeful note, urging viewers to value the present, understand their emotions and seek help when distressed. It emphasizes that every life matters, encouraging those in despair to seek assistance.

As I could not go to the forest myself, in 2020, a good friend, L.J. Hoshino, offered to visit, take photos and share her experiences. In the company of an experienced hiker friend, Ken, and dressed appropriately in warm clothing and sturdy hiking boots, L.J. embarked on a journey by car from her home in Setagaya, a ward of Tokyo. On their way, they stopped at a 7-Eleven, a last stop for many who venture into the forest with morbid intentions.

L.J. noted: "The storefront and sign of this particular 7-Eleven is in muted colours. They are dark brown, almost black. Several establishments in Japan do this in areas of natural or historic significance to help them blend into their surroundings. The dark colours are only coincidence, of course, but it still felt oddly sombre, given that extra context we had of this particular store."

On arriving at a parking lot near the trailhead into the forest, L.J. was surprised to see a bus full of children disembarking for a day hike along one of the trails. Aside from that group, L.J. and Ken did not encounter anyone else inside the forest or on the trails, an observation they attributed to the ongoing pandemic at the time.

L.J.'s senses amplified as they walked deeper into the forest and toward the area where people usually go to end their lives. Almost immediately, she felt a unique energy emanating from the surroundings. She wrote to me: "While Ken didn't perceive or feel much of anything as we walked, I felt something odd. It was not unlike walking alongside a huge aquarium where your perception of depth is off, and something large is moving behind the glass. Whatever was there had energy and power. I looked in, and I felt a presence. It paid us no mind but seemed aware, somehow, nevertheless."

The forest looked nothing like the woods of her childhood in the British countryside, L.J. said. She was struck by its unique landscape—wet from recent rainfall, slippery because of the moss and fallen branches, and treacherous because of the volcanic rock. The forest seemed to have a unique life of its own.

L.J. observed that Aokigahara did look like its famous nickname, the Sea of Trees. "I heard that [the nickname] is due to how it appears from above, but equally, it could be how it looks on the ground from within. The volcanic rocks crest and fall, and the thousands of slender trees cling to these waves, their roots crawling across the ground, looking for purchase and for what little nutrients the rocky forest floor has to provide. It's not flat. Rather, it undulates like waves. The softness of the landscape is cut with the sharp edges of broken trees and jutting rocks, disrupting the otherwise smooth curves of rock, twisted roots and moss. The whole place looks like a camouflage pattern, seemingly there to trick your eyes and disorientate you. And it does so very quickly."

The isolation and quietness struck L.J. as she and her friend ventured further into the Aokigahara Forest. Once they left the roadside, it quickly disappeared from sight, and the hum of traffic faded away. They found themselves surrounded by steep rocks and a dense expanse of trees. In the forest's depths, L.J. experienced an unusual sensation. She said that even though they were in the open, she felt completely enveloped by the forest's silence and stillness. After taking some time to absorb the environment, she and Ken decided to backtrack to the road because they realized they needed to find the official hiking trail.

"Once we made our way to the trail," L.J. said, "we saw the beginnings of the things I'd seen in various documentaries and on websites."

L.J. took a photo of the sign on the trail into Aokigahara, written in Japanese, which reads "Life is a precious gift given by your parents. Quietly, once more, think about your parents, siblings and children. Don't suffer alone. Please talk to someone." The sign included information about who to contact for help.

They walked for a while, enjoying the landscape, and then the trail abruptly ended. It was roped off because this was the entrance to the suicide area of the forest.

Ken and L.J. ignored the signs and ventured deeper, where they discovered various markers like yellow plastic tape tied to branches, which were believed to be breadcrumbs for those who may change their mind about suicide to find their way back. They found disturbing signs as well; one sign, tacked to a tree, featured a man who had presumably died by suicide. It read "Cuco will always exist" and seemed to be a plea against suicide.

They decided to turn back.

L.J. says she feels drawn to the place and wants to return someday, but she will take a hiking partner because the terrain within Aokigahara is disorienting, and Ken had to redirect her back onto the path many times.

I plan to visit Aokigahara one day. But I pledge to approach this area with profound respect, understanding and sensitivity. Aokigahara Forest is a place of natural beauty and historical significance. And it remains an area that also carries deep cultural and emotional weight. If you ever visit Aokigahara Forest, please do so with the utmost compassion, empathy and understanding.

IF YOU OR someone you know is struggling with thoughts of suicide or self-harm, it's crucial to reach out for help immediately. Please remember you're not alone, and there are professionals ready to provide the necessary support.

For those in Canada, you can contact the Canada Suicide Prevention Service at 1-833-456-4566, available 24/7. You can text 45645 from 4:00 p.m. to midnight eastern time. Go to the website talksuicide.ca for more information and resources.

For those in the United States, the National Suicide Prevention Lifeline is available 24/7 at 1-800-273-TALK (1-800-273-8255), or you can contact the Crisis Text Line by texting HOME to 741741. Go to the website crisistextline.org for more information and resources.

If you are in immediate danger, call emergency services in your country right away.

CHAPTER 11

A Brief History of Lost Civilizations:
Atlantis and Others

In March 1977, when I was eight years old, a series of sci-fi TV
movies called *Man from Atlantis* debuted. The movies were the
precursor to the TV series, which came later that fall with the
same cast. The story of both revolved around a character named
Mark Harris, a man with amnesia found near death on a beach. He
claimed to be the final living citizen of the lost continent of Atlantis
(referred to as simply "a city" in the show). Harris had unique capabilities; he was able to breathe underwater, could endure extreme
deep-sea pressures and possessed superhuman strength. His webbed
hands and feet suggested his Atlantean heritage, as did his sensitivity
to light and distinctive swimming technique—arms to his side cou-
pled with something resembling a butterfly or dolphin kick. After
his discovery, Mark Harris was enlisted by the Foundation for Oce-
anic Research, a covert government organization that performed
secret research and exploration of the ocean using a sophisticated
submarine known as the *Cetacean*.

I thought this was the best show ever, but perhaps I was the only one. The series was cancelled. (Critics called it childish.)

While I was disappointed with the program's cancellation, watching it led to my interest in lost civilizations, like Atlantis, which I'll cover in this chapter. Their existence is one of my favourite subjects to ponder.

Atlantis was first mentioned by the Greek philosopher Plato in two dialogues, *Timaeus* and *Critias*, from around 360 BCE. Plato described Atlantis as a powerful and advanced kingdom that existed 9,000 years before the time of Solon, an Athenian statesman. The information about Atlantis was passed down to Solon by Egyptian priests during his visit to the city of Sais. The priests spoke of cataclysmic events periodically wiping out advanced civilizations, and with them, great ancient knowledge. Atlantis was cited as an example of one of these lost civilizations.

The kingdom of Atlantis was said to be located beyond the Pillars of Hercules (the modern-day Strait of Gibraltar) and had more land mass than Asia and Libya combined. The Atlanteans were believed to be a mighty civilization with advanced technical capabilities. They had conquered many parts of Western Europe and Africa, asserting their dominance and showcasing their might.

However, their ambition led to their downfall. The Atlanteans attempted to enslave the Athenians, who resisted and managed to defeat them. Following this conflict, Atlantis faced divine retribution. Violent earthquakes and floods struck the city, and in a single day and night, the entire island sank into the sea, disappearing forever. The once mighty civilization was lost, leaving only the tale of its existence and downfall. Thus, Atlantis has remained as a cautionary tale about the dangers of unchecked ambition, the rise and fall of civilizations, and the way knowledge can be lost forever.

The fact that two brief mentions of a place that most likely never existed have remained relevant for more than 2,000 years is astonishing. The enduring allure of Atlantis is rooted in its mysterious nature and humanity's fascination with lost civilizations. The tale of this advanced society that mysteriously disappeared is intriguing, and its location remains unknown. Despite the absence of concrete archaeological evidence, the possibility of discovering Atlantis is tantalizing and continues to pique people's interest. It is fun to contemplate uncovering hidden secrets from past civilizations, especially ones as advanced as Atlantis. This story has inspired philosophers, writers (including Francis Bacon) and countless other artists throughout history. Plato's story of Atlantis inspired Sir Thomas More's 1516 book *Utopia*.

But other than Plato's dialogues, there are no primary accounts of Atlantis. Numerous ancient philosophers considered the kingdom a myth, including Aristotle. However, ever since Plato first mentioned Atlantis, many have believed the civilization truly existed.

In ancient times, scholars like Crantor and Proclus believed in the existence of Atlantis. Crantor, a student of Plato's student Xenocrates, claimed to have found hieroglyph-inscribed pillars in Egypt detailing Atlantis's history. However, this claim has been disputed. In his commentary on Plato's *Timaeus*, Proclus describes Atlantis's geography, which is clearly based on other authors' accounts. He mentions several islands, including a large one remembered as Atlantis, which dominated all of the islands in the Atlantic.

Over the centuries, many have speculated about the possible real-world location of Atlantis.

Some of the most popular theories about its location include:

- Mediterranean: Because of its proximity to Egypt, many believe
  Atlantis was located nearby, which is why Egyptian priests spoke
  about it so knowledgeably. The sites where people think Atlantis
  may have been located include the Island of Pharos, the Island of
  Thera (also known as Santorini) and Lake Copais in Greece.
- Cyprus Basin: Robert Sarmast, an American architect, claims that
  Atlantis is situated at the bottom of the eastern Mediterranean
  within the Cyprus Basin. He believes there are certain underwater
  features in the area that look like human-made structures, which
  could be a part of the vanished city.
- Helike: Some academics suggest that the earthquake and subsequent tsunami that annihilated Helike in 373 BC could have
  inspired Plato's Atlantis tale.
- Sardinia: Some people see a correlation between the island of
  Sardinia, with its Bronze Age culture, and Plato's descriptions of
  Atlantis.
- Malta: Because of its strategic position and the presence of some
  of the world's oldest human-made structures, Malta is believed to
  be a potential location for Atlantis.
- Turkey and Troy: Certain theories equate Atlantis with the kingdom of Zippasla in Asia Minor or with the city-state of Troy.
- Black Sea: German researchers Siegfried and Christian Schoppe
  hypothesized that Atlantis may be situated in the Black Sea.
- Pillars of Hercules (Gibraltar): There are many suggested locations in this vicinity, including Andalusia, the Spartel Bank and
  Northwest Africa (specifically Morocco and the Richat Structure
  in Mauritania).

- Azores Islands: Some speculate that these islands could be remnants of the lost civilization's mountaintops.
- Atlantic Ocean: Perhaps most obviously, theorists propose that Plato's reference to the Sea of Atlantis could have been in the location of what we now know as the Atlantic Ocean.

In the mid-1800s, speculation about the Mesoamerican Maya people's origins led scholars like Brasseur de Bourbourg and Augustus Le Plongeon to link Atlantis to Maya culture. DeBourbourg claimed that Maya descended from Atlantis, and it cost him his credibility. At the same time, Le Plongeon fabricated stories that tied himself, his wife and Egyptian deities to Atlantis and another fictitious kingdom called Mu.

The "Land of Mu" originates from Augustus Le Plongeon's investigations of Maya ruins. He claimed to have translated *Popol Vuh*, a sacred K'iche' book. The K'iche' are Indigenous people from the Americas, belonging to the broader Maya group. Their language, also called K'iche', is part of the Mayan language family and is spoken in Central America. During the time before the Europeans arrived, the K'iche' had powerful states in the highlands that were part of the ancient Maya civilization. They were most influential around 950 to 1539 AD. The word *K'iche'* means "many trees" in their language, and this word also led to the name Guatemala, which comes from the Nahuatl language meaning "Place of the Many Trees." There's a region named Quiché Department after them. Rigoberta Menchú Tum, who won the Nobel Peace Prize in 1992 for her work on behalf of Indigenous rights, is one of the most famous K'iche' individuals.

Popol Vuh suggested that Yucatán's civilization was older than Greece's and Egypt's and mentioned an even older continent's story called "Mu." The name *Mu* was sourced from de Bourbourg's mis-translation of the *Troano Codex*, hinting at a submerged land.

The *Troano Codex*, also known as the *Tro-Cortesianus Codex*, is one of the three surviving Maya books from the postclassic period (around 900–1521 AD). It is kept at the Museo de América in Madrid and is a highlight of their collection. Because of its delicate condition, visitors see a replica instead of the original. Originally divided into two parts named *Codex Troano* and *Codex Cortesianus*, they were combined in the 1880s by ethnologist Léon de Rosny. This combined version, now in Madrid, is commonly referred to as the *Madrid Codex*.

Le Plongeon equated this sunken area, Mu, with Atlantis. He also claimed that Queen Moo, a mythical Maya queen, established ancient Egypt and was a survivor of Mu's destruction, while other refugees became the Maya.

Loyola Donnelly on Atlantis: A famous account of a factual Atlantis was also made by Ignatius Loyola Donnelly (1831–1901). Donnelly was a notable American figure who wore many hats—a Republican politician, a writer, a skilled speaker and a social reform-ist. He started his writing career with *Atlantis: The Antediluvian World*. In this book, Donnelly argued that all ancient civilizations descended from the technologically superior Atlantis, which was located in the Atlantic, around 10,000 years ago. The book and Donnelly's theories were largely dismissed by academics as pseudo-archaeological, yet the work has greatly influenced the public's fascination with Atlantis.

In the first chapter, Donnelly claimed that the description of Atlantis given by Plato is not a fable but a historical recounting and that Atlantis was a large island in the Atlantic Ocean, opposite the mouth of the Mediterranean Sea. He suggested that Atlantis was the region where humanity first rose from a state of barbarism to civilization and became a single populous and mighty nation. He also proposed that the kingdom was the original seat of the Aryan or Indo-European family of nations, the Semitic peoples and possibly the Turanian races. Donnelly believed that Atlantis perished in a terrible catastrophe, where the island sank into the ocean with nearly all its inhabitants. A few survivors escaped in ships and on rafts and carried the story of Atlantis to the nations east and west.

In the book, Donnelly cited geological evidence that could've led to the disappearance of Atlantis. He explained that the Earth's surface had experienced numerous risings and fallings and suggested that the continents we know today were once under water. He also posited that the Australian Archipelago is the remaining mountain-top of a drowned continent, which he referred to as "Lemuria," the third in the triad of the three alleged lost continents, joining Atlantis and Mu.

The term *Lemuria* was first coined by British zoologist Philip Sclater in the middle of the 19th century. Sclater introduced this concept to explain the unusual distribution of lemur fossils discovered in Madagascar and India, but not in Africa or the Middle East. He suggested that these regions were once linked by a now submerged landmass that he dubbed "Lemuria," after the lemurs he was studying.

Some have come to believe that Lemuria was somewhere closer to the west coast of the United States. Mount Shasta, located in Northern California, is often associated with Lemuria in various New Age and mystical beliefs. According to these traditions, Lemuria is thought to have been an ancient civilization with advanced spiritual knowledge that some believe sank into the Pacific Ocean. Mount Shasta is considered a spiritual hot spot where the Lemurians are said to have retreated underground to continue their existence. This mountain is thus revered as a portal to higher dimensions and a meeting point of earthly and cosmic energies, attracting many spiritual seekers who come to experience its purported mystical properties and to connect with the Lemurian wisdom.

Donnelly also recounted several significant historical geological changes, including the sudden emergence and subsequent disappearance of islands due to severe earthquakes and volcanic eruptions. He believed that this geological evidence supports the existence of a landmass where Plato located Atlantis and that its sudden destruction and subsequent sinking after an earthquake is plausible.

Donnelly linked global flood legends to Atlantis's demise, seeing these stories as evidence of its advanced civilization. He argued that modern cultures inherited from Atlantis, citing similarities in artifacts, language, myths and agricultural practices as proof of ancient contact between the Americas and Europe or Atlantis. Donnelly also interpreted various symbols and myths, including pyramids and the Garden of Eden, as Atlantean references, and identified civilizations across the world as Atlantean colonies. He suggested Atlantis was a highly advanced society, with its influence and legacy awaiting further discovery.

Madame Blavatsky on Atlantis: Donnelly's book is an excellent exercise in pseudoscience and creative writing, but some have taken his concepts and run with them again. In 1883, only a year after the publication of Donnelly's book, the Russian mystic Madame Helena Petrovna (H.P.) Blavatsky (who was referenced in the chapter about Brother XII) mentions Atlantis and its race of Atlanteans as a critical feature in the belief system of the Theosophical Society, which Blavatsky co-founded in 1875.

In her books, Blavatsky wrote about concepts relating to Atlantis and the Atlantean race. She also incorporated Lemuria into her writings, which she envisioned as an immense continent and society inhabited by humans who were spiritually and psychically more evolved than current humans. Blavatsky claimed Lemurian society was matriarchal, spiritually enlightened and harmoniously balanced with nature. Like Atlantis in similar stories, it met a disastrous end, leaving behind remnants that make up present-day Australia, New Zealand and certain Pacific islands.

Blavatsky expanded on these ideas in her 1888 work, *The Secret Doctrine*; considered a significant text in theosophy, it is based on the mysterious *Book of Dzyan*, which was supposedly composed in Atlantis in the forgotten language of Senzar. The book includes quotations from the Dzyan people along with Blavatsky's commentaries on criticisms against "materialistic" science and "dogmatic" religion. But her writings about Atlantis, along with the work of other theosophists like Rudolf Steiner, perpetuated the myth of the lost civilization as a reality.

Theosophists loved writing about Atlantis and credited Atlanteans for various feats of human achievement, like the building of the pyramids. In his 1896 book *The Story of Atlantis*, theosophist William Scott-Elliot mentioned the arrival of initiated priests and followers in Scandinavian Europe around 100,000 years ago. He claimed these individuals reportedly founded Stonehenge in response to Atlantis's excessively ornate temples.

On October 20, 1912, the *New York American*, one of William Randolph Hearst's newspapers known for sensationalist journalism, published a story from Dr. Paul Schliemann, grandson of famed archaeologist Heinrich Schliemann, who claimed, thanks to clues left by his grandfather, that he had found the lost location of Atlantis.

Dr. Schliemann claimed his grandfather had devoted his life to researching the mysterious civilization of Atlantis, and Paul wanted to carry on his legacy. He made this decision when he opened a sealed envelope left by his grandfather that contained intriguing photos and documents suggesting Atlantis's actual existence and its role as the root of all known civilizations.

Among the intriguing items mentioned in these documents was a bronze vase retrieved from the Troy ruins. It held various items including a script with the words "From the King Chronos of Atlantis." Paul Schliemann also claimed there were references to Atlantis in various historical texts, such as ancient papyrus scrolls in a St. Petersburg museum, an inscription at Mycenae's Lion Gate in southern Greece and the *Troano* manuscript in the British Museum. These references, he said, indicated that Atlantis was real and significantly influenced ancient civilizations.

Fuelled by these findings, Dr. Schliemann undertook wide-ranging research in various locations like Egypt and Central and South America and examined worldwide archaeological collections for more clues to Atlantis. He claimed to have found an intriguing artifact, an owl-headed vase holding a piece of white, silver-like metal adorned with unusual figures and an inscription. This item, among others, he said, was part of a hidden collection in Paris and was suspected to be from Atlantis.

Schliemann's research journey took him to diverse locations worldwide, including the ruins of the Temple of Sais, the Chacuna Valley in America and Africa's west coast. There he said he found a variety of artifacts and geological proof that also backed the existence of Atlantis.

Dr. Schliemann's article concluded with a promise to reveal more evidence supporting Atlantis's existence in his forthcoming book. But no artifacts were produced, and those close to his grandfather, Heinrich, confirmed he never expressed interest in Atlantis. The article was filled with archaeological inaccuracies and overdramatic writing. Many believed the article was not written by an archaeologist at all but was a piece of creative writing by one of the paper's many reporters.

Another figure, Colonel James Churchward, a friend of the previously mentioned Augustus Le Plongeon, became an authority on Mu, Atlantis's sister lost continent. James Churchward was born in Devon, England, and moved to London at 18 following his father's death. He later immigrated to the United States in the 1890s, which is where he came into contact with Le Plongeon and learned about the fascinating subject of Mu.

In 1926, Churchward wrote *The Lost Continent of Mu*, in which he asserted that the now sunken continent of Mu, in the Pacific Ocean, was the cradle of all civilizations and the actual location of the Biblical Garden of Eden. He said his theories were based on his translations of ancient tablets discovered in India, which claimed the creation of man in Mu and the existence of a civilization there 50,000 years ago. While his book makes for interesting reading, he consistently failed to provide sources for any of his claims.

Edgar Cayce on Atlantis: A favourite figure of mine who claims knowledge of Atlantis as a real place is Edgar Cayce (1877–1945). Cayce was a prominent American psychic renowned for his trance readings, where he provided diagnoses and remedies for medical conditions. He is also known for his influential psychic readings that described past lives and predicted future events and for his discussions on philosophical, metaphysical and astrological subjects.

Born in 1877 in a small town in Kentucky, Edgar Cayce claimed to possess psychic abilities from a very young age. His professional life was diverse, including stints in farming, insurance and photography, but

he gained renown for his trance-induced readings, which he originally undertook to diagnose medical conditions in people and suggest treatments. His career as a psychic healer started when a self-ad-
ministered reading remedied his vocal cord paralysis. He came to
the public's attention after successfully treating a child experiencing
frequent seizures.

Cayce remained dedicated to his psychic readings throughout various personal and professional adversities, including his wife's illness,
the loss of their child and dishonest business associates. A *New York
Times* feature on him expanded his fame, leading him to dedicate
himself entirely to his psychic work.

Cayce's reading method earned him the nickname "the Sleeping
Prophet." According to the website edgarcayce.org, Cayce would put
himself into a trance by reclining on a sofa, closing his eyes and crossing his hands over his stomach. In this altered state of consciousness, he claimed to be able to tap into the universal consciousness or
super-conscious mind, giving him access to all time and space. From
this state, he would answer questions from people nationwide. His
wife, Gertrude, usually conducted these sessions, posing the questions,
while his secretary, Gladys Davis, documented each session.

The topic of Atlantis came up in various readings for people whom
Cayce said had been Atlanteans in past lives and provided insight into
the lost civilization. In a reading on February 16, 1932, Cayce spoke
about Atlantis, saying it was a peaceful, harmonious civilization that
advanced swiftly and developed what we would today categorize as
technologies linked to aviation and electricity.

According to Cayce, the decline of Atlantis was self-inflicted
because of improper exploitation of natural resources, resulting in
catastrophic geological disturbances. One such incident caused a part

of Atlantis to submerge near the current location of the Sargasso Sea. Despite their catastrophic ending, the influence of the Atlanteans permeated various corners of the world, and Atlantean wisdom was conserved and disseminated among numerous ancient societies.

In 1931, Cayce created the Association for Research and Enlightenment, which is still operational today and still boasts many followers. Sadly, the marked increase in readings in the 1940s strained Cayce's health, leading to a stroke that claimed his life in 1945.

Other Mythical Places

Although Atlantis and its counterparts Lemuria and Mu are the best-known lost civilizations, several other mythical "vanished" places have sparked historical interest and speculation. Some of these are discussed here.

EL DORADO: This mythical city of gold attracted many European explorers during the era of exploration. Initially, the legend started with a story about a tribal leader from South America who used to dust himself with gold. However, as time passed, the story evolved into a narrative about a city made entirely of gold.

SHANGRI-LA: This place is a fictional creation from James Hilton's 1933 novel *Lost Horizon*. It was portrayed as a utopian paradise nestled in the Himalayas, where residents led extraordinarily long, peaceful and harmonious lives.

AVALON: In the Arthurian legends, Avalon is a mythical island to which King Arthur was taken to heal from his wounds after his final battle. It's often linked with mysticism and magic and is occasionally portrayed as a utopia.

HYPERBOREA: In Greek mythology, Hyperborea was a utopia located in the distant north, beyond the reach of the north wind. The inhabitants of Hyperborea were described as extremely happy and reputed to live for 1,000 years.

THULE: Initially mentioned by the ancient Greek geographer Pytheas, Thule was thought to be the most northern point of the ancient habitable world. Over time, it evolved into a mythical concept often linked with a remote land in the far, frigid north.

LYONESSE: This mythical land is believed to have existed between Land's End and the Scilly Isles, off the coast of Cornwall in the UK. It's most known in Arthurian legend as the homeland of Tristan, one of King Arthur's Knights of the Round Table. Folklore says that Lyonesse sunk into the sea overnight.

Real Lost Places

If it's real history you're after, numerous historical civilizations have disappeared or been "lost" in the sense that their existence was either forgotten or their cultures significantly diminished. Here are a few examples:

MAYA CIVILIZATION: Mentioned previously as connected to Atlantis and located in Central America, the Maya were known for their sophisticated writing system, architecture, and mathematical and astronomical systems. Despite their achievements, the civilization mysteriously collapsed in the 8th or 9th century.

INDUS VALLEY CIVILIZATION: This civilization, also known as the Harappan civilization, was located in Pakistan and Northwest India. It was notable for its advanced urban planning and architecture but declined around 1900 BC for reasons still not completely understood.

MINOAN CIVILIZATION: The Minoans lived on the island of Crete and were known for their palaces and artwork. The civilization disappeared around 1450 BC, possibly after a volcanic eruption, invasion or internal social unrest.

ANASAZI (ANCESTRAL PUEBLOANS): This civilization in the Southwest United States was known for its impressive cliff dwellings. The Anasazi civilization mysteriously declined around AD 1300, likely because of climatic changes and social factors.

KHMER EMPIRE: Based in Cambodia, the Khmer Empire was one of the most powerful empires in Southeast Asia. It was known for constructing Angkor Wat, one of the most significant religious monuments in the world. Internal strife and external pressures led to the decline of the empire in the 15th century.

EASTER ISLAND CIVILIZATION (RAPA NUI): Famous for the giant stone statues known as Moai, the civilization that once thrived on Easter Island in the Pacific Ocean eventually collapsed because of environmental degradation and deforestation.

IN THIS CHAPTER, we've embarked on a captivating journey through the myths and legends of three elusive civilizations: Atlantis, Lemuria and Mu. Whether these "lost continents" are real or not, their distinct narratives have enthralled people for centuries. From the sophisticated society and tragic fate of Atlantis to the spiritual characteristics of Lemuria and the intriguing enigma of Mu, each location reflects the potency of mythology and our enduring quest to decode our ancient past. While there's a distinct lack of empirical evidence substantiating existence of these places, these tales underscore humanity's fascination with vanished worlds and our persistent longing to unveil their secrets.

Part 3

THINGS

THE THIRD SECTION is a journey into another ambiguous territory of the paranormal and unexplained phenomena, traversing the borders of human understanding and belief.

First, we delve into the mysterious case of "the Van Meter Visitor," an extraordinary tale from the small town of Van Meter, Iowa. In 1903, citizens were terrorized by an unidentified nocturnal creature for several nights, leaving unanswered questions. Our exploration deciphers the accounts, the newspaper clippings and the modern resurgence of interest in this creature, teasing out the fine line between local folklore and genuine supernatural events.

Next, we turn our gaze to the eerie case of "Popper the Poltergeist." This chilling account from the 1950s details a series of inexplicable happenings in the Herrmann family's Seaford, Long Island, home that may challenge our understanding of the physical world. Through this narrative, we explore poltergeist phenomena, the potential psychological explanations and the inscrutable nature of the events that seem to defy our current understanding of physics and reality.

Our journey continues with "the Vampires of Highgate Cemetery," which allegedly haunted the Highgate Cemetery in London during the 1970s. This exploration delves into the Gothic allure of vampiric folklore, the cultural hysteria it generated and its implications on the human psyche's susceptibility to fear and superstition. What does our fascination with such entities reveal about us, and how much is rooted in fact versus fiction?

We then ponder "the Philip experiment," a 1970s-era parapsychological experiment conducted in Toronto. Designed to create a fictitious ghost through collective belief and imagination, this tale illuminates our propensity for crafting narratives, lending credibility to the intangible and blurring the boundaries of our perceived realities.

The ending of this book includes the most personal of all these stories. "What's Next? Death, Dying and the Afterlife" includes my own experiences with the end of life and what leads up to it. The chapter delves into the mysteries of death, including the enigmatic phenomena surrounding near-death experiences, focusing on the personal experience of neurosurgeon Eben Alexander.

CHAPTER 12

The Monster of Van Meter, Iowa

The Van Meter Visitor is a mysterious and eerie part of American folklore, specifically stemming from a series of events that occurred in 1903 in Van Meter, Iowa. According to local accounts, this small community was terrorized over several nights by a bizarre creature described as being exceptionally large, with bat-like wings and capable of emitting a powerful beam of light from its forehead.

The story of this creature was first brought to me by my *Supernatural Circumstances* co-host, Morgan Knudsen, and cryptozoologist Chad Lewis, who is an expert on the Van Meter Visitor. Lewis (chadlewisresearch.com) is a renowned researcher, author and lecturer dedicated to exploring and investigating the realms of the strange and unusual. With a background in psychology, he completed both his bachelor's and master's degrees in the field. However, his insatiable curiosity and passion for uncovering extraordinary tales and the world's mysteries led him on a different path.

For nearly three decades, Lewis has embarked on captivating journeys across the globe, tirelessly seeking out the most unique and bizarre stories and untangling the threads of history. With an unwavering commitment to his craft, he has delved into the depths of diverse cultures and landscapes, always searching for the extraordinary and the inexplicable.

Through his extensive research, Lewis has become a trusted authority in the field of anomalous phenomena. His insightful investigations have shed light on many subjects, including paranormal encounters, cryptozoology, UFO sightings and strange occurrences that challenge conventional understanding. His expertise and dedication have earned him the respect of fellow researchers and enthusiastic audiences who eagerly attend his captivating lectures and presentations.

With a wealth of knowledge and a genuine passion for the mysterious, Lewis continues to unravel the enigmas that lie beyond the boundaries of the ordinary. Through his books, lectures and explorations, he invites us to question the limits of our understanding and embrace the wonder that exists in the world, waiting for discovery.

In 2013, Lewis's book, *The Van Meter Visitor: A True and Mysterious Encounter with the Unknown*, co-authored by Noah Voss and Kevin Nelson, was released.

While making a guest appearance on the podcast *Supernatural Circumstances* (season 1, episode 17), Lewis said he had stumbled onto the Van Meter story while flipping through articles in an old newspaper archive. Having already written several books, he and his co-authors were looking to visit Iowa to investigate other legends of the region. UFOs and haunted cemeteries were mainly their focus.

"I started coming across these articles again about this giant winged monster terrorizing the small town in Iowa," he explained. "So we kind of dropped all our other plans and said, 'Let's go here and see what this thing's all about.'"

Finding out about the creature, however, was easier said than done.

"Out of all the places I've ever researched, Van Meter, Iowa, has the worst record of their history of anywhere I can think of," Lewis said. "We know that a newspaper existed in Van Meter at that time, but nobody's ever seen one. Nobody has copies of it. The library doesn't have any copies of it; not just of that year when this occurred, but of the paper in general. So it's that kind of thing where when I went there, I was expecting everybody to know the story; to have all kinds of stories about how grandma and grandpa used to talk about it, maybe even, you know, the great uncle's journal about that time . . . and there was nothing . . . A lot of the people we spoke with on our original trip there had no idea what we were talking about.

"In 1903, people in Iowa, even in the small town of Van Meter," he continued, "would have been well acquainted with stories of weird things in the sky [such as] the airship flap of the 1890s about weird lights." Chad said that although 1903 newspapers from around the country had picked up on the Van Meter story, there had been no further follow-up after the initial reports.

"It's amazing because you would think at some point the people of Van Meter would have said, 'Hey, remember that time when the giant bat-like creature attacked our town?' But it was like, 'Oh, this happened. Let's forget about it and never talk about it again.'

"When you dig through the old newspaper accounts, you can see there were all kinds of stories about just odd lights, haunted places, weird monstrosities being born on farms, two-headed cows and all these other anomalies. So they weren't ignorant of these things. They knew of legends and folklore, but somehow, [the bat-like creature] just wasn't collected."

When he visited Van Meter, Lewis learned that the residents had been upset that this story had leaked beyond the town's borders and was creating a stir. The town's sentiment, according to Lewis, was "Stay away, don't come here. The story's exaggerated. You're not going to find anything . . . Yes, there's been some weird things going on, but you don't need to come here."

The story remained alive thanks to word of mouth and tales passed down from older generations.

As Chad investigated, he began to sense that it was not a hoax. The people involved in the sightings had no reason to lie—they were respected businesspeople and engaged in the community. Some of them even became elected officials later on. He could not determine what they had to gain by making the whole thing up. A motive always precedes a lie, but there does not appear to be one in this case. These people were staking their reputations on their stories and risked the wider community's shunning them and labelling them lunatics.

First settled in 1869, the city of Van Meter is situated in Dallas County, Iowa, approximately 31 kilometres (19 miles) southwest of Des Moines. The community was named for Jacob Rhodes Van Meter, a settler from the Dutch village of Meteren. Incorporated as a township on December 29, 1877, Van Meter's population in 1880 was 376. It has never grown any more extensive than its current population, which according to the 2020 census was 1,484.

Its location, nestled amid the Raccoon River and Bulger Creek forks, offered early settlers excellent water resources to drive its local timber mills. With its rolling terrain and fertile soil, the area boasted a mix of prairie farming land and river bottom land, which made it ideal for agriculture. Over the years, it has witnessed significant settlement and development, with stock and grain farms and comfortable living conditions for its residents. Van Meter is also notable for being the first settlement in Dallas County, which has a rich history of pioneers and early infrastructure such as schools, churches, bridges, mills and quarries.

The laid-back, quaint, pastoral feel of Van Meter is like that of many small Midwestern towns in the United States, full of God-fearing, honest and hardworking folks. Like many of those other places, Van Meter has its own unique stories and folklore. However, this story involves the unexplained visitation of a strange creature. Over a few days in September and October of 1903, Van Meter played host to a mysterious winged, bat-like humanoid, seen by many of the terrified townsfolk of the day.

It all started in the wee hours of September 29. A respected travelling farming-equipment salesperson, 35-year-old Ulysses G. Griffith, who worked for Griffith Brothers Implement, a company he owned and had founded with his brother, arrived back in town sometime after 1:00 a.m. The streets were empty, the homes and businesses in darkness; the town was asleep. Griffith believed he was the only person awake at that lonely hour.

As he walked through the town, something caught his attention out of the corner of his eye, an eerie light he had never seen before atop the Mather & Gregg building. He thought perhaps there was a burglary in progress and decided to investigate. As he neared the building, the light seemed to leap across the street in a swift movement, coming to rest on the roof of another building. Only moments later, as Griffith watched in stunned silence, the light moved again, crossing back to the other side of the street before disappearing altogether. Griffith watched for a few minutes to see if the light would reappear, but it did not, so he went home. Understandably, Ulysses had trouble sleeping that night, wondering if he was losing his mind.

The following day, Griffith told other locals about seeing the light and how it had leapt effortlessly across the street several times. Ulysses was not known for his flights of fancy. He was known for impeccable integrity and was a respected business owner who served on the local council. He was an active participant in local governance and decision-making, and townsfolk trusted him implicitly. Moreover, he took pride in his membership in both the Masonic Lodge and the Modern Woodmen, organizations that fostered camaraderie, community service and mutual support among their members.

Local papers picked up on the story. At first, they printed it as an amusing and exciting, albeit unexplained, anecdote. However, the newspaper articles soon became more serious over the next few days as the horrifying encounters continued.

The next person to have an encounter was reportedly a doctor named Alcott, whose personal details, including his first name, are lost to history.

According to Dr. Alcott, on the morning of September 30, at almost the same time that Griffith had his encounter the night before, he was jolted awake by a blindingly bright light shining through his bedroom window. Suspecting a possible intruder, the terrified doctor grabbed his gun and cautiously went outside to investigate the source of the light. What he saw shook him to his core.

Dr. Alcott was confronted with a perplexing and otherworldly sight on a rooftop above him, silhouetted against an overcast sky. The light was emanating from the head of a creature that defied comprehension. It appeared to be a hybrid of human and animal, unlike anything he had ever seen or heard of. It had strange characteristics, such as enormous bat-like wings. Alcott noticed that the light that had startled him awake came from a blunt horn on the creature's forehead. Dr. Alcott was so terrified that he could not think of any other thing to do but to shoot at the beast. He fired five shots at the monster. Shaky as he was, he could not have missed at that distance, but none of the bullets had any noticeable effect.

Realizing the futility of his actions and with only one shot remaining, and in a heightened state of anxiety, the doctor hastily retreated into the safety of his office and secured the doors and windows. He stayed awake for the rest of the night, too afraid to sleep and too terrified to look outside.

After sunrise, Dr. Alcott braved a look. The thing was nowhere to be seen. As the town awakened, the doctor, as Griffith had the day before, told of his encounter with a hideous creature and the same fast-moving light that Griffith had mentioned. Hearing escalating stories from two respected men caused a great level of concern for the townsfolk. Everyone wondered what the heck the two men had seen.

The next sighting occurred at almost precisely 1:00 a.m. the next night. This time it was a well-loved cashier at the local bank, Clarence (Peter) Dunn, who had a nerve-shattering experience with the strange creature. Having heard of the events of the two previous nights, Dunn, thinking perhaps bandits were responsible, sat up that night in the bank, with a shotgun at his side.

Dunn said he first heard strange noises that resembled guttural gasps, like a person or animal in respiratory distress. When he went to the window to investigate, he was stunned by a dazzling bright light but could discern what appeared to be a large creature as the source of the light. It was too close for comfort. Dunn shot at the creature with his shotgun, but it seemed unaffected.

The creature vanished as swiftly as it had appeared, leaving only a few tracks behind in the mud. Despite conducting a thorough search as the day broke, searchers found no trace of the beast except for some distinct three-toed tracks, which Dunn preserved with a plaster cast.

While some townsfolk still believed the occurrences were either nonsense or had a very rational explanation, others believed something otherworldly was attacking their little town. But what was it, and why?

The next person to see the creature was a local businessman named O.V. White, the co-owner of Fisher & White, a furniture and hardware store in town. Mr. White, who lived in an apartment above his store, was jarred from sleep by the same sounds described by Mr. Dunn the previous night, but louder. He claimed the sound went through him like nails on a chalkboard and made his nerves jangle. He grabbed his gun and went to the window, where he saw a large winged creature, with light emanating from a horn, perched atop a telephone pole in the darkness just 5 metres (15 feet) away.

White shot at it, but again, the creature appeared to be unfazed. It did, however, turn to look in White's direction. The bright light disoriented him, and he detected a horrific odour that made his head swim with confusion. At this point, his memory of the evening's events ended, and he could not recall what else happened after that.

White was not alone in this encounter. Another local store owner, Sidney Gregg, had been startled awake across the street by White's shotgun blast. He went outside to see what was causing the commotion, and his jaw dropped when he saw the strange beast sitting on top of the telephone pole. As he watched, the creature began to descend, using its feet and enormous pointed beak to gain purchase on the wooden pole.

The creature stood upright as it reached the ground. Gregg estimated its height was at least 244 centimetres (8 feet) tall. Its forehead emitted a bright light that darted about in a searching motion. Mr. Gregg, still in disbelief, told reporters that he observed the monster flapping its featherless, skin-covered wings, which looked like long arms with claws at the end. The creature leapt about like a crazed kangaroo, eventually taking flight and gliding away into the dark sky. Gregg said it seemed headed toward the abandoned coal mine some distance from town.

The following day, fellow townspeople listened, horrified, as Gregg and White shared the tales of their encounters. The town went into a state of panic. Some felt it was just a matter of time before the creature attacked someone and possibly killed them. Bullets and buckshot did not seem to affect it, so what could they do to protect themselves? Gregg spoke about the direction the creature had gone, toward the coal mine, positing that as every sighting was at night, perhaps that was where it went in the day to hide from the sun. The mine had not been operational for several years and would make the perfect hideout.

A posse set out on the evening of Friday, October 2, 1903. The group headed toward the coal mine, which stood close to an operational brick factory managed by J.L. Pratt. He'd also managed the coal mine before its closure and knew its layout and hazards, including sudden drop-offs, unstable tunnels and the potential for deadly underground gases. The well-armed group set up around the mine and awaited nightfall.

At 1:00 a.m. on Saturday, October 3, 1903, the group heard horrible sounds from deep within the mine from something that seemed to be approaching the entrance. Suddenly, the creature appeared at the mine's opening, but this time it was accompanied by a smaller creature of the same shape. The infernal things emitted a blinding, mesmerizing light and a terrible smell. Workers from the nearby tile and brick factory also caught sight of the monsters. Observing their horn-like protrusions radiating the extraordinary ray of light, Mr. Pratt and his fellow witnesses watched as the creatures flew away into the darkness. News of the sighting quickly spread.

The townspeople organized a plan to ambush and capture the creatures at the mine. Armed with their weapons, they gathered near the entrance and illuminated the town with their new electric lights, which recently replaced the gas-fuelled lights that had previously lit the streets. The hope was that the bright lights would intimidate the monsters. They waited in the rain, speculating fearfully about what might happen next.

The group waited for hours but there was no sign of the creatures. Around quarter to six, just before the sun peeked over the horizon, the giant creature appeared in the sky with the smaller one following. The townsfolk unleashed a barrage of gunfire toward the monsters. They seemed immune to the bullets but responded with screams so loud and high pitched that the sound seemed to tear into the psyches of those present. Before the sun came up, the creatures flew back into the mine opening and the darkness below. No one was willing to follow them.

The citizens of Van Meter were now sure the creature was using the mine as its lair, and worse yet, now there were two, so they decided their only course of action was to seal up the mine.

Knowing they had only until that night to complete the task, they immediately set to work. By sundown, the workers had sealed the mouth of the mine. There were no more sightings after that. Although many claimed the sightings were genuine, some who had lived through the frenzy of events that fall contended it had all been a hoax perpetrated by a few of the town's businesspeople in the hope of attracting visitors to the town to drive sales for their businesses.

If these creatures really did exist, what were they? There have been endless theories over the years.

One popular theory was that they were prehistoric creatures, perhaps a pterodactyl or Pteranodon. According to the University of California Museum of Paleontology at Berkeley, Pteranodon is a giant crested pterosaur that lived during the Cretaceous period in regions like Kansas and Nebraska. Pterosaurs were flying reptiles closely related to dinosaurs but distinct from birds. Like pelicans today, Pteranodon was a fish eater that soared over shallow seas and coast-lines. While it's uncertain if Pteranodon had a pouch like pelicans, paleontologists have discovered some skeletons with fish remains.

The first discovery of Pteranodon bones came in the 1860s. It wasn't until the early 20th century that paleontologists formed a more complete understanding of the creature. Because of the thin and hollow nature of its bones, researchers typically found their often incomplete skeletons flattened by the weight of rock and earth. Mul-tiple specimens were necessary to reconstruct Pteranodon accurately. An imposing sight, a full-grown Pteranodon was believed to have a wingspan of more than 6.7 metres (22 feet).

The idea that some prehistoric creature could have survived in a mine for eons undetected stretches one's imagination. Could these things have existed for thousands of years somewhere below the Earth's surface, and the coal mining in the area had unintentionally freed them from a cavernous subterranean prison?

On season 4, episode 2 of the Discovery show *Expedition X*, field biologist Phil Torres and paranormal researcher Jessica Chobot spec-ulated on the possibilities. They posited that perhaps people had mis-identified a blue heron, a turkey vulture or a sandhill crane. It could have been a large bat illuminated by the town's recently installed electric lighting casting shadows against the buildings, thus creating the optical illusion of a massive creature. The shadow theory could also explain the beast's seeming imperviousness to gunfire. Although plausible, these theories do not explain all the features of the alleged sightings.

Morgan Knudsen wondered if someone in Van Meter had been indulging in occult practices. She thought it might be possible someone had been dabbling where they should not have been and had unwittingly unleashed the beast on the little town. If this thing was a demon or supernatural entity, it would also explain its being bulletproof. Chad Lewis said that, although it was a possibility, he could find no evidence in his research to support this theory.

Some have tied the Van Meter Visitor to UFO sightings in the area, although no UFO sightings were reported during the 1903 occurrences. Other speculators believe the huge, strange-smelling, bat-winged creature with an LED-like light shining from the horn on its head could be from another world or even another dimension. They explain that the creature's invulnerability to bullets might stem from advanced technology we cannot understand.

Still others think the creature in Van Meter may have been a Thunderbird. The Thunderbird is significant in Native American mythology and symbolizes power and protection across the United States and Canada. This supernatural bird, known for its immense size and strength, emits thunderous sounds with its wings and shoots lightning from its eyes. While the Thunderbird brings rain and storms, its blessings can bring both benefit and destruction, as it is associated with nourishing crops but also with devastating wind, floods and fires caused by lightning. Various tribes have different oral traditions accounting for the Thunderbird, and all respect and fear its extraordinary powers.

There's also the question of the plaster cast, allegedly collected by Peter Dunn on the third night of the sightings. According to Chad Lewis's book *The Van Meter Visitor: A True and Mysterious Encounter with the Unknown,* no one knows the whereabouts of the alleged plaster cast. Lewis's attempts to find the impression were fruitless, and there is no record of its existence after the first reports. If it ever truly existed, Lewis figured, it might have come into the possession of some unknown person, or perhaps even a museum, for safekeeping and has long been forgotten. Maybe the plaster cast still exists in some darkened corner in an unused basement or attic, or perhaps it was thrown away at some point, incorrectly tagged as unimportant detritus.

Cryptozoologists have gathered plaster casts of the alleged footprints of numerous other cryptids after sightings worldwide. I've seen some myself, allegedly those of a Sasquatch as collected by John Green. John Willison Green (1927–2016) was a prominent Canadian journalist and a renowned investigator of the Bigfoot phenomenon. With educational backgrounds from the University of British Columbia and Columbia University, Green dedicated his efforts to researching and documenting encounters with Bigfoot. His extensive work included compiling a comprehensive database containing over 3,000 reports of sightings and tracks related to the elusive creature. Throughout his career, Green made significant contributions to the field of cryptozoology and played a pivotal role in advancing our understanding of Bigfoot.

A few of the casts collected by Green reside at the Kilby Historic Site in Harrison Mills, BC, in a small display room within the museum, where I saw them. Anyone interested in Sasquatch has seen them in photographs, but viewing them in person is another thing. There is nothing like seeing what may or may not be the footprint of one of the world's most elusive creatures. I read a T-shirt once that said "Bigfoot: World Champion Hide-and-Seek Player."

If a plaster cast of the Van Meter Visitor's footprint does indeed exist, it would at least offer physical proof of the encounter for scientists to consider.

Recently, there have been more sightings of unexplained creatures in Iowa. One night in June 2015, Joey Perales, a high school student, and his girlfriend, Tia Stauffer, had a terrifying and memorable experience. The couple was off to spend a quiet night at Terry Trueblood Lake, a recreational area on the southern outskirts of Iowa City and a 10-minute drive from Joey's home.

Terry Trueblood Lake lies within the Terry Trueblood Recreation Area, which was once a sand and gravel quarry located along the Iowa River at the southern edge of Iowa City. The lake offers a range of activities for visitors to enjoy. Fishing, boating, kayaking, paddle boating and even ice skating during winter are popular options. Additionally, a bike trail encircles the lake, providing a scenic route that connects to the trail along the river, offering miles of biking opportunities.

After Chad Lewis connected us, Joey shared his story with me. Perales said there were two parking lots to choose from at the lake. They typically chose the larger lot closer to the paddle boat rentals. However, on this occasion, their desire to stargaze led them to the smaller parking lot on the far side of the lake, which had limited lighting. Joey and Tia enjoyed the serene night atmosphere and headed toward their chosen spot with a blanket, which Tia wrapped around herself, and a lantern to light their way.

As they walked along the path—the lake on one side and an old highway on the other—a dense wall of tall grass stood between them and the lake. They had travelled halfway to their destination, about

200 metres or yards, when they had their encounter. They heard something moving fast through the grass. Tia was frightened.

Joey recounted their experience: "Having taken about 10 steps after hearing the noise, we heard it again. This time it was closer and sounded louder from all the grass that was being pushed as [the creature] quickly moved through the grass. We both stopped at the same time, hearing it get closer and closer and then nothing. Just silence. Now I was getting a little freaked out, but I kept my cool because my brain was just reminding me it was a deer or some kind of animal."

Tia held up their lantern, hoping to illuminate whatever they were hearing in the dark. For a few moments, there was only silence. All they could see was the path ahead of them and the grass.

Then it happened.

Joey continued: "This thing shot out of the grass, not looking at us but staring in a different direction. We were in shock, just standing there frozen on the path. Its neck slowly moves in our direction, with its body still in the other direction. Tia saw it but ... was holding up the lantern, which almost blinded her, so she couldn't see it as well as I did. Looking at this creature, it was like no animal I've ever seen. It was tall, taller than me, standing perfectly balanced. It had a long face with blackness behind it that blended into the dark lake. Wings, I thought, of some kind, and the lantern showed me it was white in colour with small black eyes and something I couldn't really see on the top of its head. Looking into the face of this creature felt like a terrifying eternity but was honestly more like two or three seconds."

They froze until Joey told Tia to run, and they did. Joey checked over his shoulder to ensure the thing was not chasing them. The blanket slipped, causing Tia to trip and fall, hitting her head on the concrete path. She quickly got up, dropped the lantern and started running again, screaming in terror. They rushed to the car, panicked, and sped away. Tia had a bleeding head wound and a large bump over her right eye. Both were frightened and shaken. As they drove down the old highway, they could see the abandoned path, with the discarded blanket and flickering lantern.

Joey and Tia also shared their story with Discovery's *Expedition X* investigation team. Tia told the show's presenters that the creature had enormous, tucked-in, leathery "bat-like wings" and looked directly at them. It was significantly taller than Joey, with a beak-like snout. She said that as they ran, it kept pace, parallel to them, but when they got to the car, it was gone. Tia, who had worked at a zoo and been around many exotic animals, said it was unlike any animal she had ever seen.

Another eyewitness interviewed on the show was Mike Evans. He had grown up in Iowa, and only weeks before the show's recording, he had seen a massive creature flying in the sky above a hilltop, near Colfax, Iowa, heading toward Red Rock. It was 2 to 2.5 metres (6 to 8 feet) long and had bat-like wings, a tail and a face that appeared reptilian. Evans, a lifelong birdwatcher and hunter, was familiar with every animal there is to see in Iowa, but what he saw that night left him wondering.

In the end, no one seems able to explain the creature that appeared in Van Meter and, more recently, in the surrounding areas.

The town has a festival each year called the Van Meter Visitor Festival. If you want to visit the area and learn more about this strange creature, you can find the details online.

CHAPTER 13

Popper the Poltergeist

When one thinks of Long Island, New York, and the supernatural, typically what jumps to mind are the terrifying events that allegedly occurred in a distinctive house in the peaceful town of Amityville, located on the south coast of the island. There, on the night of November 13, 1974, Ronald (Butch) DeFeo Jr., a distressed 23-year-old man, rushed into a local bar and claimed that his entire family, including his parents and four siblings, had been brutally murdered in their spacious Dutch Colonial house at 112 Ocean Avenue.

However, investigations later revealed that it was Butch himself who had committed the heinous act, wiping out his entire family. He was convicted on six counts of second-degree murder and received a sentence of 25 years to life in prison for the gruesome slaying of his sleeping family members.

Only a month after Butch's conviction, the Lutz family (Kathy, George and their three children) decided to move into the house where the DeFeos had been murdered. They had acquired the large residence for only $80,000 because of the tragedy that had happened there. However, their stay at 112 Ocean Avenue turned into a nightmarish ordeal that lasted only 28 days. The Lutz family hastily abandoned their new home, asserting that an unseen presence, which they believed to be demonic, had subjected them to relentless psychic torment and rendered their life in the house unbearable.

The events surrounding the Lutz family's harrowing experience gained widespread attention when author Jay Anson published a book in 1977 on the case titled *The Amityville Horror*. A film adaptation in 1979 further popularized the story and captivated audiences worldwide. The Amityville Horror has become one of history's most famous and extensively covered tales of haunting and alleged demonic possession. Nevertheless, the veracity of the claims remains controversial and hotly debated among skeptics and believers.

Less than 8 kilometres (5 miles) to the east, 16 years before the initial events in Amityville, the widely publicized Herrmann House in Seaford was considered the most intensely investigated poltergeist case in American history. The case was so compelling it inspired Steven Spielberg to write and produce the hit 1982 film *Poltergeist*.

The word *poltergeist* refers to a phenomenon characterized by unexplained disturbances, such as knocking noises and movement of objects. The term comes from the German words for *crash* and *ghost*. Poltergeist activity has traditionally been associated with mischievous spirits, but some people believe the activity results from repressed emotions in a living person, particularly children, or is caused by natural events like seismic activity. Reports of poltergeist activity date back centuries, but evidence supporting the involvement of supernatural entities is often lacking.

At the Herrmann house, parapsychological researchers William G. Roll and J. Gaither Pratt recorded at least 67 anomalous poltergeist incidents between February 3 and March 10, 1958. Many strange incidents occurred while the investigators were in the house with members of the Herrmann family.

The house at 1648 Redwood Path was a small, unassuming three-bedroom bungalow with a semi-finished basement that belonged to James Herrmann Sr., an Air France liaison officer. The family had lived in the house since 1952. Herrmann Sr. was a respected member of the Seaford community; he volunteered as a Boy Scout master and was involved in the parent-teacher association at his children's school. Lucille Herrmann Sr. was a homemaker and doting mother to their two children: 12-year-old James (Jimmy) Herrmann Jr. and 13-year-old Lucille Herrmann Jr.

Young Jimmy Jr. arrived home from school on Monday, February 3, 1958, around 3:30 p.m. and was shocked to find a broken ceramic doll smashed into a model ship, which was also broken, on the dresser in his bedroom. Jimmy was upset and asked his mother and sister what had happened to his toys, but both denied knowing anything about it.

Wondering what was going on, Mrs. Herrmann checked the rest of the rooms in the house. To her surprise, a bottle of holy water had toppled over on her dresser. Its cap was off, and the holy water was spilled all over. Mrs. Herrmann had been home all afternoon and claimed she had not heard any commotion from either room.

As Mrs. Herrmann cleaned up the holy water in her bedroom, she began hearing strange noises in different areas of the house. Intermittently, over the next 45 minutes, mysterious sounds echoed throughout the home. Fearing an intruder, Mrs. Herrmann followed each sound to investigate. When she arrived at each room, she found bottles of various household sundries emptied of their contents, their tops removed.

She found two spilled bottles in the bathroom cabinet under the sink—one bottle of rubbing alcohol and another of peroxide. Their screw caps lay beside them.

A similar scenario played out in the kitchen, where a starch bottle had been opened under the sink, resulting in another messy spill. But the peculiar events didn't stop there. In the unfinished portion of the basement, right under the kitchen, Jimmy and his mother discovered a cardboard box that had formerly been on a shelf. The heavy box had somehow made its way onto the floor. As they approached, a half-gallon of bleach seemingly leapt out of the box, crashed onto the floor and broke into pieces. They were only 2 metres (6 feet) away when this uncanny incident happened. They couldn't believe what they were seeing.

When James Herrmann Sr. arrived home after a long day of work, his wife and children met him in a panic over what they had witnessed that afternoon. As Mrs. Herrmann and the children led him through the house, excitedly explaining what had gone on, Mr. Herrmann thought they had collectively lost their minds. He assumed there had to be a logical explanation, but as he pondered it, he could not develop one.

The family cleaned up the messes and either replaced the bottle caps or poured the contents into fresh containers. Because the smell from some of the spilled chemicals was overwhelming, they opened all the windows to air out the house despite the cold temperatures outside.

Everything returned to normal until the afternoon of Thursday, February 6, between 3:30 and 4:30 p.m. That afternoon, Jimmy and Lucille Jr. were the only family members home. Suddenly, they heard noises reminiscent of the unsettling sounds they'd heard three days previously. In a perplexing repeat, two bottles stored in the bathroom cabinet were found with their caps mysteriously unscrewed and emptied of their contents.

In the cellar, the site of the prior bleach bottle incident, another bottle of bleach seemed to propel itself out of a 20-centimetre (8 inch) box, colliding violently with the cement floor and shattering. Upstairs in the linen cupboard, the family found an open bottle of wine that was tipped over and had stained all the items in the surrounding area.

The next day, Friday, February 7, at the same time, between 3:30 and 4:15 p.m., Jimmy was home from school alone. In a troubling continuation of these unexplained phenomena, a bottle of ammonia stored under the kitchen sink was found with its lid off and the contents spilled all over.

Mr. and Mrs. Herrmann listened to their children's stories of what had happened but suspected perhaps the kids had fabricated the most recent events. Lucille and Jimmy were adamant that they were telling the truth.

Then, on Sunday, February 9, at 10:15 a.m., the Herrmann family was in the dining room. Their collective peace was disturbed by a series of noises from various rooms throughout the house. Upon investigation, they discovered a chain of disturbances similar to the previous ones.

A holy water bottle on Mr. Herrmann's dresser in the primary bedroom had been tampered with; its cap was unscrewed, and the water had spilled all over. Similarly, Mrs. Herrmann found a bottle of perfume on her dresser on its side with its screw cap and rubber stopper removed. The contents had made a mess on the dresser.

In the kitchen, the family found an open bottle of starch with its contents spilled out. Then they found a new gallon can of paint thinner tipped over on the basement floor.

At around 10:30 a.m., a peculiar incident occurred right in front of Mr. Herrmann's eyes. While he stood in the bathroom doorway, watching James brush his teeth, he witnessed a bottle of Kaopectate and a shampoo bottle, both placed on top of the vanity, inexplicably move in different directions and topple off the table. The frequent removal of bottle caps and spilling of liquids during these encounters was a pattern, eventually leading to the nickname we now know, Popper the Poltergeist.

The Herrmanns, now very concerned, decided to contact the police.

The next day, February 10, while the family and Patrolman James Hughes were in the living room, a noise came from the bathroom. Upon inspection, they discovered yet another bottle, which had been sitting on the vanity, turned over, adding to the growing list of mysterious containers that had spilled open.

In those days, involving the police in anything almost always ensured attention from the press. The following day, newspapers throughout the United States carried stories about the bottle-tipping entity in the Herrmann family's home. News reporters from all over called on the Herrmanns for comments. Newspaper, radio and television journalists all wanted a piece of the story.

Among the scores of news outlets reporting the same story, the *Chicago Tribune* reported that, in an attempt to understand the bizarre occurrences, James Herrmann Sr. considered that maybe nuclear radiation was responsible.

In the mid to late 20th century, strange events in the United States were often attributed to nuclear radiation thanks to a mix of factors: limited public understanding of radiation, Cold War anxieties, pop culture representations of radiation as a source of mutation and apocalypse, real nuclear accidents highlighting radiation's risks, and inconsistent information from authorities. These elements combined to make nuclear radiation a go-to explanation for the unexplained, reflecting deep public mistrust and curiosity.

Motivated by these fears, Herrmann contacted Dr. Donald Hughes from Brookhaven National Laboratory, an atomic energy facility, but Hughes could not identify a cause for these phenomena. Dr. Hughes noted that it was plausible some bottles would explode from the overdevelopment of gases within, but he dismissed any connection to radioactivity.

Amid all the press attention, strange incidents continued to occur in the house.

On the afternoon of Tuesday, February 11, between 3:30 and 5:25 p.m., a perfume atomizer formerly resting undisturbed on Mrs. Herrmann's dresser spontaneously opened, tipped over and discharged perfume onto the dresser.

Simultaneously, a top on a container of paint thinner in the cellar became unscrewed, spilling smelly paint thinner onto the floor.

Suspecting the children might be responsible, Joseph Tozzi, a Nassau County Police detective assigned to the case, interviewed the Herrmann kids on February 12. Tozzi told them there would be severe consequences if he discovered they had created a hoax. Both denied responsibility for the occurrences. Tozzi focused much of his attention on young Jimmy, who had been the only person home during several incidents. Still, Jimmy steadfastly maintained his innocence.

The next day, on Thursday, February 13, another bewildering incident occurred between 6:45 and 7:25 a.m. With Jimmy, Lucille and Mrs. Herrmann at home (Mr. Herrmann had left the premises at 7:10), the holy water bottle on Mr. Herrmann's dresser again acted strangely. It opened by itself, fell and spilled its contents. Suspecting possible electrical interference, the Long Island Lighting Company attended the Herrmann home and placed an oscillograph in the cellar. The device showed no anomalies, and the lighting company removed it the next day.

Then, another episode occurred on Saturday, February 15, at 5:50 p.m., while the entire family was home. Jimmy, Lucille Jr. and Mr. Herrmann found the holy water bottle on Mr. Herrmann's dresser open yet again, with the contents spilled out. When Mrs. Herrmann went to clean up the water, she noted it was hot to the touch. Similarly, when Mr. Herrmann picked up the perfume bottle from his wife's dresser, he noticed it was warm, which was a new development.

Later in the evening, at 7:40 p.m., Jimmy, Lucille and Miss Marie Murtha, Mr. Herrmann's cousin, were gathered in the living room. Mr. and Mrs. Herrmann were elsewhere in the house. Miss Murtha witnessed an extraordinary event. A porcelain figurine, which had been sitting motionless on an end table, started to "wiggle" before it left the table and moved, on its own, approximately 60 centimetres (24 inches) across the room.

By the middle of February, numerous news reports had made their way to the attention of world-renowned J.B. Rhine at his Parapsychology Laboratory at Duke University in Durham, North Carolina. Dr. Rhine is considered by many the founder of modern parapsychology.

Joseph Banks Rhine, born in rural Pennsylvania on September 29, 1895, was the second child of five born to a travelling schoolteacher and merchant. He self-financed his education at Ohio Northern University and the College of Wooster but left after his faith was challenged by a few of his science courses, thus ending his plans for a religious ministry. After this life-altering experience, Rhine served in the Marines during the First World War for two years, where he reassessed his future.

He decided to pursue science as a career and returned to Ohio to marry his high school friend Louisa Weckesser. In 1920, the couple moved to the University of Chicago, where Louisa studied plant physiology. They both received their master's and doctoral degrees in botany from the university.

Inspired by a lecture by Sir Arthur Conan Doyle and an intriguing clairvoyance anecdote, the Rhines transitioned their careers from botany to psychical research. Their work led to the exposure of a fraudulent medium, and later, under the guidance of psychologist William McDougall at Duke University, they explored the psychic realm with innovative testing methods. Despite initial setbacks, J.B. Rhine's experiments provided significant evidence for psychic abilities. He coined the term *extrasensory perception* (ESP) and published a landmark monograph on it in 1934.

Dr. Rhine felt the Herrmann family claims were worth investigating and assigned Dr. J. Gaither Pratt to look into the strange events.

Joseph Gaither Pratt (1910–1979) was a renowned American psychologist and parapsychologist recognized for his experiments and research in ESP. Born and raised on a farm in North Carolina, Pratt initially aspired to be a minister before shifting his focus to psychology during his studies at Duke University, where he later worked under J.B. Rhine in the parapsychology department.

Pratt achieved his master's and doctorate in psychology by 1936 and subsequently took a faculty position at Duke. He also spent two years at Columbia University, writing his PhD thesis and publishing his first book on ESP testing.

Thanks to police reports, the events unfolding in the Herrmann house had already been documented, which is unusual for a possible haunting. Often, the story is told to investigators only by the family and other tangential witnesses; officials like police detectives are not usually involved. Dr. Pratt immersed himself in the case, reading all he could and speaking with other witnesses.

The Long Island Lighting Company returned on February 17 and thoroughly checked the home's wiring—from top to bottom. Again, nothing electrically unusual was noted. The lighting company returned for further tests several times throughout the investigation but found nothing significant.

The police didn't use fingerprinting during the investigation because of the frequent handling of the objects in question. Instead, on February 19, they marked five previously disturbed bottles with a fluorescent powder without the family's knowledge. Tozzi instructed everyone not to touch the bottles in the hope of catching a hoaxer. However, none of these marked bottles experienced further disturbances.

An event labelled number 37 in Pratt's report took place on the evening of Thursday, February 20, and was particularly violent. At around 9:45 p.m., Mrs. Herrmann was on the phone in the dining room, with Jimmy nearby and Lucille in the bedroom. Jimmy was storing his books when he heard a loud pop, and an ink bottle on the table unscrewed itself and flew in a northeasterly direction into the living room, spilling ink on a chair, the floor and wallpaper by the front door. Mrs. Herrmann immediately hung up and called the police, who had just left the house around 10 minutes before.

While waiting in the hallway with her children for the police detective's arrival, Mrs. Herrmann heard another loud noise emanating from the living room at approximately 9:50 p.m. Upon entering the room, they found that a figurine had left its spot on an end table, flown about 3 metres (10 feet) through the air and hit the desk 15 centimetres (6 inches) to the east of where it had previously sat. The figurine broke into many pieces after hitting the desk. No one was in the room when it happened. If this last incident occurred as Mrs. Herrmann described it, Jimmy and Lucille were with her then and could not have been involved.

The Herrmann family were now having trouble sleeping. They lay awake at night, worried by thoughts of what might happen next. They just wanted an explanation.

The Herrmanns were Catholic and wanted to rule out demonic possession, especially since several of the events appeared focused on their holy water. On February 24, Detective Tozzi consulted with a Catholic priest who was also an engineer. Tozzi asked whether there were potential natural causes for the Herrmann family's disturbances. The priest suggested what was happening might not have a natural cause. When asked about the possibility of a demon and conducting an exorcism, the priest clarified that exorcism typically applies to desecrated church property or possessed individuals, not cases like this.

On the evening of February 25, around 7:30 p.m., while Gaither Pratt was present in the home, Mr. Herrmann was engaged on a call, and other family members along with investigators were occupied in various sections of the residence, a disturbance upstairs prompted the discovery of a lamp tipped over in the master bedroom. Concurrently, in the dining room where Jimmy was dining solo, a plate of bread set on a cupboard inexplicably ended up on the floor. Mrs. Herrmann stumbled upon this after she had been outside observing firefighters gauge the depth of water in a well, an investigation initiated by Detective Tozzi to determine if fluctuations in the groundwater level might be linked to the ongoing anomalies. Jimmy reported that he did not witness the plate's movement but had been startled by the sound of its impact with the floor. While it would've been easy for Jimmy to have pushed the bread, his terrified reaction raised doubts. Nevertheless, this incident alone does not provide significant evidence for a parapsychological explanation.

The next day, historical maps confirmed that no water bodies existed in the area before the house's construction. Tests for unusual radio frequencies around the house found nothing. An inspection found the home structurally sound, with only normal settling cracks in the basement floor.

Dr. Pratt was overwhelmed by the level of attention required for the investigation and decided he needed another pair of hands. At the beginning of March, Rhine assigned a 22-year-old parapsychologist named William G. Roll to help him investigate the case.

William George Roll Jr. (1926–2012) was born in Germany to an American vice-consul and a Danish mother; he experienced a challenging childhood, marked by his parents' divorce and his mother's death. Roll experienced out-of-body phenomena following his mother's passing, which piqued his interest in parapsychology.

In his youth, Roll participated in the Danish resistance during the Second World War and later reunited with his father, who was working on restoring American embassies in Scandinavia as part of General Eisenhower's staff. He moved to the United States and pursued psychology, philosophy and sociology studies at the University of California, Berkeley. However, his primary fascination remained with parapsychology, which led him to study under Harry Price at Oxford University. Although his thesis was considered inadequate for a PhD, he was awarded a Master of Letters degree and had his work published.

Roll's interest in parapsychology drew the attention of J.B. Rhine, leading him to join the parapsychology lab staff at Duke University in 1957. He'd been on the job for less than a year before being tasked to work with Dr. Pratt on the Herrmann case, Roll's first serious investigation. Roll would end up becoming one of the most famous parapsychologists of the 20th century.

Pratt and Roll vowed to leave no stone unturned. They desperately wanted to solve the mystery of the Herrmann house and, hopefully, provide peace to the family. They determined there were three questions that needed to be answered from a scientific perspective.

First: Were the disruptions due to known physical phenomena or the result of PK? PK, or psychokinesis, also known as telekinesis, is a parapsychological concept that involves the influence of the mind on physical objects, resulting in movement or change in the object due to an observer's mental focus. Examples of psychokinetic effects include levitation and metal bending, although these demonstrations are often fraudulently performed in stage magic.

Second and third: If the evidence suggested the cause was parapsychological, which psychological elements could illuminate the nature of these specific psychokinetic occurrences and the concept of psychokinesis overall?

On March 1, a team of engineers visited the Herrmann home to investigate the disturbances but found nothing unusual. Data regarding plane departures from Mitchell Airfield, facing the Herrmann house, was gathered on March 3, but the investigators could not establish links between the disturbances and flights. They removed the TV antenna from the chimney and repaired a small crack in the foundation on March 4 to reduce potential vibrations. On March 5, plumbing checks revealed minor vibrations from a circulator, although a nearby house exhibited significantly more intense vibrations.

On March 2, several disturbances occurred in the Herrmann house at different times. At 4:40 p.m., a glass bowl fell off a bench in the dining room in front of a family friend. At the same time, they discovered a lamp tipped over in Mrs. Herrmann's bedroom. Later, at 7:30 p.m., after Mr. Herrmann, Jimmy and Mr. Herrmann's brother returned from a store run, they found a globe from the bookcase in Jimmy's room in the middle of his bed. Other occurrences that evening also took place in Jimmy's room. At 9:45 p.m., a picture fell off the wall, and at 10:10 p.m., a night table fell over, causing a brass lamp on the table to crash to the floor, breaking the globe around the bulb and bending the base.

On March 4, yet another series of strange events occurred in the Herrmann house. At 4:50 p.m., a flashbulb flew off an end table in a hallway and hit the wall, as witnessed by Mr. John Gold of the *London Evening News*. At the time, Mrs. Herrmann was in the living room and Jimmy was in the cellar. Ten minutes later, they heard four loud bangs, and a bleach bottle in the basement was found knocked over on the floor with the cap off. Jimmy was in the bathroom, and Mrs. Herrmann and Mr. Gold were in the living room at the time of this disturbance.

At 5:10 p.m., a loud crash upstairs led to the discovery that a glass bowl from the dining room table had flown into a corner cabinet, damaging the frame. Jimmy was still in the bathroom, and Mrs. Herrmann and Mr. Gold were in the basement. Finally, at 5:12 p.m., they heard another loud crash and found a bookcase in the unfinished part of the basement tipped over. Jimmy was with Mrs. Herrmann and Mr. Gold in another part of the basement at the time.

On March 5, at 10:20 p.m., while both children were in bed, Mr. and Mrs. Herrmann and a family friend were in the kitchen and heard a noise from the hall. Upon investigation, they found the globe from Jimmy's room outside his door. The following morning at 7:20, while both children were in their bedrooms and Mrs. Herrmann was in the kitchen (Mr. Herrmann had already left for work), they heard another loud noise from the living room. The coffee table in front of the sofa was found overturned, flipped on its top.

On Sunday, March 9, at 9:40 p.m., while both children were in bed, Mrs. Herrmann was in the kitchen, Mr. Herrmann and William Roll were in the dining room, and Dr. Pratt was in the living room, they all heard a thumping noise originating from near Jimmy's room. The noise grew louder at 9:45 p.m. The cause was undetermined, and the children appeared to have slept through the whole thing.

Pratt and Roll were also in the house when the last event, a bottle popping, occurred on March 10. A bleach bottle in the cellar had its cap off and was found tilted in a box. The bottle was only partially full, and no bleach had spilled. The cap was discovered on the floor, and it was wet inside, with a damp spot underneath it. The investigators had been performing a PK experiment with dice with Jimmy for the preceding half hour, so they knew he hadn't been in the basement. The investigators reasoned that since the wet spot was fresh, it proved that Jimmy hadn't staged the bottle earlier.

After the incident with the bleach bottle, there were no more unusual events. The whole thing stopped as fast as it had begun, and life went back to normal for the Herrmann family.

After spending 10 days investigating the goings-on in the Herr-mann house, Pratt and Roll published a 45-page report in the *Journal of Parapsychology* outlining what they had learned about the myste-rious incidents and providing their theories. They dismissed numer-ous potential physical explanations based on expert tests, includ-ing interference from high-frequency radio waves, unusual ground movements, presence of foreign matter in bottles, electrical or other malfunctions, downdrafts from a chimney, changes in air circulation or groundwater levels, structural problems with the house, vibrations from nearby airplanes and vibrations in the plumbing system.

Pratt and Roll acknowledged the possibility that many of the strange incidents reported by the Herrmann family could have been faked, especially by the children, Jimmy or Lucille Jr. They admit-ted that some of these occurrences could have been the work of an "audacious trickster" even when a third person was present.

However, they also documented 17 incidents where they could verify the children's locations, and the children could not have manipulated the objects that had moved, which was harder to explain. Despite thorough questioning, even under emotional distress, Jimmy consistently denied causing the disturbances. The possibility that Jimmy could have learned complex magic to simulate these events was deemed unlikely.

Incidents witnessed by non–family members and the involvement of the police refuted the theory that the entire series of events was an elaborate hoax by the family. The Herrmanns, however, declined to undergo lie detector tests to further verify their accounts.

Pratt and Roll favoured the explanation of recurrent spontaneous psychokinesis (RSPK), which is hypothesized as an "unconscious expression of repressed psychological force leading to physical acts." This theory was particularly relevant given the focus on Jimmy and the pattern of incidents involving objects belonging to the parents, suggesting the incidents were a manifestation of unmet emotional needs.

The Herrmann house poltergeist case is one of the 20th century's most widely publicized and unexplained incidents, and it greatly influenced parapsychological research. It also led to investigations of other similar cases by Pratt and Roll.

CHAPTER 14

The Vampires of Highgate Cemetery

As long as I knew her, my grandmother lived next door to a funeral home—there was always a hearse parked outside her dining room window. After studying architectural drafting in my early 20s, I was hired by the Town of Bridgewater's Engineering Department to survey the award-winning Brookside Cemetery in order to update the cemetery's maps with accurate locations of all the graves. It was quite an undertaking (pun intended), and while there, I became friendly with the cemetery staff, particularly the superintendent, Melvin Crouse. After the mapping was complete, Melvin offered me a job as a seasonal employee, the duties for which included landscaping and, most interestingly, tending and digging graves. I learned a lot at Brookside, including a genuine appreciation for cemeteries.

When I travel, I spend lots of my time in cemeteries, burial grounds and graveyards. They are places of beauty, reflection and solitude and are excellent for meditation. Memorials and crypts, typically created using stone and metal by skilled artisans, tell fascinating and sometimes enigmatic stories of people long gone. While I was in England in 2022, among other famous burial sites like Westminster Abbey, the group of cemeteries called "the Magnificent Seven" was on my list of places to go.

According to the London Natural History Society, the Magnificent Seven are seven Victorian Gothic garden cemeteries, mostly overgrown, all located within 9 kilometres (5.6 miles) of St. Paul's Cathedral. They represent some of the few large green spaces near central London, and they consist of woodland and rough grassland that also support local wildlife. The seven cemeteries are Abney Park, Brompton, Highgate, Kensal Green, Nunhead, Tower Hamlets and West Norwood.

During a population boom in London during the 1800s, over-crowded churchyards led to sanitation issues and the spread of disease. More places were required to bury the city's dead. Parliament responded by authorizing private garden cemeteries. The city established the Magnificent Seven between 1832 and 1841. However, the cemeteries fell into disrepair by the 20th century, and nature reclaimed them. In recent decades, there has been renewed interest in these cemeteries for their architectural, historical and environmental value. They are all worth a visit for cemetery buffs.

I recently travelled to London and visited the historic Highgate Cemetery, where a peculiar story took root in the 1970s. Residents and visitors recounted tales of an enigmatic entity that allegedly haunted the grounds, eerily similar to a vampire. The unusual happenings, sightings and encounters with this entity rapidly piqued public curiosity and drew significant media coverage. Many people claimed to have had personal experiences with this being, and it was subsequently dubbed "the Highgate Vampire."

Referred to by some as a city of the dead, Highgate was established in May 1839 by the Bishop of London. Highgate Cemetery is one of the world's most famous, architecturally elaborate and beautiful cemeteries. With the Victorians' romantic attitudes toward dying, death and all things funerary, burial in Highgate became so fashionable in 1854 that the city expanded the east side of the property to facilitate those wishing to use the cemetery as their final resting place.

More than 170,000 people lie buried at Highgate, and believe it or not, there's still room for more. One of the most memorable features of the west side of Highgate is Egyptian Avenue, which, as its name suggests, is influenced by ancient Egyptian architecture. Marked by vine-covered obelisks at the entrance, it comprises a columned, darkened walkway lined with 16 vaults, each sealed with a stone door featuring an inverted torch symbol. The avenue leads to the Circle of Lebanon, a circle of tombs built around an old cedar of Lebanon tree, embodying the 19th-century interest in ancient civilizations and the afterlife.

My afternoon exploring Highgate with my friend was a highlight of my trip. We took in a lot that afternoon wandering the quiet, darkened paths, but one thing we did not see any evidence of was the infamous Highgate Vampire.

The concept of the vampire as an actual entity has existed since ancient times, but where the word itself comes from is still being determined. In her 1985 paper "The History of the Word 'Vampire,'" Katharina M. Wilson disputed the common belief that the term is of Hungarian or Transylvanian origin. Instead, she presented four main theories suggesting that the word has Turkish, Greek, Hebrew or Hungarian roots. Its first appearances in major European languages go as far back as 1679 (English), 1721 (German) and 1737 (French). Wilson noted that the adoption of the term across languages remains complex and ambiguous.

The most famous fictional vampire is, of course, Bram Stoker's Dracula. The classic 19th-century horror novel, written as a series of letters, diary entries and other fragments of communication, chronicles the story of Count Dracula's endeavour to relocate from Transylvania to England, where he intended to propagate his undead plague of vampirism. The tale begins with a young English lawyer, Jonathan Harker, visiting Dracula's castle in the Carpathian Mountains to help with property acquisition, only to discover that he is not free to leave and is now a prisoner. Upon Dracula's relocation to England, he starts victimizing the innocent, including Mina, Harker's fiancée, and her friend Lucy. The plot intensifies as a dramatic struggle unfolds between the rising horror caused by Dracula and the group determined to defeat him, led by Professor Abraham Van Helsing.

The initial series of events that led to the legend of the Vampire of Highgate Cemetery occurred in 1869, only 30 years after the cemetery's opening, and involved two artists, English poet, illustrator, painter and translator Dante Gabriel Rossetti and his wife and muse, Elizabeth Siddal, who was an artist in her own right.

Elizabeth Siddal, often called Lizzie, was a prominent figure in the 19th-century Pre-Raphaelite art movement. She had been working in a London milliner's shop when artist Walter Howell Deverell initially discovered her. She became a muse for many artists within the Pre-Raphaelite Brotherhood, including John Everett Millais and Dante Gabriel Rossetti, whom she later married. Her unconventional beauty, marked by her tall frame, slender features and striking red hair, defied the typical beauty norms of her era.

Perhaps the most famous painting Elizabeth Siddal modelled for is *Ophelia*, created by British artist Sir John Everett Millais between 1851 and 1852 and now housed in Tate London. The haunting painting portrays Ophelia, a character from Shakespeare's *Hamlet*, floating in the water just before she succumbs to her death by drowning.

Beyond being a model, Elizabeth Siddal was also a talented artist and poet. In 1857, she was the only female exhibitor at the Pre-Raphaelite exhibition in London.

Despite her beauty and artistic success, Siddal had a difficult life. She and Rossetti had been engaged for 10 years before they finally married. Their relationship was stormy and fraught with passionate arguments and tragedy. She experienced depression, especially after giving birth to a stillborn child.

Elizabeth killed her emotional pain by consuming the opiate laudanum and became hopelessly addicted to the powerful drug. She eventually died from an overdose at her home at 14 Chatham Place on the morning of February 11, 1862, a few months shy of her 33rd birthday. Her death was ruled accidental, but the overdose may have been intentional. She had expressed the wish to die in the days leading up to her death, and her body was found with a note pinned to her nightclothes imploring her family to care for her intellectually challenged younger brother, Harry. Had Elizabeth's death been determined suicide in those days, she would not have been given a Christian burial, so it's likely her possible suicide was covered up.

Regardless of how Elizabeth had passed away, Dante Rossetti was inconsolable. His muse, the great love of his life, was dead after only two years of marriage. Rossetti was so distraught at Elizabeth's funeral that he placed a manuscript of some of his best poems into her coffin and buried it with her. Elizabeth was interred in the Rossetti family plot on the west side of Highgate.

Just seven years after Elizabeth's passing, Dante Gabriel Rossetti had a change of heart about the manuscript he had buried with her and became obsessed with retrieving it. He worried that some of his most important work lay mouldering in Lizzie's grave. Pressured by his business agent, Charles Augustus Howell, Rossetti agreed to have Lizzie exhumed so he could retrieve his valuable book of poems. As Rossetti was unwilling and unable to do the work himself, Howell made the arrangements to exhume her body. After acquiring permission from the proper authorities, a date was set for a cool October night in 1869. The disinterment was to occur under the cover of darkness to protect the public's prying eyes from the gruesome scene and to prevent any upset of Rossetti's family since his father lay buried in the same grave.

In Janet Camp Troxell's paper "Collecting the Rossettis," she spoke about the manuscripts, poems and letters in her collection, which includes the note given to Charles Howell by Rossetti, describing the manuscript Howell was to find in Elizabeth's grave.

Rossetti wrote to Howell, "The book is bound in rough grey calf and has, I'm almost sure, red edges to the leaves. This would distinguish it from the Bible also there, as I told you."

In compliance with legal requirements, a solicitor and a doctor witnessed the exhumation of Elizabeth Siddal's grave on October 5, 1869, to ensure no crime or fraud occurred. Workers unearthed the coffin and retrieved the book of poetry. Troxell reported that, besides the manuscript, there was Rossetti's Bible, as he'd indicated. A dead dove was present as well. The most shocking sight, however, was Elizabeth Siddal herself. Her skin, it was said, appeared as fresh as it had on the day she died. Her thick, luxurious red hair had allegedly grown after death, filling the coffin. The lid was quickly placed on the coffin and it was reburied.

It is unclear whether there were murmurs of vampirism at the time, but the story of how Elizabeth looked in her grave made its way around and she became the first vampire of Highgate Cemetery. Some even believe that the story of Elizabeth in her grave inspired the character of Lucy in Bram Stoker's *Dracula*. However, this remains unconfirmed.

A controversial figure named David Robert Farrant, a 24-year-old tobacconist, was the first to publicly claim he had seen what he believed was a vampire in Highgate Cemetery. Born in Highgate, Farrant was the president of the British Psychic and Occult Society and was known in the community for his interest in the supernatural.

According to a 1982 documentary called *The Vampire of Highgate*, Farrant had been raised around occult practice and mysticism, as his mother was actively involved with an occult organization and claimed to be a medium and a clairvoyant. After his mother's death when David was just 13, his interest in the occult grew. By 18, he had fallen in with the same organization, and they initiated him into what he called "the old religion," or Wicca. David was instrumental in the founding of the British Psychic and Occult Society in 1967, which he then came to lead. His group used Highgate Cemetery for their various rituals, often entering secretly (and illegally) at night.

In the summer of 1969, Farrant learned of a strange occurrence in Highgate Cemetery near the Circle of Lebanon. A man using the pseudonym Thornton, a chartered accountant who wished to remain anonymous, had a peculiar experience in the cemetery.

Thornton spent the day walking around and photographing Highgate's monuments and other features. When the bell rang, signalling the cemetery's closing, he sensed a presence behind him. Thornton turned to look and saw a tall, dark spectre hovering just above the ground. He couldn't move and said it felt like a powerful "hypnotic force" had sapped his energy. Time seemed to stand still, and he could not focus on anything other than the strange sight before him. He stood frozen but terrified for several minutes before the spectre abruptly vanished. Once he slowly regained his senses, he fled to his car, which was parked outside the cemetery gates. As he sped away, Thornton, a skeptic of things supernatural, wondered what had just happened.

A month after Thornton's experience, another story was reported to Farrant about a strange occurrence in Highgate Cemetery. In September 1969, an older woman living near Swains Lane had a frightening encounter while walking her dog near the cemetery's main gates. She reported seeing a "tall, dark man" floating above the ground inside the cemetery, his eyes glinting and seemingly lit from within. The thing vanished as quickly as it appeared.

On the night of December 21, 1969, the eve of the winter solstice, David Farrant decided to check out the cemetery for himself. He headed out to Highgate at around 11:00 p.m. Despite his initial skepticism, Farrant sensed "an alien presence" as he walked beside the cemetery wall along the street. He claimed that as he prepared to scale the wall, a humanoid figure, about 213 centimetres (7 feet) tall, materialized in front of him. As the dark, featureless figure approached, the surrounding area turned icy cold, and Farrant noticed two faint points of light where the figure's face should have been. He felt that the entity was evil and that he was under psychic attack. Farrant claimed he then recited a Qabbalistic incantation he knew, which is often used to negate malignant influences. This incantation seemed to disturb the entity, after which it retreated, and the temperature returned to normal.

After Farrant's sighting, members of his group, the British Psychic and Occult Society, were determined to investigate further and attended Highgate Cemetery. There were two other sightings near the same spot in late December 1969 and again in January 1970. The cemetery's history was rife with tales of dark apparitions dating back to the Victorian era, many with vampiric overtones, especially Elizabeth Siddal's exhumation story, and the reported feeling of psychic attack during several of the sightings made many of the occult group believe the entity might be a vampire.

The public became aware of the sightings when a letter written by Farrant appeared in the *Hampstead and Highgate Express*, known locally as the *Ham & High*, on February 6, 1970. Farrant described the creature and the encounters in the letter and suggested the thing might be a vampire. He even referenced Bram Stoker's *Dracula* and Lizzie Siddal. The story caused quite a stir, and there were subsequent interviews with Farrant in that paper and others. In one interview, Farrant attributed the deaths of foxes within the cemetery to the vampire.

After David Farrant was featured in an interview about the case on the BBC, interest in the Highgate Cemetery vampire exploded. Farrant vowed to put a stake through the thing's heart to dispatch it. Much to the dismay of cemetery staff and police, groups of people, primarily local youth, flocked to Highgate Cemetery on March 13, 1970, trespassing in the hope of seeing the vampire and watching Farrant kill the creature.

Around 100 people gathered for the vampire hunt. A significant police presence, reportedly 40 officers, was needed to manage the crowd. Amid the frenzy, some reported seeing a suspicious "crawling" entity in the dark. Alan Blood, a 25-year-old teacher from Chelmsford, joined the hunt, ready to stake the supposed vampire with a wooden cross.

After another night of vampire hunting in Highgate Cemetery in August 1970, David Farrant was arrested and charged with illegally being in an enclosed area within the cemetery. Farrant reported to police that he believed a vampire lurked in the cemetery's catacombs. This vampire, he claimed, would rise from its grave to feast on human blood, and he aimed to eliminate the creature, armed with a crucifix marked with a black-magic symbol. He planned to search St. Michael's Churchyard at midnight for the vampire. If not for the police's intervention, he would have looked into the coffins in the catacombs, intending to find and stake the creature's heart.

When apprehended, Farrant was carrying candles, incense, charcoal, a camera, chalk and a carved piece of wood with a white satin cord. Farrant said the cord was so he could make a protective circle. However, in court, the police presented the wooden stake without the cord to show it as an implement of vampire hunting. David was found not guilty after his defence attorney successfully argued that where police caught Farrant did not meet the legal definition of an enclosed area.

After his acquittal, David Farrant kept up his antics within Highgate Cemetery, but the authorities were watching. He was implicated in three additional court cases between 1970 and 1974. At the last court appearance in 1974, Farrant was finally convicted. A psychiatric evaluation revealed he had no identifiable mental illness. The psychiatrist testifying at the trial noted that Farrant's fascination with the supernatural could lead to a mental breakdown if not properly managed.

David Farrant received a sentence of four years and eight months in prison for crimes related to the cemetery, which included damaging a memorial, breaking into catacombs, interfering with remains, firearm possession, theft and attempting to intimidate police officers with threatening objects. He served three years behind bars and claimed his actions were justified. He blamed media attention for thwarting his efforts to dispatch the evil and dangerous vampire.

In Farrant's later writings and media interviews, he continued trying to explain the vampire's presence in Highgate Cemetery. In his 1991 book *Beyond the Highgate Vampire*, Farrant also posited that the appearance of the entity around the time of the ringing of the cemetery's closing bell is congruent with the time that in 1856 a man named Henri Feuhonlet died by suicide, shooting himself in the head with a pistol as the bell sounded.

An article published in *The Illustrated London News* on December 6, 1856, titled "Love and Suicide," tells the sad story.

The body of a gentleman was found on Monday evening with the right side of the face and head completely blown away. In his right hand, the deceased grasped the stock of a pistol, and the barrel, which had been blown off by the force of the explosion, lay some distance from the body. Mr. Broadbent immediately went off to inform the police, who found that he was dressed in dark clothing and appeared to be a gentleman. He had a gold ring with a white stone in it on his finger, a serpent ring through which his neckerchief was passed, and a gold pin in his shirt. His linen was marked "Henri Feuhonlet," while under the lining of his hat were also found the initials "H.F." in ink. Two sealed letters were likewise found in his pocket, the one addressed to a "Miss Patridge" while the other, on being opened, began, "My dear father and mother"; they were both signed "Henri Feuhonlet" but bore no address or date. The letters were written in a good plain legible hand, and in the one addressed "My dear father and mother," the writer spoke of great mental afflictions on account of some love affair and ended by saying, "I can write no more." The deceased, who seemed to be about twenty-five years, and had something the appearance of a foreigner, has not yet been identified.

Farrant remained a colourful character in the media for years. In a 1978 election, he was the sole candidate of the Wicca Workers Party in Hornsey, advocating for a variety of policies, including nudity, free sex, reinstating the Wiccan creed, establishing state-run brothels, banning communism and leaving the European Common Market. He lost his bid for office.

On April 24, 2019, the *Ham & High* reported David Farrant's passing. Senior reporter Samuel Volpe wrote that despite the controversy and his time in prison, Farrant remained fascinated with the occult and paranormal and continued to hold talks and write about occult phenomena. In the article, his wife, Della, described David as a kind, loving and somewhat shy man who was very much a people person and always interested in how the world works.

The enduring Highgate vampire story is a captivating blend of folklore, urban legend and media influence. This saga reflects societal fears, mass hysteria and the power of legends in shaping communities. Perhaps the next time I visit, I'll stick around until the closing bell. Who knows what I'll see?

CHAPTER 15

The Philip Experiment

I first learned about this fascinating case from my co-host, author and parapsychological researcher Morgan Knudsen, in the first episode of our podcast, *Supernatural Circumstances*. My involvement in that podcast has affected me so much that I wanted to include a few of those stories in this book. Being a relative newcomer to the science of parapsychological investigation and massively skeptical, I had doubts about the podcast project when we first began. However, when Morgan introduced me to the "fake" ghost named "Philip," the story blew my mind.

In their quest to explore the boundaries of the paranormal, the Toronto Society for Psychical Research (TSPR) embarked on a unique group experiment. In 1973, they set out to create their own "ghost"—a fictional entity named Philip. The experiment was designed to test the theory of collective hallucinations and the power of suggestion in a group setting. The society's members, aware that Philip was purely a product of their imagination, sought to manifest this invented character through controlled experiments. Those involved were surprised by the experiment's outcome. And they learned much more than they had expected.

As this book's chapter on Popper the Poltergeist mentioned, Dr. J.B. Rhine's highly controlled and successful telepathy and psychokinesis experiments helped legitimize parapsychology. His team investigated paranormal phenomena across various disciplines. Rhine's initial experiments, detailed in his book *Extrasensory Perception*, demonstrated significant evidence for clairvoyant and telepathic perception over numerous trials. Rhine also initiated the study of psychokinesis, or mind–matter interactions, at Duke University in 1933, using dice-throwing as a lab test. After nine years and 18 separate investigations, Rhine's team strove to answer the question: Can minds influence matter? In all their experiments, subjects attempted to control the outcome of dice throws. Despite measures ensuring randomness, some individuals, who claimed the ability to affect matter with their minds, displayed statistically significant deviations over hundreds of thousands of throws, hinting at a possible physical effect, driven by mental intention, the outcomes of which were consistent, despite safeguards, peer reviews and transparent methods.

Rhine also explored the effects of drugs, distance and other variables on scoring rates. While his book was well received, it also faced criticism from academics. Critics argued that subjects could see the symbols on the ESP cards and that scoring and recording errors inflated results. These criticisms led to minor data collection and analysis changes but didn't majorly alter positive experimental results. Rhine's attention to detail and commitment to the scientific exploration of strange phenomena cemented his place as an important contributor to the modern history of parapsychological study.

Rhine's work led in part to the 1970 founding of the Toronto Society for Psychical Research (TSPR). This organization delved into the lesser-known aspects of human experience using parapsychology. Their main focus was the scientific examination of phenomena like telepathy, clairvoyance, precognition and paranormal investigation.

Planning the Philip experiment posed two challenges. First, unlike with previous telepathy experiments, the group decided that no participant should claim previous psychic abilities. Second, the team had to figure out how to create an environment conducive to achieving their goal of manifesting an entity.

To create such an environment, the team crafted a detailed backstory for Philip, encompassing his 1600s life, his personality and the drama surrounding his death, to enhance believability and focus. Regular group sessions were held where participants immersed themselves in Philip's narrative, employing traditional seance techniques such as dimming lights, sitting around a table and meditating to summon him. The participants' belief in the experiment's potential and their emotional investment in Philip's story were crucial, aiming to unify their intentions and energy toward manifesting the entity. This unique blend of belief, narrative immersion and traditional spiritualist practices led to unexplained phenomena attributed to Philip, showcasing the experiment as a study on the power of collective thought, the ideomotor effect or the dynamics of group psychology.

For clarification, the ideomotor effect is a psychological phenomenon where individuals unconsciously move or act in response to suggestions, expectations or thoughts, without being aware of these movements' origins. It explains unconscious movements during activities like using a pendulum or Ouija board, where people attribute the movement to supernatural forces instead of their own subconscious actions. This effect underscores the mind–body connection, showing how mental processes can influence physical behaviour without conscious intent.

The TSPR carefully chose a group of eight members to be involved.

The group's eight diverse individuals were:

- Al: a practical and commonsensical heating engineer interested in scouting and photography.
- Lorne: an industrial designer passionate about bushido, ancient history, Oriental philosophies and astronomy.
- Andy: Lorne's wife, a homemaker with an artistic flair. She had a keen interest in astronomy and a love for animals.
- Bernice: an accountant with an artistic side who enjoyed philosophy and outdoor activities.
- Dorothy: a homemaker and Cub Scout leader with a keen interest in parapsychology and a background in bookkeeping.
- Sidney: the group's youngest member; a college student studying sociology who took a break to travel and work as a salesperson.
- Sue: a mother of three and the chair of Mensa for Canada. She was a nurse before her marriage.
- Iris: an author who was deeply interested in paranormal experiences. The oldest group member, she worked as a nurse and social worker and was actively involved in women's work in the United Church of Canada. After the experiment's completion, Iris wrote a book titled *Conjuring Up Philip* that was published in 1976.

One of the two non-participating observers of the experiment was George (A.R.G.) Owen, Iris's husband, who had co-founded the TSPR with her. He was also the director of the New Horizons Research Foundation (1970-1984), a non-profit entity based in Toronto that was committed to fostering scientific exploration and spreading knowledge. New Horizons was strongly connected with the TSPR, as George and Iris Owen were the key researchers in both organizations.

During its 14 years of existence, New Horizons generated a series of 53 research documents, papers, proposals, briefs, notes and reviews, primarily authored by George and/or Iris Owen. These works spanned a variety of subjects, from unidentified flying objects and lunar effects to parapsychology and sociology. The foundation also partnered with other researchers and institutions, including students from the Princeton Engineering Anomalies Research laboratory at Princeton University.

The second observer was Dr. Joel Lloyd Whitton (1945–2017), a renowned psychiatrist based in Toronto. He held the prestigious position of professor emeritus at the University of Toronto, York University and Guelph University and was also a staff member at a Toronto hospital. His medical expertise was primarily in the areas of migraine, chronic pain, head injuries and trauma.

However, his unique research into past lives and reincarnation is particularly interesting. Using hypnosis, Dr. Whitton guided his patients back into their previous lives to uncover the roots of traumas and neuroses that were affecting them in their current lives. He was also a member of the TSPR, where he honed his interest in exploring the boundaries of human consciousness and experience.

The group decided on the name Philip as the imaginary ghost they hoped to summon during their experiment. According to Iris Owen's book, group member Sue was responsible for creating

Philip's interesting and fictitious biography. Philip was imagined as a 17th-century English nobleman during Cromwell's rule. He was a Catholic and royal supporter married to the beautiful but cold Dorothea. After falling for Margo, a stunning gypsy girl, he secretly housed her in Diddington Manor's gatehouse. When Dorothea discovered the affair and accused Margo of witchcraft and adultery, Philip, to protect his reputation and wealth, didn't defend her, leading to Margo's execution. Consumed by guilt, Philip spiralled into despair, frequently wandering Diddington's battlements until his suspected suicide, after his body was discovered at the base of the battlements.

The group agreed Philip's "biography" was perfect for what might have been a real ghost. They set out to collectively hallucinate a visible form of him. To achieve this, they discussed Philip's backstory, physical characteristics, personality and relationships in detail, creating a comprehensive mental image they all agreed on. This image was further solidified through a drawing by group member Andy. The drawing of Philip depicts a strong-looking Caucasian man with rugged features, shoulder-length hair, a full beard and kind eyes. For additional accuracy, they also researched details of Philip's historical period.

The group then began the experiment using meditation, typically sitting in a circle around a picture of Philip with hopes of materializing him. They experimented with lighting and held two meditation sessions per meeting, sharing their experiences and feelings in between. Unlike many seances seen in Hollywood films, the group never met in complete darkness, though sometimes they used coloured lights or candles to illuminate the sessions. During their meditations, they visualized Philip in their minds, with the drawing of him on the table in front of them to help with their manifestation. Additionally, they set an aluminium cardboard square on the ground, aiming to incite Philip to materialize on its surface.

The group adhered to a simple routine: meditate, share experiences and then meditate again, gradually extending the sessions' length as they grew accustomed to the practice. Throughout their discussions, they refined Philip's character, eventually feeling like he was a real historical figure. However, despite a year of diligent effort, they witnessed no significant manifestations. Philip had not appeared, nor had anything happened that would have proven to be a psychokinetic, or PK, event.

Undaunted, they were determined to move forward and continue the experiment, but they knew something had to change. Up to this point, the whole affair had been a rather joyless experience. They had been engaged in nothing but a dry and serious business in trying to manifest Philip. Iris Owen pored over papers published by other parapsychologists who had been more successful in their attempts to conjure spirits. In a few of these reports, Iris noticed a common thread that struck her. These people were having fun during their sessions. They were much more lighthearted than her group had been in the first year of the Philip experiment.

Iris learned that multiple researchers had suggested that anyone with the right mindset could acquire psychokinetic skills, and such talents were not restricted to mediums. Researchers believed these abilities were enhanced by belief and expectation and would, conversely, be hampered by skepticism. Belief in what one was doing seemed critical to a successful experiment.

Studies in psychokinesis continue to this day. According to Heather Warner-Angel's 2017 clinical psychology master's thesis at Eastern Illinois University, it's been scientifically established by various studies that a belief in psi phenomena, including telepathy, precognition, clairvoyance and psychokinesis, has a substantial impact on an individual's performance on related tasks. This influence is often called the sheep–goat effect. Individuals who believe in psi phenomena (labelled as "sheep") tend to perform better in psi tasks, often scoring above chance. Conversely, those who don't believe in psi phenomena (called "goats") tend to score below chance levels. This effect was explored in several studies, including ones conducted at Harvard from 1942 to 1945, where participants with high belief ratings (the "sheep") consistently outperformed those with low belief ratings (the "goats") in clairvoyance tasks involving ESP cards.

This correlation is particularly noticeable in participants with low religiosity. Moreover, belief in personal luck strongly correlates with psi task performance. Therefore, individuals with a high belief in psi or luck tend to excel in psi tasks, while skeptics often perform below chance levels.

In other pioneering experiments in macro-psychokinesis in the 1960s and 1970s conducted by British psychologist Kenneth (K.J.) Batcheldor, the Philip group found that elements like joy, conviviality and amusement were integral to his successful experiments. With belief in what they were doing top of mind, Batcheldor and his team performed experiments that produced physical phenomena like table rapping and movements without visual apparitions.

Batcheldor suggested employing methods from Victorian seances, which were often social, relaxed events, contrary to the Philip group's more solemn meditation techniques. Victorian seances, however, were typically conducted in dim light or darkness, and only one participant, the medium, was responsible for any phenomena that occurred. The phenomena were often attributed to spirits, which were identified as friends or relatives of the participants. These conditions made it difficult for serious researchers to validate the results, especially when there was a strong desire for contact with the departed among the participants and motivation from the medium to provide proof of their existence.

However, Batcheldor did not believe that a professional medium was necessary to get results, and he proved it. His team in England successfully levitated a heavy table in an experiment, highlighting the role of belief and expectancy in psychokinesis. This approach, rooted in the idea that psychokinesis is a learnable skill, influenced the group's perspective. The discovery led to tensions between spiritualists, who are focused on spirit communication, and parapsychologists interested in the manifestation of psychical phenomena.

The Philip experiment continued, and their new sessions were filled with discussion and study, inspired by Batcheldor's experiment. They aimed to create a relaxed, social atmosphere they hoped would be more conducive to manifesting paranormal events. Over their first few meetings, the group felt awkward and self-conscious as they tried to maintain casual conversations, tell jokes and sing songs while focusing on conjuring Philip's ghost. After a few weeks, they relaxed, becoming more comfortable with their new approach. There were no results in the first weeks, but they kept going, feeling new resolve and wanting to give the experiment a good chance to work.

The group reserved the room used for the experiment strictly for their activity. They decorated the space with various objects related to Philip, including the portrait drawn by Andy, fencing foils and photos of meaningful locations from his life. In addition to the main room, there was a small adjacent alcove where they played music records from Philip's determined era during sessions.

It took only a few sittings before the new method began to show positive results. It was either the third or fourth session that something started to happen. Group members felt, rather than heard, the first occurrence as the table began intermittently vibrating while they were talking to each other. There was a bit of back and forth as members accused one another of somehow causing the disturbance. Everyone denied responsibility, but all agreed they had felt it.

Excited, they continued the session and began to hear sounds like knocking on the table, which also resulted in the same feelings of vibration. Again, each group member looked at the others, asking whether they were the source of the rapping sounds. And again, no one admitted to causing them. Even though the group were aware of similar occurrences from earlier studies, they were shocked when the table moved randomly across the room. Early doubts that group members might be unconsciously moving the table were quickly ruled out.

Table raps and unexplained movements of seance tables have long been a feature of spiritualist sessions aiming to communicate with the deceased. The Society of Psychical Research defines spiritualism as the belief that human personalities continue to exist after death and that it is provable by gathering messages from entities who no longer possess a physical body. People seek this type of communication for comfort after loss, for insights into the afterlife or to obtain guidance in their lives. Often after wars and plagues, there are spikes in spiritualist interest as survivors seek closure through communication with their deceased relatives, hoping to learn they are still around, albeit in another dimension or realm.

A spiritualism session, or seance, requires a small- to medium-sized wooden table, two or more friends, a quiet room with dimmed lights and an open mind. Participants sit around the table, place their hands on it and concentrate on the answers they seek from "the other world." After asking the spirits a question, they wait for the knocks on the table or for it to move or tilt, which is the spirits' response. Before the advent of spirit boards, rapping was considered a valid communication tool between seance participants and the entities they believed they had conjured.

The most famous early instance of table-rapping communication involved the Fox sisters, mentioned in the earlier chapter about Harry Houdini, who claimed they were frauds. The siblings were outed by one of the sisters in a later-life confession.

Even though the case of the Fox sisters might have been fraudulent, the Philip group devised a similar method to communicate with whatever was causing the table's movement and the rapping sounds— one rap signified "yes" and two "no." They focused on asking binary questions to avoid the laborious process of spelling out responses through raps. Early on, the raps confirmed that this was "Philip," a wholly fabricated spirit with whom they communicated.

They used a typical plastic-topped card table for their sessions, with each session beginning with greetings to Philip. It was noted that the raps most often came under the hand of the person addressing Philip, as if responding to the individual speaking.

During a typical session, the group would greet each other and then say hello to Philip, and often receive a responsive rap to the greeting. After several successful sessions, they found no need for warming up or relaxation exercises. They got right into it. They did learn, though, that they had to keep the tone of the sittings jovial and had to take regular breaks, where they would talk, sing and tell jokes. Philip would often respond to a particularly funny joke with rapid raps. It became increasingly important to maintain a relaxed atmosphere, as too much intensity seemed to suppress the unusual occurrences. Any accidental sounds or movements caused by the group were readily admitted, ensuring that the results were not tampered with in any way. The interactions were also recorded on audiotapes.

Over the following sessions, through table raps, Philip began to share his story with the group, making him even more real to them, although they remained aware he was a concoction. Philip's responses, in the form of knocks or scratches, were often what the questioner expected. Doubtful questions received hesitant knocks, and overly personal inquiries were met with scratching sounds, interpreted as Philip's refusal to answer. During these sessions, the group conversed with Philip as if he were an actual guest despite his limited means of communication. Mistakes occurred when the group asked questions requiring more than a yes/no answer, prompting Philip to produce scratching sounds instead. A particularly amusing instance happened when Philip simultaneously rapped under everyone's hand upon a group member's jesting request.

Philip was questioned on his religious affiliations, his personal relationships and his role in the Civil War. His responses included contradictions like wavering between Catholic and Protestant, then declaring he was an Anglo-Catholic—a denomination nonexistent in his time. When asked about his role in the Civil War, he said he led a regiment and participated in espionage but seemed hesitant when asked about his loyalty to King Charles I. The group assumed that maybe Philip switched sides when Oliver Cromwell came to power but received no definitive answer.

In one recorded meeting, the group sang songs for Philip and discussed his personal likes and dislikes, covering topics from his favourite horse to his alleged indulgences in London's chocolate houses. Though playful and entertaining, these narratives were not always historically accurate, such as the mention of chocolate houses, which didn't exist during Philip's supposed lifetime.

Rapping was not the only physical phenomenon encountered during the experiment. Often, the table creaked and groaned, which was presumed to be the buildup of some form of energy or force. The group sensed shifts in the table's feel before the phenomena occurred.

The sitting room also featured a lighting panel, which intriguingly appeared to respond to verbal commands thought to be from Philip. It would occasionally flicker in sync with the instructions, yet no physical interference was evident. While it was possible that changes in power supply could explain the lighting anomalies, the group leaned toward attributing these events to Philip and the paranormal realm.

On a few occasions, the table moved significantly, including standing on one leg, moving around the room and turning on its side, seemingly in response to the group. These movements were often unpredictable and resulted in the table moving to different corners of the room or to the doorway. In one instance, the table used one of its legs to scratch out answers on the wall. At one point, the group felt tired and requested that Philip flip the table. The table then flipped over. (See notes for a link to the video on YouTube.)

While singing the nonsense song "99 Bottles of Beer," the group noted that the table responded by bouncing, shaking and rapping in time with the music. Some members believed the table achieved complete levitation during the song. At the end of the song, as the session concluded, each member said good night to Philip, with the table responding to each goodbye with a distinct rap.

The group discovered that Philip did have limitations. While they reported that Philip could accurately answer questions about his historical era, his knowledge did not surpass the group's collective understanding, suggesting his responses came from their subconscious. They recorded no audible responses, hinting that any perceived whispers were imagined. Physical phenomena, which included moving objects or flickering lights, relied on the group's focused belief and ceased when this wavered, again underlining the psychological nature of these occurrences.

Besides table rapping and other noises, Philip supposedly made lights blink and even levitated the table half an inch above the ground, a feat witnessed by those present but not captured on film because of the dim lighting.

It was hard to keep the meetings a secret. Word of the strange events surrounding the group leaked out, and the media soon got wind of the experiment. In November 1974, the group agreed to participate in an episode of the CBC documentary program *Man Alive*. The Philip experiment attracted significant media attention, leading to an hour-long documentary called *Philip, the Imaginary Ghost* by the CBC, which is now available on DVD. In their show *World of the Unexplained*, Toronto's CITY-TV featured the experiment as a live seance for an audience of 50 and a film crew, which marked the experiment's peak. These videos are viewable on YouTube, showcasing a complete table levitation and forceful raps as responses as the group chatter among themselves and sing silly songs. Another video includes interviews with Iris Owen and Joel Whitton and demonstrations of table movements and raps. In the United States, portions of the video *Philip, the Imaginary Ghost* were featured on the popular TV program *That's Incredible!*

It is unclear how this group created what appeared to be a physical force that could be heard and recorded. The group members were adamant that no one was physically moving the table during the sessions. Still, even direct observers doubted the experiment's veracity despite the participants' hands being in full view. Iris Owen stuck to her claims that the events were not a hoax. She later wrote that the group determined that manually reproducing the table movements was impossible. As for the rapping phenomenon, this also seemed unfeasible to produce via fraud. There remains no definitive understanding of how the raps and table movements were created.

A second experiment, also initiated by the Toronto Society for Psychical Research, was designed to mimic the original Philip experiment and prove its replicability. The group involved in this test were entirely different people from the original group, and they conceived a character named "Lilith." Lilith was imagined to be a French-Canadian girl involved with the French resistance during the Second World War, who was eventually apprehended and executed as a spy.

Only five weeks after they started their sessions, the participants began to notice the table moving, similar to the happenings of the Philip experiment. Soon after, rapping noises started, and they would respond to the group's questions in a way consistent with the fabricated character. The replication of these strange occurrences in this second experiment underscored the assertion that any group of people, given the right conditions, could produce such phenomena.

Iris's husband, Dr. George Owen, interpreted these findings as evidence that a group's collective will, anticipation and emotional engagement can manifest as physical phenomena. The results suggest that group belief and imagination could potentially create or influence apparent paranormal occurrences. However, these interpretations remain contentious within the scientific community, and many argue that further, more meticulous research is required.

Other experiments have attempted to replicate the Philip experiment and Lilith experiment with varying degrees of success. The method used in the Philip experiment, termed "PK by committee" by parapsychologist D. Scott Rogo, has been reproduced in other settings, with imaginary figures like the Artful Dodger, Santa Claus and others creating similar effects.

In 1994, a professor and eight undergraduate students from Franklin Pierce College in New Hampshire conducted a 10-week experiment to attempt to produce the "PK by committee" effect. They created a fictitious entity named "Alexander," a Confederate army officer. The group, including their character Alexander, tried to influence a candle flame. The flame seemed to respond to the group's discussions. When the group discussed lighthearted or enjoyable topics, the flame flared up higher and brighter, but when they talked about darker subjects, the flame seemed to shrink, nearly extinguishing.

In 2002, a team of professional and amateur paranormal researchers in Adelaide, South Australia, established the Spenser group. They named the group after a fictional British sea captain, Spenser Blake. Like the Philip and Batcheldor groups, the Spenser group aimed to generate psychic phenomena, also known as psi phenomena, from the collective consciousness rather than an actual entity.

The group tried to affect a candle flame with psychokinetic energy, as the Franklin Pierce College group had attempted. They also incorporated telepathy, video and audio recordings, and table raps and taps, in addition to the candle flame manipulation.

During their sessions, they noticed various occurrences. They reported and, in some cases, recorded table creaks, raps, taps and scratches, while other noises were faint or not recorded but confirmed by the members present. The participants also reported feeling vibrations from the table. The group noted that these noises could not conclusively be attributed to psi phenomena, as similar sounds could be caused by tapping a chair leg or foot on the floor.

Most participants reported various bodily sensations such as hot hands, a poking sensation on their palms, sensations of being touched and throbbing or tingling fingertips. One participant claimed to have been poked in the leg. Other incidents include a participant feeling grabbed on the leg, smelling an aniseed scent and feeling like she was getting injections in her arms. A guest participant felt a cold breeze across her hands. One participant felt like a needle was sticking into his finger and arm. Another participant reported the sensation of her chair being grabbed. Unpleasant experiences also included unusual head sensations, a heavy feeling around the head and shoulders, and feelings of sickness when standing up and sitting down.

Also significant, four participants reported observing unusual lights. One saw small flashes, a blue dot and a floating white light. Another noticed flickering light in the room and a grid of red lights, coinciding with a third seeing a white triangle flash. A fourth member saw a white light moving toward the table and sparkling lights near another's hands. In a semi-dark session recorded with infrared light, orbs were seen moving across the wall, possibly due to reflected light from dust particles.

Spenser group members experimented with ways to produce the raps and taps they were observing mechanically. They discovered they could consistently make similar taps by slightly pulling their hands toward themselves while on the table, even using only fingertips. Further, the frequency of the taps decreased with less hand contact. No taps occurred when hands were entirely off the table, leading them to hypothesize that many of the taps they had previously attributed to paranormal phenomena may have been unconsciously produced by group members manipulating the table. They didn't rule out the possibility of some paranormal effects but suggested a non-paranormal explanation for some observed phenomena.

Morgan Knudsen has made astute observations about the Philip experiment and what we can learn from its early failures and later successes.

In her book *Teaching the Living*, Morgan suggests that a critical element in turning the Philip experiment into a success was the active cultivation of joy. The experiment's members found it fascinating and felt fulfilled and bonded after each session, creating a culture centred on happiness, leading to the observation that those with less emotional negativity often experience more positive encounters with paranormal phenomena. However, she also reminds us that our projections can often attract similar phenomena. Knudsen uses the analogy of a radio dial with negative emotions on one end and positive ones on the other. Individuals tend to resonate consistently on this spectrum, attracting phenomena that align with their emotional state.

For example, despite having a seemingly happy life, one of Morgan's clients was terrorized by a violent entity. Intriguingly, this client admitted to having unresolved emotional trauma from a past abusive relationship. When a person addresses such emotional wounds, the associated aggressive phenomena often disappear.

Not everyone wishes to confront and heal their emotional pain, as it's often more familiar than the uncertain path to happiness. As spiritual beings living a human experience, we can reshape our reality by shifting our paradigms. Morgan believes that although it varies across individuals and cultures, joy bridges them all, and it's essential for those dealing with other realms to guide, not dictate, the journey of self-discovery. Despite its challenges, commitment to this journey is ultimately an individual decision but one worth undertaking.

There are many takeaways from the Philip experiment. By successfully creating a fictional ghost through group focus and imagination, the experiment demonstrated how belief, expectation and the ideomotor effect can produce physical manifestations, such as knocks and object movements, attributed to a non-existent entity. These outcomes suggest that the human mind plays a significant role in the perception and creation of paranormal experiences, highlighting the fact that psychological and social dynamics may be the source of seemingly supernatural events. This experiment challenges our understanding of reality and the paranormal, indicating that the boundaries between mind and matter may be more intertwined than previously thought.

CHAPTER 16

What's Next? Death, Dying and the Afterlife

As far as we know, humans are the only animals capable of under-standing that all of us, good eggs and bad apples alike, will inev-itably die. In his book *The Varieties of Religious Experience*, philosopher William James said, "Back of everything is the great spectre of uni-versal death, the all-encompassing blackness." James called this idea "the worm at the core" of human existence, a bit of inescapable rot in an otherwise amazing apple. The idea of our eventual death is unavoidable. One day, we will all upgrade to the cloud version from our physical edition.

American cultural anthropologist Ernest Becker expanded on James's ideas in his 1974 Pulitzer Prize–winning book, *The Denial of Death*. Becker explored how people and cultures respond to death, suggesting that human civilization is essentially a defence against our awareness of mortality. This awareness motivates everything we do, from our interests and art creation to having children to pass on our genes. According to Becker, our deep desire for immortality drives us to leave a mark on the world to achieve a sense of lasting presence.

Ever since I can remember, I've been both fascinated and terrified by the idea of dying. This fear makes me wonder about what happens after we die. This massive question leads to many others: Is the idea of an afterlife something we've created to make ourselves feel better about dying, or is there absolute proof that something of us lives on? Different cultures and religions have beliefs about what comes after death, from ancient myths to spiritual teachings. These questions leave us thinking more deeply about life and death and push us to live better, thinking about the mark we want to leave in the world.

My most notable experience with mortality happened at Vancouver General Hospital. There, while working in my role as a security guard, I witnessed the sudden passing of a colleague.

It was early in my shift when I first met a new guard, whom I'll call Jimmy Johnson, on his first day. At 43 years old, Jimmy was about my height and had a round, red face framed by strawberry-blond curls. The site supervisor training Jimmy showed him the patrol routes I had learned months before.

In the early hours, less than halfway through the shift, a fire alarm sounded on the sixth floor of the Centennial Pavilion. Following protocol, all guards rushed to the alarm location. When I arrived, I found Jimmy looking awful. He had difficulty catching his breath and had a pale, grey and sweaty complexion. I mentioned concern for Jimmy's health to the site supervisor, but we pressed on.

After confirming the alarm was false, the site supervisor, Tim, informed the other guards to return to their regular patrols. Tim asked Jimmy and me to join him; he wanted to teach us how to reset the alarm system. So we headed to the fourth floor, the central hub for the building's alarms. This particular floor in the Centennial Pavilion, known as an interstitial floor, is off-limits to visitors. It mainly stores patient records and contains the mechanical gear that runs the building's systems.

The elevator door opened to a darkened and quiet environment. At night especially, there are not many reasons other than why we were there to be on that floor then. I was told to stay near the elevator while Jimmy and Tim entered a mechanical room to reset the alarm. Only moments later, Tim radioed me to come and help him in the mechanical room double-time. He sounded shaken, unusual for him.

When I entered the room, I saw Jimmy on the floor, struggling for breath, his face turning a ghastly purple. While Tim performed CPR, I called for EMTs, who arrived within moments, accompanied by other security officers. Despite the best efforts of the EMTs and the quickly arriving hospital cardiac team, Jimmy passed away. We later learned it was from a massive heart attack caused by known cardiac issues.

In that critical moment when Jimmy's life slipped away, I sensed an indescribable presence departing from him. It's challenging to pinpoint precisely what it was—a change in his gaze, a subtle aura or perhaps a certain feeling that permeated the air around us. Still, an evident change marked the shift from being alive to no longer living. Jimmy was with us one instant, a living being filled with life; the next, an eerie stillness prevailed, marking his absence. This profound shift wasn't just about the cessation of breath or heartbeat; it felt like the essence that made Jimmy who he was just disappeared into the unknown.

I noticed the same thing when viewing my grandmother's body after she died in 2000. The body was the one I recognized as having housed her personality and spirit, but she was no longer present. I've had this feeling every time I have seen the body of someone I have known in life. Something had gone, but where?

Belief in an afterlife is common across numerous religions, each presenting a unique vision influenced by their cultural understanding of the cosmos, earthly life and the human soul. Different societies imagine the afterlife in various ways, influenced by their religious beliefs and other societal factors. Some believe in reincarnation, where the soul enters a new body upon conception. While some religions, like Christianity, emphasize individual immortality and life after death, others focus more on earthly life, leaving the concept of the afterlife less defined.

Many cultures depict the passage to the afterlife as a journey. This journey can take different forms, such as crossing a symbolic river, traversing a dangerous road or following a predetermined path. The Inuit culture, for example, talks about a specific path that the deceased need to travel on, which coincides with the Milky Way. Wiccans believe in a place called the Summerland, where souls rest and reflect on their life experiences before being reincarnated with no memory of their past lives.

The geographical location of the afterlife also differs vastly across cultures, usually categorized into three main possibilities—on Earth, beneath it or in the heavenly realms. Some cultures believe the domain of the dead is situated on Earth but inaccessible to and distanced from the living. In contrast, others conceive an underworld beneath the Earth or under water, often portrayed as a dimly lit realm or a place of retribution. And some cultures associate the afterlife with heavenly spheres, often idealized versions of our living world.

Scientific research has explored the possibility of life after death, significantly focusing on near-death experiences (NDEs). NDEs are unusual psychological occurrences reported by individuals who have narrowly escaped death from a severe accident or illness. While such experiences have been documented sporadically throughout history, they gained significant public interest in the late 1970s, coinciding with advancements in resuscitation techniques.

The term *near-death experience* was brought into the mainstream in 1975 by Raymond Moody, a psychologist and physician, through his book *Life After Life*. The book details 150 instances of personal experiences that transpired during life-threatening situations. These experiences often start with an abrupt sensation of departing from the body and viewing it from an external perspective, accompanied by feelings of ecstasy, tranquility and joy. Common elements include journeying through a tunnel toward a light, encountering deceased loved ones or a "being of light," and experiencing a rapid review of one's life.

After such an event, individuals often report profound life changes, such as a newfound lack of fear of death, diminished interest in material wealth, increased empathy and love for others, a rejuvenated appreciation for loved ones and nature, and significant shifts in career and personal relationships. Physical changes, including unexplainable self-healing, heightened intuition and even the development of psychic abilities, have also been documented.

People have also reported having negative and distressing experiences during NDEs. These unsettling experiences can involve feelings of being trapped in a void, eternal darkness or being pulled into hell by demonic entities. Despite the frightening nature of these incidents, some researchers suggest they can also lead to positive behavioural changes in the individuals who experience them.

On a recent podcast episode of *Supernatural Circumstances*, Morgan Knudsen and I had the pleasure of talking with Dr. Eben Alexander, who had his own NDE. Dr. Alexander's NDE is unique because of his specialized medical training and extensive experience. Before his NDE, he had dedicated more than two and a half decades to his career as an academic neurosurgeon.

Dr. Alexander, a University of North Carolina at Chapel Hill alumnus, earned his medical degree from Duke University School of Medicine in 1980. During his 15 years as a neurosurgery instructor at Harvard Medical School, he has performed over 4,000 neurosurgical procedures. Throughout his career, he has contributed to more than 150 peer-reviewed journal articles and chapters, authored or edited five books on radiosurgery and neurosurgery, and delivered more than 230 presentations globally.

His tenure at Brigham and Women's Hospital, the Children's Hospital and Harvard Medical School in Boston saw him managing numerous patients who faced significant disruptions to their con-sciousness. These disruptions often resulted from various causes such as trauma, brain tumours, aneurysm ruptures, infections or strokes, leaving many in a comatose state. From this extensive experience, he believed he had developed a comprehensive understanding of how the brain produces consciousness and our notions of mind and spirit.

His perceptions were profoundly shaken in the early morning hours of November 10, 2008. It started at around 4:30 a.m. with severe back pain and a throbbing headache followed by delirium and grand mal seizures. Right there at home, Dr. Alexander began his descent into a deep coma.

A 2018 report by Surbhi Khanna, MD, Lauren E. Moore, MD, and Bruce Greyson, MD, detailed Dr. Alexander's medical condition. He didn't have any history of brain or immune system problems. At the hospital, he was very confused, sometimes agitated, and showing signs of high fever and fast breathing, which suggested a severe bacterial infection. His blood pressure was high, and he was partly unconscious, with a test score indicating moderate brain damage. Despite his serious condition, his heart appeared normal. Physically, he seemed fine except for his inability to respond or speak.

Tests showed a high white blood cell count (indicating a bacterial infection), other signs of acid buildup in his body and abnormal breathing patterns. A scan of his head showed signs of meningitis, a severe infection of the brain's protective membranes, which was confirmed by further tests, including an emergency spinal tap and a computed tomography (CT) scan. The diagnosis was Escherichia coli meningitis, a grim prognosis typically associated with high mortality rates and neurological complications.

Dr. Alexander's condition fluctuated significantly, with Glasgow Coma Scale scores varying between 6 (severe brain injury) and 11 throughout his hospital stay. The Glasgow Coma Scale is a tool used to measure a person's level of consciousness and the severity of their brain injury, with lower scores pointing to more severe injuries. As his family watched helplessly, Dr. Alexander was intubated and placed on a ventilator to breathe for him before being taken to the ICU.

While in the ICU, he was treated with antibiotics and seen by specialists in neurology, infectious disease and physical medicine. In the following days, his condition included being sedated and on a ventilator, barely responding to pain and having very small pupils—a sign of potential brain stem damage. He showed some involuntary movements in his arms. Although his reflexes were weak, they were the same on both sides, but one specific reflex suggested damage to his brain. Despite experiencing seizures before arriving at the hospital, no further seizures were observed after sedation. A brain activity test (EEG) was not performed; he was in such critical condition that

it was believed the procedure wouldn't help in deciding his treatment. Imaging revealed swelling in both the membranes enveloping
the brain and the cerebral cortex's folds due to an accumulation of
pus, putting pressure on the brain tissue. Tests on his cerebrospinal
fluid confirmed a bacterial infection caused by a type of bacteria
that is an uncommon cause of meningitis in adults and typically
leads to death or severe, lasting brain damage. Dr. Alexander was not
expected to recover.

On his sixth day in the hospital, however, he surprised everyone by starting to wake up. He was removed from the ventilator
and was awake but seemed confused. Dr. Alexander was in what
he referred to on our podcast as a "36-hour paranoid delusional
psychotic nightmare" of which he has no lasting memory. By the
seventh day, his condition had improved noticeably; he recognized
his family and co-workers, although he kept asking the same questions about his sickness, indicating that his short-term memory was
temporarily affected.

He was transferred to a unit for patients needing less intensive
neurological care, remaining alert but disoriented. A physical checkup
showed he was awkward using his left arm and leg, but his muscle
strength was normal. Miraculously, there were no signs of specific
neurological issues by the time he left the hospital.

On the ninth day, after his sudden improvement, Dr. Alexander
first shared that he had had a near-death experience, claiming to see
events from outside his body, like observing people who weren't
family members praying for him on the fifth day while he was deeply
comatose. This observation, confirmed by family and hospital staff,
was surprising because, typically, only family could visit the ICU.
The accurate details he provided about his coma period, from days

1 to 5, suggest his experience happened then. During those days, his Glasgow Coma Scale scores, which were recorded twice daily, showed he was severely brain impaired, with scores between 6 and 7.

Remarkably, in just a few months, he achieved a recovery that astonished his neurologists, who described it as "complete and remarkable." They concurred that his condition could have been lethal, yet he recovered fully without any lasting neurological harm.

Dr. Alexander gave Morgan and me a fascinating overview of his NDE. Severely affected by meningoencephalitis, he emerged from the coma devoid of any memories from his past life, including language and knowledge of the world. Amid this blank slate, he underwent a profound spiritual journey, transcending space and time to a realm that felt like the genesis of existence itself.

He said, "First, there was the earthworm's eye view of primitive cores. A kind of unresponsive underground realm rescued from that by the slowly spinning white light that came packaged with a perfect musical melody. It opened up into this rich, ultra-real gateway valley, which had many Earth-like and spiritual features. It was much more real than this world.

"Information flows in that realm; it's what I call knowledge through identification, where you become the grander and greater aspects of the scene you're witnessing. And this knowledge through identification is very difficult to put into words when you come back here because it's so foreign to our normal way of acquiring information."

Dr. Alexander believes it is in this liminal realm where life reviews occur. A life review is a phenomenon often reported in NDEs, where the person's life flashes before their eyes. This includes the entirety of one's life, from birth to death, with every moment being simultaneously displayed and relived rather than merely remembered.

Furthermore, these experiences are not limited to one's own perspective but are relived from the viewpoints of all involved parties. Dr. Alexander said that in his case, a life review could not occur because he was suffering from amnesia at the time. Despite this, he experienced life reviews in a more general, expansive way through evolving visions.

He continued: "In this gateway valley, I was a speck of awareness on a butterfly wing, millions of other butterflies looping and spiralling in vast formations. There were thousands of beings in the meadow below us dancing. This meadow was perfect. Forests surrounded it, and waterfalls flowed into crystal blue pools. It was a world of perfection in so many ways."

To assist in describing the place, Dr. Alexander often uses the analogy that it resembles Plato's world of ideals, but tailored for the individual soul. In this realm, people re-experience their life events, surrounded by radiant light and profound love. Actions perceived as selfish, greedy or causing pain and suffering to others appear particularly negative during the life review. This process is a powerful motivator, subtly encouraging individuals toward greater love, kindness, compassion and mercy. The principle guiding this experience is that the treatment of others is reflected and revisited in the life review, directly impacting the individual.

He said, "I wasn't alone there. Those who've read my book, *Proof of Heaven*, will recognize I had a beautiful guardian angel, a spiritual guide, a beautiful young woman with sparkling blue eyes, high cheekbones, a high forehead and a broad smile. She looked at me with a look of pure love. Never said a word—didn't have to—but her emotional truth and awareness came deeply into my own."

He experienced a profound sense of being deeply loved and valued eternally, reassured that there was nothing to fear and that he was being looked after. The impact of this message at that time was incredibly refreshing and freeing.

"I'll never forget that guardian angel, you know, her face and everything about her. Then, everything accelerated to new levels. I remember . . . angelic choirs above that were swooping and emanating these chants, anthems and hymns that would thunder through my awareness."

The festivities and joy observed in the valley were powered by musical portals that led to increasingly higher realms. These experiences included a vision of the material world's four-dimensional space–time collapsing, leading to a spiritual domain and what is referred to as "deep time." This concept of time vastly differs from our usual understanding, permitting birth, death and all life events to occur simultaneously, representing a much more advanced order of time.

Dr. Alexander described a profound journey beyond the material world's dualities, like good and bad or light and darkness, into a realm of oneness he calls "the core." This core realm epitomizes universal love and oneness, where he felt his consciousness merge with a divine force that underpins existence. He emphasized that while the material world is fraught with conflict and darkness, the core represents a state of pure peace and love, a common revelation in NDEs. Throughout his experience, he navigated various spiritual levels, guided by the melody of music and a guardian angel, learning lessons of love and interconnectedness.

Eventually, when he could no longer return to the higher realms using the melody, he felt a deep sadness yet trusted in being cared for, reflecting on his journey's affirmations of being loved.

Remarkably, even in the lowest level of his experience, surrounded by thousands of beings emitting comforting energy, he felt the same love as in the higher realms, attributing this to the power of prayer. Six faces appeared toward his journey's end, providing temporal anchors to his real-world coma experience, underscoring his journey's profound, non-local and universal nature. Among these faces was a family friend who, though not physically present, supported him through channelling, challenging Dr. Alexander's preconceived notions about such phenomena.

It was his 10-year-old son who called him back to consciousness from that fantastic realm.

"The last of the faces got me back to this world. And it was a 10-year-old boy. Turns out it was my son, Bond. Amnesia still powerful, I did not recognize him. I had no idea who he was. And yet he was pleading with me. The doctors had held a family conference that morning, saying I'd gone from a 10 percent chance of survival down to 2 percent now but with no chance of recovery."

Doctors were suggesting that Dr. Alexander be removed from the ventilator and taken off three powerful antibiotics, essentially to let him pass away. Upon hearing this, Bond realized the severity of his father's condition, which had been previously shielded from him, and understood that matters were far graver than he had been informed. In a rush of urgency, Bond sprinted down the hallway, reached his dad and forcefully opened his eyelids—finding both eyes askew, with neither pupil reacting to light. This condition is universally recognized in the medical field as dire. Despite this, Dr. Alexander asserts that even though he could not physically see or hear his son, the earnest pleas he made reached him.

The length of Dr. Alexander's near-death experience, along with his professional background as a respected neuroscientist, provides a unique and compelling perspective on the phenomenon of NDEs. Typically, NDEs are fleeting experiences that individuals struggle to describe and quantify. However, Dr. Alexander's was notably extensive and detailed, offering a richer dataset from which to draw insights and hypotheses about the nature of consciousness, the brain and what might lie beyond death.

Dr. Alexander's scientific background further amplifies the significance of his experience. As a neuroscientist, he deeply understands the brain's functions and mechanisms, mainly how it processes experiences like consciousness and perceptions of reality. This expertise lends credibility to his interpretations and reflections on his NDE, enabling him to analyze his experience through neuroscientific knowledge.

Moreover, the rarity of a neuroscientist experiencing such a profound and well-documented NDE adds another layer of importance. It challenges the conventional scientific skepticism surrounding NDEs, often dismissed as hallucinations or neurological anomalies. Dr. Alexander's experience suggests that current understandings of brain function and consciousness might only partially explain these phenomena. His account pushes the boundaries of scientific inquiry into areas traditionally considered metaphysical or spiritual.

His story provides a significant insight into the nature of reality and consciousness, potentially transforming our perspectives on spirituality, the soul and the non-material world. By examining his experience and its scientific and broad implications, he anticipates a greater integration of science and spirituality.

Since his recovery, Dr. Alexander has dedicated his life to sharing his experience and educating others with the insights gained from his unique NDE. His latest book exploring consciousness and reality, *Living in a Mindful Universe: A Neurosurgeon's Journey into the Heart of Consciousness*, co-authored with Karen Newell, was released in 2017. His debut, *Proof of Heaven*, topped the *New York Times* bestseller list and received notable nods, including that of Oprah Winfrey. It was followed by *The Map of Heaven*, which examines the intersection of science, religion and human spirituality across history, suggesting a collective awakening to our true nature and destiny. His insights on near-death experiences have been featured in numerous publications, emphasizing the mind–body debate and reality's nature.

The stories shared by those who have journeyed through NDEs open our hearts and minds, challenging what we think we know about the very essence of consciousness and the fabric of our reality. While some may dismiss these accounts as brain vanomalies, the depth and consistency of these experiences across different cultures and medical backgrounds whisper of a reality beyond our physical one.

In the shared tales of individuals like Dr. Alexander, we find not just stories but windows into the possibilities of the soul's journey beyond this life. As we continue to untangle the complex web of consciousness and its ties to the physical world, NDEs serve as a beacon, illuminating the vast potential of our consciousness to transcend the finality of death and touch upon the eternal, offering us a glimpse of what's next.

Acknowledgements

A MOTLEY CREW of generous souls have been instrumental in turning this labour of love into a reality. Since my last literary endeavour, I've weathered some tumultuous life storms, and I couldn't have done it without my friends. My family, meanwhile, to coin a nautical phrase, has been my lighthouse—Marion (Mom), Ted (Dad) and Rachel (the best sister a guy could hope for) Browne. And a special mention to Dianne Ashton, my birth mother, who didn't just give me life; she has given me a fair bit of sanity recently.

Then there's my partner in crime, Mathew Stockton, co-host of the *Dark Poutine* podcast. His grand entrance into my life at its gloomiest hour was akin to a knight in shining armour riding into battle, except instead of a steed, he has a microphone, and his lance is his invaluable contribution to our show. (Oh dear, that was a little more flowery than I intended. Anyway, thank you, my friend.)

Morgan Knudsen, fellow explorer of the unknown on *Supernatural Circumstances*, deserves a standing ovation for her help decrypting this book's enigmas. She's my decoder ring for the supernatural.

A rousing salute to my UK entourage, who put up with me during my research journey and played integral roles in it. Anna Frederiksen, who played tour guide through the labyrinth of London; Michael J. Buchanan-Dunne, creator and host of the *Murder Mile UK True-Crime Podcast* and one of the funniest people I've met, put together a meet-up, and I still owe him a round of drinks; and Jen Pollard, who helped me gain access to the hallowed halls of Cambridge University's library, where we then went elbow-deep into the Society for Psychical Research archives.

To L.J. Hoshino, who not only braved the ethereal and eerie woods of Aokigahara Jukai in Japan but also gifted me with her compassionate insight and hauntingly beautiful photographs of her expedition. Thank you, L.J., for being such a courageous and kindred spirit.

Cathy Leimanis, my ever-ready sounding board and bookkeeper, thank you for your relentless support and for weathering my mental tempests.

Janice Zawerbny has braved the wild terrain of editing not one but two of my books. I owe you a bottle of the strongest headache medication, a truckload of gratitude and some fabulous lunch dates.

After the wild ride of my first book, *Murder, Madness and Mayhem*, I must tip my hat to every reader, reviewer and advocate. Your excitement for that adventure has fuelled this one.

A hearty huzzah to every member of our virtual tribe, particularly the inhabitants of our flagship Facebook group, Dark Poutine's Yumber Yard. You all are the crème de la crème of online buddies.

And lastly, to my legion of friends, who shall, according to tradition, remain anonymous. You are my human compasses, reminding me "one day at a time" to stick to the path and keep on trucking. Without you, I'd probably be lost somewhere in the Bermuda Triangle or worse.

Thank you all from the bottom of my word processing software. (I use an amazing app for Mac called Bear, with which I have written hundreds of podcast episodes and now two books.)

Sources

Introduction: A Lifetime of Obsession with the Weird

Clancy, C.J. "Roy Sullivan: Struck by Lightning Seven Times." IrishCentral, 10 July 2023. www.irishcentral.com/opinion/others/roy-sullivan-struck-lightning -seven-times.

"Twins Reared Apart: A Living Lab." *New York Times*, 9 December 1979. www .nytimes.com/1979/12/09/archives/twins-reared-apart-a-living-lab.html.

"The Mysterious Death of Mary Hardy Reeser." *The Dead History*, 13 August 2020. https://web.archive.org/web/20220120161246/https://thedeadhistory .com
/blog/the-mysterious-death-of-mary-hardy-reeser.

"Bermuda Triangle Demystified?" *New York Times* archive, 2006. https://archive .nytimes.com/www.nytimes.com/fodors/top/features/travel/destinations /bermudaandcaribbean/bermuda/fdrs_feat_29_8.html?n=Top/Features /Travel/Destinations/Bermuda.

Part 1: People

Chapter 1: Harry Houdini: Escape Artist, Illusionist and Debunker

Wehrstein, K.M. "Harry Houdini." Psi Encyclopedia, 30 May 2022. https://psi -encyclopedia.spr.ac.uk/articles/harry-houdini.

Kalush, William, and Larry Sloman. *The Secret Life of Houdini*. New York: Simon & Schuster, 2008.

Meyer, Bernard C. *Houdini: A Mind in Chains*. New York: Dutton, 1976.

Houdini, Harry. *A Magician Among the Spirits*. New York: Harper & Brothers, 1924.

Houdini, Harry. *The Right Way to Do Wrong*. New York: Dover, 2019.

"Harry Houdini: American Magician." Biography. Britannica, 25 March 2024. www.britannica.com/biography/Harry-Houdini.

Cox, John. "Wild About Harry." 2015. www.wildabouthoudini.com.

"The Great Harry Houdini." Houdini: His Life and His Art, 2024. www.thegreatharryhoudini.com.

"The Unmasking of Robert-Houdin by Harry Houdini." Project Gutenberg, 16 May 2013. www.gutenberg.org/ebooks/42723.

Lee, Evie. "Ptomaine Poisoning." CPD Online College, 25 November 2021. https://cpdonline.co.uk/knowledge-base/food-hygiene/ptomaine-poisoning.

Harnisch, Larry. "Harry Houdini: An Interview by Marcet Haldeman-Julius, October 1925." *The Daily Mirror*, 1 June 2015. https://ladailymirror.com/2015/06/01/harry-houdini-an-interview-by-marcet-haldeman-julius-october-1925.

Tymn, Michael. "Margery (Mina Stinson Crandon)." Psi Encyclopedia, 11 September 2022. https://psi-encyclopedia.spr.ac.uk/articles/margery-mina-stinson-crandon.

Mikkelson, David. "Did Houdini Die from a Punch to the Stomach?" Snopes, 2 May 2001. www.snopes.com/fact-check/death-of-houdini.

"Houdini 1936 Final Official Seance." houdinimuseum. YouTube, 30 October 2010. www.youtube.com/watch?v=xnmY0kX8U6s.

"Hardeen Dead, 69; Houdini's Brother; Illusionist, Escape Artist, a Founder of Magician's Guild—Gave Last Show May 29. *New York Times*, 13 June 1945. www.nytimes.com/1945/06/13/archives/hardeen-dead-69-houdinis-brother-illusionist-escape-artist-a.html.

Gayle, Damien. "Rescuers Revive Escape Artist After 'Buried Alive' Stunt Goes Wrong." *The Guardian*, 8 September 2015. www.theguardian.com/uk-news/2015/sep/08/escape-artist-buried-alive-stunt-yorkshire#:~:text=In%201992%20a%2032%2Dyear,helpers%20to%20pour%20on%20top.

The Windbridge Institute, LLC: Normalize, Optimize, Utilize Psi. 2024. https://windbridgeinstitute.com.

"Are All Mediums Frauds?" Windbridge Research Center, 2015. www.windbridge.org/are-all-mediums-frauds.

Chapter 2: Kaspar Hauser: The Nuremberg Stranger

von Feuerbach, Anselm. *Caspar Hauser: An Account*. Boston: Allen and Ticknor, 1832.

Duchess of Cleveland (Wilhelmina Powlett). *The True Story of Kaspar Hauser, from Official Documents*. London: Macmillan, 1893.

Stanhope, Philip Henry, Earl. *Tracts Relating to Caspar Hauser*. London: Hodson, 1836.

Kitchen, Martin. *Kaspar Hauser: Europe's Child*. New York: Springer, 2001.

Valbert, M.G. "The History of a Delusion." *Popular Science Monthly*, 30 April 1887. Wikisource, 2018. https://en.wikisource.org/wiki/Popular_Science_Monthly /Volume_30/April_1887/The_History_of_a_Delusion.

Letter Kaspar Hauser was carrying. Wikimedia Foundation, 29 July 2006. https:// commons.wikimedia.org/wiki/Kaspar_Hauser#/media/File:Adresse_des _Geleitbriefs.jpg.

Letter Kaspar Hauser was carrying. Wikimedia Foundation, 29 July, 2006. https://commons.wikimedia.org/wiki/Kaspar_Hauser#/media/File: Geleitbrief.jpg.

Letter Kaspar Hauser was carrying. Wikimedia Foundation, 29 July 2006. https:// commons.wikimedia.org/wiki/Kaspar_Hauser#/media/File:Maegdleinzettel.jpg.

Letter Kaspar Hauser was carrying. Wikimedia Foundation, 29 July 2006. https:// commons.wikimedia.org/wiki/Kaspar_Hauser#/media/File:Faksimile_des _Spiegelschriftzettels_(gespiegelt).png.

Chapter 3: Jerome, the Legless Man of Sandy Cove

Mooney Jr., Fraser. *Jerome: Solving the Mystery of Nova Scotia's Silent Castaway*. Halifax: Nimbus, 2008.

"The Mystery of the Man at Meteghan," *St. John Daily Sun*, 8 September 1905.

Hill, Harriet. "Mystery Fascinates." *Montreal Gazette*, 14 June 1963.

MacDonald, Andrea. "Legless-Man Mystery Revealed." *Halifax Daily News*, 30 August 2006.

Flemming, Brian. "Maritime Mysteries Still Enthrall." *Halifax Daily News*, 5 September 2006.

Richler, Noah. "The Legless Castaway." Literary Review of Canada, 1 March 2009.

Cameron, Ian. "The Frozen Man of Queens County." *Canadian Family Physician*, August 2009.

MacGowan, Doug. "Jerome of Sandy Cove, Nova Scotia." Historic Mysteries, 13 May 2012. www.historicmysteries.com/history/jerome-of-sandy -cove/2187.

Comeau, Tina. "The Story of Jerome: The Southwestern N.S. Mystery That Never Ends, Even 110 Years After His Death." Saltwire Network, 2022. www.saltwire.com/atlantic-canada/news/the-story-of-jerome-the -southwestern-ns-mystery-that-never-ends-even-110-years-after -his-death-100717898.

November 15, 1898: *The Evening Mail* from Halifax, Nova Scotia, Canada · 2. Newspapers.com, 2024. www.newspapers.com/image/776161145/?terms =jerome%20mystery&match=1.

November 17, 1898: *The Evening Mail* from Halifax, Nova Scotia, Canada · 7. Newspapers.com, 2024. www.newspapers.com/image/776161242/?terms =jerome%20mystery&match=1.

September 28, 1905: *Nanaimo Daily News* from Nanaimo, British Columbia, Canada · 3. Newspapers.com, 2024. www.newspapers.com/ image/325669381/?terms=Jerome%20%22Sandy%20Cove%22&match=1.

April 16, 2007: *Whitehorse Daily Star* from Whitehorse, Yukon, Canada · 14. Newspapers.com, 2024. www.newspapers.com/image/579101014/?terms =Jerome%20%22Sandy%20Cove%22&match=1.

Chapter 4: The Mysterious Brother XII and His Missing Treasure

Wilson, E.A. *Foundation Letters and Teachings: Brother XII.* Vancouver: Sun Publishing, 1927.

Wilson, E.A. *The Aquarian Foundation: A Movement for the Unification of All Men of Good Will.* Vancouver: Sun Publishing, 1927.

Wilson, E.A. *The Three Truths: A Simple Statement of the Fundamental Philosophy of Life.* Vancouver: Sun Publishing, 1927.

Wilson, E.A. *Unsigned Letters from an Elder Brother.* London: Fowler, 1930.

Oliphant, John. *Brother XII.* Halifax: Twelfth House Press, 2006.

Definition of Irvingites. New Advent. Catholic Encyclopedia. www.newadvent .org/cathen/08174a.htm.

Sullivan, Charles A. "The Irvingites and the Gift of Tongues." 17 October 2020. https://charlesasullivan.com/1826/the-irvingites-and-the-gift-of-tongues.

Lovegrove, Donald. "De Courcy Island." BritishColumbia.com, 2024. https://britishcolumbia.com/plan-your-trip/regions-and-towns/vancouver -island-bc-islands/de-courcy-island.

Azpiri, Jon. "'He Could Look into Your Soul': The Bizarre Mystery Behind a B.C. Cult Leader and His Missing Gold." Global News, 12 May 2019. https://globalnews.ca/news/5264892/brother-xii-gold.

O'Hagan, Howard. "The Weird and Savage Cult of Brother 12." *Macleans*, 23 April 1960. archive.macleans.ca/article/1960/4/23/the-weird-and-savage-cult-of-brother-12.

Scott, Andrew. *The Promise of Paradise: Utopian Communities in British Columbia.* Madeira Park, BC: Harbour Publishing, 2017.

"Theosophy." The Theosophical Society in America, 2024. www.theosophical .org/about/theosophy.

Chapter 5: Giants, a.k.a. the Exceptionally Tall: Myths and Reality

Scott, Jess. "Who Are the Jötnar in Norse Mythology?" Life in Norway, 8 October 2021. www.lifeinnorway.net/jotnar-norse-mythology-giants/#:~:text=In%20 Norse%20mythology%2C%20the%20J%C3%B6tnar,the%20end%20of%20 the%20world.

"Ispolin." Wikipedia, 15 June 2023. https://en.wikipedia.org/wiki/Ispolin.

Antonio, Edward. "What Were the Nephilim in the Bible?" Christianity.com. Salem Web Network, 17 January 2024. www.christianity.com/wiki/angels-and -demons/who-were-the-nephilim-in-the-bible.html.

"The Bulgarian Stonehenge—the Gate of Mother Goddess: The Megalith Near the Village of Buzovgrad." Park Hotel, Stara Zagora, 2024. https:// hotelstarazagora.eu/en/landmarks/the-bulgarian-stonehenge-the-gate-of -mother-goddess-the-megalith-near-the-village-of-buzovgrad.

"Origin Stories: Glooscap." First Peoples of Canada. Canadian Museum of History, 2024. www.historymuseum.ca/cmc/exhibitions/aborig/fp/fpz2f21e.html.

"Daidarabotchi." The Palace of the Dragon King, 2024. https://yokai.com /daidarabotchi.

"Gigantism." Cleveland Clinic, 2024. https://my.clevelandclinic.org/health /diseases/22954-gigantism.

Phillips, Jennifer. *Robert Wadlow: The Unique Life of the Boy Who Became the World's Tallest Man.* Author, 2019.

Drimmer, Frederick. *Born Different: Amazing Stories of Very Special People.* New York: Bantam, 1991.

Fadner, Frederic, with Harold F. Wadlow. *The Gentleman Giant: The Biography of Robert Pershing Wadlow.* Boston: Humphries, 1944.

Robert Pershing Wadlow (1918–1940). Find a Grave Memorial. www.findagrave
.com/memorial/1590/robert-pershing-wadlow.

"Robert Wadlow Statue—World's Tallest Man." Great Rivers & Routes, 2024.
www.riversandroutes.com/directory/robert-wadlow-statue-worlds-tallest-man.

"Robert Pershing Wadlow." Alton Museum of History and Art, 1998.
http://www.altonweb.com/history/wadlow.

Martinez Vilches, Oscar. *Chiloé misterioso: turismo, mitología chilota, leyendas.* Chile:
Ediciones de la Voz de Chiloé, 1992.

"Glooscap: 40-Foot-Tall Indian, Millbrook, Nova Scotia." RoadsideAmerica.com,
2024. www.roadsideamerica.com/story/44600.

Rossen, Jake. "Adam Rainer, the Little Person Who Became a Literal Giant." Mental
Floss, April 14, 2023. www.mentalfloss.com/posts/adam-rainer-little-person
-giant.

"Giant Macaskill Angus Mor Macaskil." Explore North Uist, 2020. www.isle-of
-north-uist.co.uk/isle-of-berneray/giant-macaskill-angus-mor-macaskil.

"Cape Breton's Giant: Angus McAskill." MacAskill.com, 2023. https://web.archive
.org/web/20100724044325/http://www.macaskill.com/GeneralTallTales/
Angus/angus2.html.

Giant MacAskill Museum. Dunvegan Museums. www.dunveganmuseums.co.uk
/GiantMacAskill.html.

Welcome to the Giant MacAskill Museum. http://giantmacaskillmuseum.com.

Chapter 6: Wannabe Spaceman:
The Disappearance of Granger Taylor

Devlin, Mike. "What Happened to Granger Taylor?" *Times Colonist*, 3 February
2019. www.timescolonist.com/islander/what-happened-to-granger
-taylor-4669648.

"World's Largest Hockey Stick & Puck." Atlas Obscura, 20 January 2010.
www.atlasobscura.com/places/worlds-largest-hockey-stick-puck.

Hooper, Tyler. "The Man Who Went to Space and Disappeared." Vice News, 1
July 2016. www.vice.com/en/article/yvwjkv/the-man-who-went-to-space
-and-disappeared-the-story-of-granger-taylor.

"Spaceman." CBC Docs, 2024. www.cbc.ca/cbcdocspov/episodes/spaceman.

Peters, Hammerson. "Granger Taylor: The Spaceman of Vancouver Island."
Mysteries of Canada, 30 May 2019. https://mysteriesofcanada.com/bc
/granger-taylor-the-spaceman-of-vancouver-island.

"UFO Hovers Outside Hospital 1970 British Columbia - Aliens Reported." ufos-upclose. YouTube, 2015. www.youtube.com/watch?v=-MbSLuTYCBc.

Barron, Robert. "Witness to Duncan UFO Doubts Prank Explanation Offered in Wake of Stamp." *Saanich News*, 29 November 2023. www.saanichnews.com /news/witness-to-duncan-ufo-doubts-prank-explanation-offered-in-wake-of -stamp-7116762.

Bainas, Lexi. "Documentary Reminds of Many Unanswered Questions About Granger Taylor's Disappearance." *Cowichan Valley Citizen*, 15 February 2019. www .cowichanvalleycitizen.com/entertainment/documentary-reminds-of-many -unanswered-questions-about-granger-taylors-disappearance-793214.

ParaResearchers of Ontario. ParaResearchers, 2024. https://pararesearchers.org.

Browne, Mike, and Scott Hemenway. "Spaceman: The Disappearance of Granger Taylor (BC)." *Dark Poutine*, episode 60, 11 February 2019. https://podcasts .apple.com/us/podcast/spaceman-the-disappearance-of-granger-taylor-bc /id1304781389?i=1000429620346.

"LSD Abuse & Addiction: Effects, Signs & Treatment." American Addiction Centers, 3 July 2023. https://americanaddictioncenters.org/lsd-abuse.

Part 2: Places

Chapter 7: Was Borley Rectory England's Most Haunted Property?

"Survey and Making of Domesday." The National Archives, 20 April 2023. https://fbcoverup.com/docs/library/2023-04-20-Survey-and-making-of -Domesday-The-National-Archives-(UK)-accessed-Apr-20-2023.pdf.

Wright, Thomas. *The History and Topography of the County of Essex*. London: Forgotten Books, 2017.

Price, Harry. *The End of Borley Rectory*. Hong Kong: Hesperides Press, 2014.

Adams, Paul, Peter Underwood, and Eddie Brazil. *The Borley Rectory Companion*. Cheltenham, UK: The History Press, 2016.

Foyster, Lionel. "The Foyster Memorandum." Foxearth and District Local History Society. www.foxearth.org.uk/TheFoysterMemorandum.html.

Foyster, Lionel. "Fifteen Months in a Haunted House." Foxearth and District Local History Society. www.foxearth.org.uk/FifteenMonthsInaHauntedHouse .html.

"The Haunted Rectory . . ." Foxearth and District Local History Society. www.foxearth.org.uk/TheHauntedRectory.html.

Morris, Richard. "The Little World of Harry Price." Foxearth and District Local History Society. www.foxearth.org.uk/HarryPrice.html.

Definition of residual haunting. Llewellyn Worldwide. www.llewellyn.com /encyclopedia/term/residual+haunting.

Willin, Melvyn. "Borley Rectory." Psi Encyclopedia, 30 March 2024. https://psi-encyclopedia.spr.ac.uk/articles/borley-rectory.

Fraser, John. "Harry Price." Psi Encyclopedia, 27 January 2024. https://psi -encyclopedia.spr.ac.uk/articles/harry-price.

Colvin, Barrie. "Poltergeists (Overview)." Psi Encyclopedia, 8 November 2023. https://psi-encyclopedia.spr.ac.uk/articles/poltergeists-overview.

"The Stone Tape Theory." The Haunted Walk. https://hauntedwalk.com/news /the-stone-tape-theory.

Definition of poltergeist. *Merriam-Webster* dictionary. www.merriam-webster .com/dictionary/poltergeist.

Chapter 8: Valley of the Headless Men

Peters, Hammerson. *Legends of the Nahanni Valley*. Illustrated edition. Author, 2018.

Nahanni National Park Reserve. Parks Canada, 30 January 2023. https://parks .canada.ca/pn-np/nt/nahanni/visit.

Crowe, Lilah. "Local Folklore: Anishinaabe Tale of the Wendigo." Ithaca County His-torical Society, 21 April 2021. https://web.archive.org/web/20231128121400 /https://www.itascahistorical.org/local-folklore-anishinaabe-tale-of-the-wendigo.

Oldak, Sean E., Anthony J. Maristany, and Brianna C. Sa. "Wendigo Psychosis and Psychiatric Perspectives of Cannibalism: A Complex Interplay of Culture, Psychology, and History." *Cureus*, 30 October 2023. https://doi.org/10.7759 /cureus.47962.

Brightman, Robert A. "The Windigo in the Material World." *Ethnohistory* 35 (4): 337-379, 1988. JSTOR. www.jstor.org/stable/482140.

Swancer, Brent. "The Mysterious Valley of the Headless Corpses." Mysterious Universe, 3 October 2014. https://mysteriousuniverse.org/2014/10/the -mysterious-valley-of-the-headless-corpses.

Hess, Brooke. "Secrets of the Nahanni: The Valley of Headless Men." *The Outdoor Journal*, 12 September 2018. www.outdoorjournal.com/secrets-nahanni -valley-headless-men.

"Mysteries of the Nahinni Park Reserve in Canada." StrangeOutdoors, 21 February 2018. www.strangeoutdoors.com/mysterious-stories-blog/2018/2/21 /mysteries-of-the-nahinni-park-reserve-in-canada.

Berge, Chloe. "The Haunting History of This Canadian National Park." Fodors Travel Guide, 9 March 2020. www.fodors.com/world/north-america /canada/experiences/news/the-haunting-history-of-this-canadian-national -park.

"Nahanni National Park." Unesco. World Heritage Convention, 2024. https://whc.unesco.org/en/list/24.

"Journeys of Discovery: Under the Midnight Sun." Nahanni River Adventures and Canadian River Expeditions, 2022. https://nahanni.com.

"Waheela." Cryptid Wiki. https://cryptidz.fandom.com/wiki/Waheela.

Chapter 9: Eerie Occurrences at Old McDonald's Farm

Graham, Monica. *Fire Spook*. Halifax: Nimbus, 2018.

Columbo, John Robert. *Ghost Stories of Canada*. Toronto: Dundurn, 2000.

Mary Ellen Spook: Fire-Spook of Caledonia Mills. www.parl.ns.ca/maryellenspook /index.asp.

The Fire-Spook of Caledonia Mills. The Town of Antigonish, 2024. www.townofantigonish.ca/folklore.html.

"Folklore of Nova Scotia." Electriccanadian.com. https://electriccanadian.com /history/novascotia/folklore/chapter11.htm.

Antigonish Heritage Museum, 2024. https://antigonishheritage.ca.

"Hobgoblin." Wikipedia, 28 February, 2024. https://en.wikipedia.org/wiki /Hobgoblin.

"Apparitions of Black Dogs." Internet Archive: Wayback Machine, 1 October 2008. https://web.archive.org/web/20090323040252/http://nli.northampton .ac.uk/ass/psych-staff/sjs/blackdog.htm.

DeLong, William. "Inside the Bone-Chilling Legend of Black Shuck, the Hell-hound of the English Countryside." All That's Interesting, 23 October, 2022. https://allthatsinteresting.com/black-shuck.

"Investigating the Antigonish Fire Spook Haunting." Wizzley, 9 December 2014. https://wizzley.com/ghost-antigonish-fire-spook.

American Society for Psychical Research. www.aspr.com.

"A Look Back at the Mysterious Haunting of an Antigonish County Farm, 100 Years Later." CBC News, 30 October 2022. www.cbc.ca/news/canada

/nova-scotia/mysterious-haunting-antigonish-county-macdonald
-farm-1.6631829.

"The Mysterious Fire Spook of Caledonia Hills." Mysterious Universe, 10 March
2021. https://mysteriousuniverse.org/2021/03/the-mysterious-fire-spook-of
-caledonia-hills.

Library of Congress. *Washington Times* (1902-1939), 2 April 1922, Sunday morning, image 15. Loc.gov, no. 1922/04/02: 3. info:lccn/sn84026749.

Grey, Orrin. "A Haunting at Caledonia Mills: The Chilling Case of the Mary
Ellen Spook Farm." The Lineup, 5 June 2017. https://the-line-up.com
/caledonia-mills-the-mary-ellen-spook-farm.

"Caledonia Mills Fire Spook." Paranormal Studies & Inquiry Canada. https://
psican.org/index.php/ghosts-a-hauntings/nova-scotia/570-caledonia-mills
-fire-spook.

Library of Congress. *New York Tribune* (1866-1924), 9 March 1922, image 51." Loc.
gov, no. 1922/03/19. info:lccn/sn83030214.

Strickler, Lon. "Fire Spook of Caledonia Mills." Phantoms & Monsters, 9 December 2013. www.phantomsandmonsters.com/2013/12/fire-spook-of-caledonia
-mills.html.

Glossary of Psi (Parapsychological) Terms (L-R). Internet Archive: Wayback
Machine, 2009. https://web.archive.org/web/20100824232035/http://
parapsych.org/glossary_l_r.html#p.

Browne, Mike, and Mathew Stockton. "The Caledonia Mills Poltergeist."
Dark Poutine, episode 247, 5 December 2019. https://darkpoutine.com
/2022/12/247-the-caledonia-mills-poltergeist.

Chapter 10: Suicide Forest: The Sea of Trees

"Aokigahara." Aokigahara Forest. www.aokigaharaforest.com.

Seward, Jack. *Hara-Kiri*. North Clarendon, VT: Tuttle, 2012.

Matsumoto, Seicho⁻. *Kuroi jukai*. Tokyo: Ko⁻dansha, 1973.

Harrington, Roger. *Suicide Forest*. Independently published, 2017.

Devlin, Tara A. *Aokigahara*. Independently published, 2019.

Wataru, Tsurumi. *The Complete Manual of Suicide*. Independently published, 2018.

Russell, Roxanne. "Views of Suicide in Modern Japanese Literature: A Positive
Portrayal in Nami No Tou." *Southeast Review of Asian Studies* 28: 199-201,
2006. https://go.gale.com/ps/i.do?p=AONE&u=anon~11506f21&id
=GALE|A165781183&v=2.1&it=r&sid=googleScholar&asid=311acee1.

Teixeira, Pedro M. "The Portrayal of Suicide in Postmodern Japanese Literature and Popular Culture Media." The University of Vermont. ScholarWorks, 2014. https://scholarworks.uvm.edu/hcoltheses/15.

Takahashi, Yoshitomo. "Aokigahara-Jukai: Suicide and Amnesia in Mt. Fuji's Black Forest." *Suicide and Life-Threatening Behavior* 18 (2): 164175, 1988. https://doi .org/10.1111/j.1943-278x.1988.tb00150.x.

Takei, Nori, and Kazuhiko Nakamura. "Is Inseki-Jisatsu, Responsibility-Driven Suicide, Culture-Bound?" *Lancet* 363 (9418): 1400, 2004. https://doi.org /10.1016/s0140-6736(04)16066-2.

"Number of Suicides per 100,000 Inhabitants in Japan from 2014 to 2023." Statista, 2024. www.statista.com/statistics/622249/japan-suicide-number-per-100-000 -inhabitants.

Chambers, Andrew. "Japan: Ending the Culture of the 'Honourable' Suicide." *The Guardian*, 3 August 2010. www.theguardian.com/commentisfree/2010/aug/03 /japan-honourable-suicide-rate.

"No Letup in Suicide Rate." Internet Archive: Wayback Machine, 10 June 2010. https://web.archive.org/web/20100911085525/http://search.japantimes.co.jp /cgi-bin/ed20100610a2.html.

Puchko, Kristy. "15 Eerie Facts About Japan's Suicide Forest." Mental Floss, 7 June 2023. www.mentalfloss.com/article/73288/15-eerie-things-about-japans -suicide-forest.

Gilhooly, Rob. "Inside Aokigahara, Japan's 'Suicide Forest.'" *The Japan Times*, 26 June 2011. www.japantimes.co.jp/life/2011/06/26/general/inside-japans -suicide-forest.

"Suicide Forest in Japan." Vice Video, 2019. https://video.vice.com/en_ca/video /suicide-forest-in-japan/55e4b8b52f12412c4b4b4ab6.

Keefe, Alexa, and Tomasz Lazar. "An Ethereal Forest Where Japanese Commit Suicide." Photography. *National Geographic*, 3 February 2017. www.nationalgeographic.com/photography/article/aokigahara-jukai -suicide-forest.

Rahman, Khaleda. Haunting images from inside Japan's Suicide Forest. *Daily Mail Online*. 14 March 2018. www.dailymail.co.uk/news/article-5499373 /Haunting-images-inside-Japans-suicide-forest.html.

Bever, Lindsey. "The Haunting Allure of Aokigahara, the Japanese 'Suicide Forest' Logan Paul Captured on Film." *Washington Post*, 2 January 2018. www .washingtonpost.com/news/worldviews/wp/2018/01/02/the-haunting-allure -of-aokigahara-the-japanese-suicide-forest-logan-paul-captured-on-film.

Park, Madison, Emily Smith, and Ray Sanchez. "YouTube Star Logan Paul Posts New Emotional Apology for Showing Video of Apparent Suicide Victim." CNN.com, 2 January 2018. https://edition.cnn.com/2018/01/02/health /logan-paul-video/index.html.

Ichihira, Mizuki, and Valeria. "Aokigahara: The Most Famous Forest in Japan." We Languages, 11 January 2024. https://we-languages.com/aokigahara.

Chapter 11: A Brief History of Lost Civilizations: Atlantis and Others

Scott-Elliot, W. *The Story of Atlantis and the Lost Lemuria*. DigiCat, 2022.

Donnelly, Ignatius. *Atlantis: The Antediluvian World*. New York: Dover, 1976.

Rawlings, Prescott. *Atlantis: The Great Flood and the Asteroid*. eBookIt.com, 2013.

Helena Petrovna Blavatsky. *Collected Writings*. Newburyport, MA: Quest Books, 1973.

Churchward, James. *The Lost Continent of Mu: The Motherland of Man*. Woodstock, VT: William Edwin Rudge, 1926.

Churchward, James. *The Sacred Symbols of Mu*. New York: Ives Washburn, 1933.

Schliemann, Paul. "How I Found the Lost Atlantis, the Source of All Civilization." *New York American*, 20 October 1912.

"Timaeus by Plato." Project Gutenberg, 1 December 1998. www.gutenberg.org /ebooks/1572.

"Critias by Plato." Project Gutenberg, 1 December 1998. www.gutenberg.org /ebooks/1571.

"Atlantis." Internet Archive: Wayback Machine, 23 February 2017. https://web .archive.org/web/20221208175602/https://www.cs.mcgill.ca/~rwest /wikispeedia/wpcd/wp/a/Atlantis.htm.

"Ignatius Donnelly: American Politician, Writer & Social Reformer." Biography. Britannica. www.britannica.com/biography/Ignatius-Donnelly.

"Atlantis and Lemuria." The Rudolf Steiner Archive, 2024. https://rsarchive.org /Books/GA011/English/TPS1911/GA011_index.html.

"Lemuria (Steiner)." Theosophy Wiki, 7 July 2017. https://theosophy.wiki/en /Lemuria_%28Steiner%29.

Roos, Dave. "Did the Lost Continent of Lemuria Ever Exist?" HowStuffWorks, 22 June 2022. https://history.howstuffworks.com/history-vs-myth/lemuria .htm.

Wehrstein, K.M. "Famous Past Life Claims." Psi Encyclopedia, 16 February 2024. https://psi-encyclopedia.spr.ac.uk/articles/famous-past-life-claims.

"Location Hypotheses of Atlantis." Wikipedia, 24 April 2024. https://en.wikipedia.org/wiki/Location_hypotheses_of_Atlantis.

Man from Atlantis. Wikipedia, 13 March 2024. https://en.wikipedia.org/wiki/Man_from_Atlantis.

Wehrstein, K.M. "Edgar Cayce." Psi Encyclopedia, 25 April 2024. https://psi-encyclopedia.spr.ac.uk/articles/edgar-cayce.

Edgar Cayce's Life and Readings. https://edgarcayce.org/edgar-cayce.

Little, Gregory L., Lora Little, and John Van Auken. *Edgar Cayce's Atlantis.* Virginia Beach, VA: A.R.E. Press, 2006.

Wehrstein, K.M. "Joe Fisher." Psi Encyclopedia, 30 December 2022. https://psi-encyclopedia.spr.ac.uk/articles/joe-fisher.

"K'iche' People." Wikipedia, 23 April 2024. https://en.wikipedia.org/wiki/K%CA%BCiche%CA%BC_people.

"Madrid Codex (Maya)." Wikipedia, 18 April 2024. https://en.wikipedia.org/wiki/Madrid_Codex_%28Maya%29.

Part 3: Things

Chapter 12: The Monster of Van Meter, Iowa

Lewis, Chad, Noah Voss, and Kevin Lee Nelson. *The Van Meter Visitor.* Eau Claire, WI: On the Road Publications, 2013.

City of Van Meter website. 2024. www.vanmeteria.gov.

"Van Meter Township History." Iagenweb. https://iagenweb.org/dallas/twp/vanmeter/vanmetertownshiphistory.htm.

"A Winged Monster." Newspapers.com, 11 October 1903. www.newspapers.com/article/-van-meter-ia-monster-oct-11-1903-pt-1/19497609.

"A Winged Monster" (continued). Newspapers.com, 11 October 1903. www.newspapers.com/image/85102469/?clipping_id=19497740.

McCormack, David. "The Unsolved Mystery of the Van Meter Visitor—A Winged Creature with a Glowing Horn That Caused . . ." *Daily Mail Online,* 4 May 2013. www.dailymail.co.uk/news/article-2319503/The-unsolved

-mystery-Van-Meter-Visitor--winged-creature-glowing-horn-caused-terror
-Iowa-town-110-years-ago.html.

Tyrrell, Ethan. "Meet the Bulletproof Bat Monster of Van Meter, Iowa." Cracked,
26 August 2021. www.cracked.com/article_31109_meet-the-bulletproof
-bat-monster-of-van-meter-iowa.html.

Logan, Malcolm. "There Be Monsters: The Outlandish Terror of the Van Meter
Visitor." *My American Odyssey: Discovering America One Town at a Time*, 10 April
2021. https://myamericanodyssey.com/the-van-meter-visitor.

UCMP. "*Pteranodon ingens* display information." Berkeley.edu. https://ucmp
.berkeley.edu/museum/public/ingensmount.html#:~:text=Pteranodon%20
is%20a%20large%20crested,ancestor%20in%20the%20Late%20Triassic.

Terry Trueblood Lake. Iowa Department of Natural Resources. www.iowadnr
.gov/idnr/Fishing/Where-to-Fish/Lakes-Ponds-Reservoirs
/Lake-Details?lakeCode=SAL52.

Carey, Liz. "Visiting with the Van Meter Visitor as the Festival Takes Shape This
Fall." The Daily Yonder, 6 August 2021. https://dailyyonder.com/visiting-with
-the-van-meter-visitor-as-the-festival-takes-shape-this-fall/2021/08/06.

"Van Meter Visitor Festival." *American Ghost Walks*, 2024.
www.americanghostwalks.com/articles/van-meter-visitor-2022.

"The Van Meter Monster." Discovery, 8 September 2021. www.discovery.com
/shows/expedition-x/3/the-van-meter-monster.

"6 Photos: Van Meter's Visitor—a 'Winged Creature' Reportedly Seen in 1903."
Des Moines Register, 24 September 2021. www.desmoinesregister.com
/picture-gallery/news/2015/07/01/6-photos-van-meters-winged-creature
-reportedly-seen-in-1903/29582693.

Browne, Mike, Morgan Knudsen, and Chad Lewis. "Did You See That? The Van
Meter Visitor (Featuring Chad Lewis)." *Supernatural Circumstances*, season 1,
episode 17, 6 June 2022. https://podcasts.apple.com/ca/podcast
/did-you-see-that-the-van-meter-visitor-featuring-chad-lewis
/id1590554538?i=1000565333567.

Chapter 13: Popper the Poltergeist

Pratt, J.G., and W.G. Roll. "The Seaford Disturbances." *Journal of Parapsychology
1958-06* 22 (2), 1958.

Roll, William G. *The Poltergeist*. New York: Cosimo, 2004.

Roll, William, and Valerie Storey. *Unleashed*. New York: Simon & Schuster, 2007.

Brady, Ralph F. *Landmarks & Historic Sites of Long Island*. Mount Pleasant, SC: Arcadia, 2012.

Anson, Jay. *The Amityville Horror*. New York: Gallery Books, 2019.

February 11, 1958: *Chicago Tribune* from Chicago, Illinois · 1. Newspapers.com, 2024. www.newspapers.com/image/372508693/?terms=Seaford%20 Herrmann&match=1.

February 17, 1958: *Tucson Citizen* from Tucson, Arizona · 7. Newspapers.com, 2024. www.newspapers.com/image/581870970/?terms=Seaford%20 Herrmann&match=1.

February 22, 1958: *Newsday* (Nassau Edition) from Hempstead, New York · 5. Newspapers.com, 2024. www.newspapers.com/image/711848224/?terms =Seaford%20Herrmann&match=1.

March 21, 1958: *The Catholic Standard and Times*. The Catholic News Archive, 2024. https://thecatholicnewsarchive.org/?a=d&d=cst19580321 -01.2.145&e=en-201txttxIN.

April 17, 1958: *Newsday* (Nassau Edition) from Hempstead, New York · 9. Newspapers.com, 2024. www.newspapers.com/image/711859197/?terms =Seaford%20Herrmann&match=1.

Wehrstein, K.M. "Seaford Poltergeist." Psi Encyclopedia, 24 January 2022. https://psi-encyclopedia.spr.ac.uk/articles/seaford-poltergeist.

Wehrstein, K.M. "William Roll." Psi Encyclopedia, 31 October 2022. https://psi-encyclopedia.spr.ac.uk/articles/william-roll.

Wehrstein, K.M. "J Gaither Pratt." Psi Encyclopedia, 28 June 2022. https://psi -encyclopedia.spr.ac.uk/articles/j-gaither-pratt.

Duggan, Michael. "Psychokinesis Research." Psi Encyclopedia, 30 June 2023. https://psi-encyclopedia.spr.ac.uk/articles/psychokinesis-research.

Colvin, Barrie. "Poltergeists (Overview)." Psi Encyclopedia, 8 November 2023. https://psi-encyclopedia.spr.ac.uk/articles/poltergeists-overview.

"Popper the Poltergeist: America's First Paranormal Reality Show." American Hauntings, 2014. www.americanhauntingsink.com/popper.

Chapter 14: The Vampires of Highgate Cemetery

Wilson, Katharina M. "The History of the Word 'Vampire.'" *Journal of the History of Ideas* 46 (4): 577-583, 1985. https://doi.org/10.2307/2709546.

Troxell, Janet Camp. "Collecting the Rossettis." *The Princeton University Library Chronicle* 33 (3): 142-145, 1972. https://doi.org/10.2307/26409951.

Farrant, Della. *Haunted Highgate*. Cheltenham, UK: The History Press, 2014.

"The Magnificent Seven." London Natural History Society, 2024. www.lnhs.org .uk/index.php/resources/locations/8-locations/554-the-magnificent-seven.

Highgate Cemetery website. 2024. https://highgatecemetery.org.

"Why Do Fans Leave Pens at Douglas Adams's Grave in London?" Quora. www.quora.com/Why-do-fans-leave-pens-at-Douglas-Adamss-grave-in -London#:~:text=In%20my%20opinion%20it%20is,have%20relevance%20 through%20his%20writing.

"Lamia." Wikipedia, 21 April 2024. https://en.wikipedia.org/wiki/Lamia.

Hawksley, Lucinda. "The Tragedy of Art's Greatest Supermodel." BBC, 31 July 2020. www.bbc.com/culture/article/20200103-the-tragedy-of-arts-greatest -supermodel.

Ian. "The Highgate Vampire—How It All Began—by David Farrant." Mysterious Britain & Ireland, 28 October 2018. www.mysteriousbritain.co.uk/hauntings /the-highgate-vampire-how-it-all-began-by-david-farrant.

Google search for "Henri Feuhonlet 1856." *The Illustrated London News* 20. Google Books. https://books.google.ca/books?id=oKq-DzQIO _kC&pg=PA561&lpg=PA561&dq=Henri+Feuhonlet+1856&source=bl&ots= _IXXCBXAzx&sig=ACfU3U381Gq_IlMhEHH-C9i53gE26hgyRA&hl =en&sa=X&ved=2ahUKEwixrvTjqamAAxVZADQIHcyFD _4Q6AF6BAgJEAM#v=onepage&q=Henri%20Feuhonlet%201856&f=false.

March 14, 1970: *Evening Post* from Bristol, Avon, England · 14. Newspapers.com, 2024. www.newspapers.com/image/876079331.

March 14, 1970: *Huddersfield Daily Examiner* from Huddersfield, West Yorkshire, England · 1. Newspapers.com, 2024. www.newspapers.com/image /941949754.

September 30, 1970: *The Guardian Journal* from Nottingham, Nottinghamshire, England · 7. Newspapers.com, 2024. www.newspapers.com/image/881787208.

July 18, 1974: *The Daily Telegraph* from London, Greater London, England · 3. Newspapers.com, 2024. www.newspapers.com/image/825608979.

"The Highgate Vampire Society." David Farrant, 2023. https://davidfarrant.org /the-highgate-vampire-society.

"Ley Lines." The Skeptic's Dictionary, 2016. www.skepdic.com/leylines.html.

Kemp, Sam. "The Strange Tale of the Highgate Vampire." *Far Out*, 4 August 2022. https://faroutmagazine.co.uk/strange-tale-of-highgate-vampire.

Volpe, Sam. "Highgate 'Vampire Hunter' Dies Half a Century After Supernatural Panic Gripped Community." *Ham & High*, 24 April 2019. www.hamhigh .co.uk/lifestyle/21353447.highgate-vampire-hunter-dies-half-century -supernatural-panic-gripped-community.

Chapter 15: The Philip Experiment

Owen, Iris M. *Conjuring Up Philip: An Adventure in Psychokinesis.* Toronto: Fitzhenry & Whiteside, 1976.

Rhine, J.B., and J.G. Pratt. *Parapsychology: Frontier Science of the Mind.* Springfield, IL: Charles C Thomas, 1957.

Wehrstein, K.M. "Philip Psychokinesis Experiments." Psi Encyclopedia, 23 November 2022. https://psi-encyclopedia.spr.ac.uk/articles/philip -psychokinesis-experiments.

Wehrstein, K.M. "Kenneth Batcheldor." Psi Encyclopedia, 25 March 2024. https://psi-encyclopedia.spr.ac.uk/articles/kenneth-batcheldor.

Mackenzie, Brian. "Joseph Banks Rhine: 1895-1980." *American Journal of Psychology* 94 (4): 649-653, 1981. http://www.jstor.org/stable/1422426.

New Horizons Research Foundation Occasional Papers. Survival Research Institute of Canada, 2024. https://survivalresearch.ca/nhrf-papers.

Palmer, John. "Pink Noise and Dice." Opinion. *Washington Post*, 7 March 1987. www.washingtonpost.com/archive/opinions/1987/03/08/pink-noise-and -dice/07dbba9f-c203-449f-9a87-298633e52cb0.

Warner-Angel, Heather L. *Psi Performance, Belief in Psi, and Competition in a Game-Show Format.* Master's thesis, Eastern Illinois University, 2017.

"Mediums, Spirits, and Spooks in the Rocky Mountains." University of Colorado Boulder. www.colorado.edu/center/west/sites/default/files/attached-files/ logan_0.pdf.

Philip, the Imaginary Ghost. CBC documentary, 1974. Available: www.amazon.ca /Philip-Imaginary-835850-Ontario-Limited/dp/B00JXQPDBS.

Storm, Lance, and Colin Mitchell. "'Are You There, Spenser?'": Attempts at 'PK by Committee' in a Seance-like Situation." *Australian Journal of Parapsychology* 3 (1), 1 June 2003.

"The Philip Experiment." SpiritSeekers. YouTube, 1 October 2010. www.youtube.com/watch?v=X2lGPT2J1cc.

"The Philip Experiment." HistoryvsHollywood." YouTube, 23 April 2014. www.youtube.com/watch?v=MzNxHLe1_SQ.

Browne, Mike, and Morgan Knudsen. "The Philip Experiment." *Supernatural Circumstances*, season 1, episode 1, 25 October 2021. https://open.spotify.com/ episode/5VgO1PD76Ogk1ZbGwUirY8?si=8873389167184471.

Knudsen, Morgan. *Teaching the Living: From Heartbreak to Happiness in a Haunted Home*. San Diego: Beyond the Fray Publishing, 2022.

Chapter 16: What's Next? Death, Dying and the Afterlife

Definition of rest in peace. Dictionary.com. www.dictionary.com/e/pop-culture /rest-in-peace.

"Hamlet, Act III, Scene I [To Be, or Not to Be]." Poets.org, 20 May 2019. https://poets.org/poem/hamlet-act-iii-scene-i-be-or-not-be.

James, William. *The Varieties of Religious Experience: A Study in Human Nature*. New York: Modern Library, 2002.

Becker, Ernest. "Illuminating Denial of Death." Ernest Becker Foundation. www.ernestbecker.org/biography.

Becker, Ernest. *The Denial of Death*. London: Souvenir Press, 1973.

"Different Religions' Views on the Afterlife." Universal Life Church, 31 October 2023. www.ulc.org/ulc-blog/different-religions-views-on-the-afterlife.

Moody, Raymond A. *Life After Life*. New York: HarperOne, 2015.

Sartori, Penny. "Near-Death Experience." Psi Encyclopedia, 24 September 2022. https://psi-encyclopedia.spr.ac.uk/articles/near -death-experience.

Khanna, Surbhi, Lauren Moore, and Bruce Greyson. "Full Neurological Recovery from Escherichia coli Meningitis Associated with Near-Death Experience." *Journal of Nervous and Mental Disease* 206 (9): 744–747, 2018.

Alexander, Eben. *Proof of Heaven: A Neurosurgeon's Journey into the Afterlife*. New York: Simon & Schuster, 2012.

Alexander, Eben, and Ptolemy Tompkins. *The Map of Heaven: A Neurosurgeon Explores the Mysteries of the Afterlife and the Truth About What Lies Beyond*. London: Piatkus, 2014.

Alexander, Eben, and Karen Newell. *Living in a Mindful Universe*. Emmaus, PA: Rodale, 2017.

Greyson, Bruce. *After*. New York: St. Martin's Essentials, 2022.

Kean, Leslie. *Surviving Death: A Journalist Investigates Evidence for an Afterlife*. New York: Three Rivers Press, 2018.

Browne, Mike, and Morgan Knudsen. "Finding Your Sanity & Soul: A Discussion with Dr. Eben Alexander." *Supernatural Circumstances*, season 2, episode 23, 29 April, 2024. https://open.spotify.com/episode/19R7wbBAWV8vm1gctnrfmV?si=88cf-55b470444c5a